Advanced Lisp Technology

Advanced Information Processing Technology

A series edited by Tadao Saito

Advanced Lisp Technology

Edited by

Taiichi Yuasa

Hiroshi G. Okuno

Graduate School of Informatics
Kyoto University

The Information Processing Society of Japan

CRC Press is an imprint of the
Taylor & Francis Group, an **informa** business

A TAYLOR & FRANCIS BOOK

First published 2002 by Taylor & Francis

Published 2019 by CRC Press
Taylor & Francis Group
6000 Broken Sound Parkway NW, Suite 300
Boca Raton, FL 33487-2742

© 2002 by Taylor & Francis Group, LLC
CRC Press is an imprint of Taylor & Francis Group, an Informa business

First issued in paperback 2019

No claim to original U.S. Government works

ISBN 13: 978-0-367-45492-0 (pbk)
ISBN 13: 978-0-415-29819-3 (hbk)

Visit the Taylor & Francis Web site at
http://www.taylorandfrancis.com

and the CRC Press Web site at
http://www.crcpress.com

This book has been prepared for camera-ready copy provided by the editors.

Every effort has been made to ensure that the advice and information in this book is true and accurate at the time of going to press. However, neither the publisher nor the authors can accept any legal responsibility or liability for any errors or omissions that may be made. In the case of drug administration, any medical procedure or the use of technical equipment mentioned in this book, you are strongly advised to consult the manufacturer's guidelines.

British Library Cataloguing in Publication Data
A catalogue record for this book is
available from the British Library

Library of Congress Cataloguing in Publication Data
A catalog record for this book has been requested

Contents

v

Series Foreword

The Information Processing Society of Japan (IPSJ) is the top academic institution in the information processing field in Japan. It has about thirty thousand members and promotes a variety of research and development activities covering all aspects of information processing and computer science.

One of the major activities of the society is publication of its transactions containing papers covering all the fields of information processing, including fundamentals, software, hardware, and applications. Some of the papers are published in English, but because the majority are in Japanese, the transactions are not suitable for non-Japanese wishing to access advanced information technology in Japan. IPSJ therefore decided to publish a book series titled "Advanced Information Technology in Japan."

The series consists of independent books, each including a collection of top quality papers, from mainly Japanese sources of a selected area in information technology. The book titles were chosen by the International Publication Committee of IPSJ so that they enable easy access to information technology from international readers. Each book contains original papers and/or those updated or translated from original papers appearing in the transactions or internationally qualified meetings. Survey papers to aid understanding of the technology in Japan in a particular area are also included.

As the chairman of the International Publication Committee of IPSJ, I sincerely hope that the books in the series will improve communication between Japanese and non-Japanese specialists for their mutual benefit.

Tadao Saito

Series Editor

Chairman
International Publication Committee
the Information Processing Society of Japan

Preface

Research and development activities related to Lisp have been quite active in Japan. Many Lisp languages and many Lisp processors have been designed and developed here.

There were three booms in Lisp research; in the early seventies, in the mid-eighties, and in the late-eighties. During the first boom, some experimental Lisp systems were developed, and some also came to be practically used. At that time, available computing power and memory space were small, as was the Lisp community. The second boom was triggered by the explosion of interest in AI, which was partly due to the Fifth Generation Computer System Project in Japan. Although the FGCS project advocated Prolog as a primary AI language, Lisp also shared the attention paid to AI research.

The third boom was caused by the emergence of Common Lisp. Available computing power and memory space increased greatly, and the Lisp community also became larger. Many Lisp systems were developed at this time. In particular, KCL (Kyoto Common Lisp) has been used not only in Japan but also in the world. Major research and development activities up to 1990 were reported in the special section on "Lisp systems in Japan" of *Journal of Information Processing* (vol.13, no.3, 1990).

Recently many parallel and distributed processors are available both experimentally and commercially, which prompts academia and industry to do research in parallel and distributed processing. This book focuses on recent activities, including parallel and distributed Lisp systems, memory managements for those systems and other related topics.

The papers in this book are organized into groups by subject:

Part I: Parallel and Distributed Lisp Systems
Part II: Language Features
Part III: Memory Management
Part IV: Programming Environments

The papers in Part I report contributions to Lisp system design and implementation on a wide variety of parallel and distributed computing environments, such as SMPs, distributed-memory parallel machines, SIMD machines, and network-connected workstations. These systems attempt various strategies to provide the base system with constructs for parallel computation, from low-level communication primitives to high-level semi-automatic parallelizing constructs.

Most language features proposed in the papers in Part II are related with parallel and distributed Lisp processors. Included features are: evaluation strategy for parallel symbolic computation, extension of first-class continuations for parallel Scheme systems, and light-weight process for real-time symbolic computation. The last paper in Part II proposes restricted but efficient first-class continuations.

Part III of this book consists of papers on memory management and garbage collection. Topics in these Papers are: parallel garbage collection for parallel Lisp systems, hybrid incremental garbage collection for parallel Lisp systems, garbage collection for Lisp systems on SIMD architectures, and stop-and-collect type of garbage collection with sliding rather than copying.

Papers in Part IV are related with programming environment. The first paper handles system's management of Lisp macros. The second paper proposes user interface for Lisp printers.

As will be clear from the collection of papers in this book, the main interest of Lisp research in Japan has been on parallel and distributed processing. The current movement is to develop new application areas, which requires high productivity, dynamic features, and efficiency of Lisp in the information network society, though it is too early to include papers along this movement in this book.

Taiichi Yuasa
Hiroshi G. Okuno
Kyoto and Tokyo
At the beginning of the 21st Century

The Authors

Yoshiji Amagai received his B.E. and M.E. degrees in computer science and communication engineering from the University of Electro-Communications in 1983, 1985. He has been in Nippon Telegraph and Telephone Corporation from 1985, and is currently working for NTT Network Innovation Laboratories.

Akihiro Fushimi was born in 1971. He received his M.E. degree from Toyohashi University. of Technology. in 1995. He has been working in NTN Corp. since 1995 and now is a system engineer of Advanced Operation Development Dept. of NTN. His current interests are network architecture and programming language implementation.

Katsumi Hatanaka was born in 1969. He received his M.E. degree from Toyohashi University. of Technology. in 1994. He has been working in OKI Electric Industry Co., Ltd. since 1994 as a database engineer. His current interests are data warehouse and knowledge discovery in databases. He is a member of IPSJ.

Mitsuru Ishida was born in 1955. He received the degree of M.E. degree in Education from Tokyo Gakugei University, Tokyo, Japan, in 1982. Since 1982, he has been a teacher of high school. He also received the B.E. degree in computer science from the University of Electro-Communications in 1992. He is now a doctoral student in computer science at the University of Electro-Communications. His current research interests include storage management of both concurrent and real-time types.

Takayasu Ito received his B.E. in electrical engineering in 1962 from Kyoto University, his M.S. in computer science in 1967 from Stanford University, and his Dr. Eng. degree in 1970 from Kyoto University. In 1962–1977 he was with Central Research Laboratory of Mitsubishi Electric Corp with on leave to AI Laboratory of Stanford University from 1965 until 1968. Since 1978 he has been a Professor at Tohoku University, and now is a Professor, Department of Computer and Mathematical Sciences, Graduate School of Informations Sciences. Since 1962 his research interests are in AI and pattern recognition, Lisp and functional languages, theories of programs and semantics. His current interests are in extensions of PaiLisp and ISLisp that he advocated, constructive theories of concurrency and execution, and design of new internet languages. He is Associate Editor of Higher-Order and Symbolic Computation, and a member of Editorial board of Information and Computation. Also, he served conference chairs of TACS'91, TACS'94, TACS'97, and IFIP TCS2000, and he is the conference chair of TACS 2001. He is one of the first IPSJ Fellows.

Teruo Iwai received his B.E. in 1988, his M.E. degrees in 1990 both in mathematics from Keio University. He is a research fellow at Keio University. His current research interests are Lisp systems and parallel processing.

Shin-ichi Kawamoto received his B.E. and M.E. in information engineering in 1991 and 1993, respectively, and his Dr. degree in information science in 1998, all from Tohoku University. He was a research associate from 1996 until 1998, working on the PaiLisp system. Since 1998 he has been with Central Research Laboratory of Hitachi Ltd., where he works on basic software systems for high-perfeormance computing architectures.

Hideki Koike received his B.E. in mechanical engineering in 1986 and his M.E. and Dr.Eng. degrees in information engineering in 1988 and 1999, respectively, all from the University of Tokyo. Currently he is an Associate Professor of Graduate School of Information Systems in University of Electro-Communications, Tokyo.

Tsuneyasu Komiya received his B.E., M.E. and Dr.Eng. degrees from Toyohashi University of Technology in 1991, 1993 and 1996, respectively. He is currently an instructor in the Graduate School of Informatics, Kyoto University. His research interests include symbolic processing languages and parallel languages. He received an IPSJ best paper award in 1997. He is a member of IPSJ.

Atusi Maeda received his B.E. in 1986, his M.E. in 1988 and his Ph.D.(Eng.) degrees in 1997 all in mathematics from Keio University. He was a Research Associate at University of Electro-Communications from 1997 to 1999. He is currently an Assistant Professor at Institute of Information Sciences and Electronics, University of Tsukuba. His research interests are in design and implementation of programming languages, compilers and parallel programming.

Shogo Matsui received his B.E. in 1982, his M.E. in 1984 and his Ph.D.(Eng.) degree in 1991 all in mathematical engineering from Keio University. He joined the faculty at Kanagawa University in 1989, and now is an Associate Professor in the Department of Information Science. His research interests are in Lisp systems including Lisp machines and parallel garbage collection.

Toshihiro Matsui received his B.E. in instrumentation engineering 1980, his M.E. in information engineering in 1982, and Dr.Eng. degrees in information engineering in 1991, all from the University of Tokyo. He joined Electrotechnical Laboratory in 1982, and conducted research on programming systems for robotics. He was a visiting scholar of Stanford University, MIT AI Lab., and Australian National University in 1991, 94 and 99. He received Research/Best-Paper Awards from International Symposium of Robotics Research (ISRR) in 1989, Robotics Society of Japan in 1989, Moto-oka Memorial in 1992, etc. He is now Senior Research Scientist of ETL and leading a research group for a mobile office robot project.

Yoshitaka Nagano was born in 1967. He received his M.E. degree from Toyohashi University. of Technology. in 1993. He has been working in NTN Corp. since 1993 and now is a system engineer of R&D Dept. of NTN. His current interest is computer vision for industrial automation.

Masakazu Nakanishi received his B.E. in 1966, his M.E. in 1968 and his Dr.Eng. all in administrative engineering from Keio University. He joined the faculty at Keio University in 1969 and now is a Professor in Department of Information and Computer Science. He died in 2000. He developed the first Lisp system in Japan. His main research interests lie in languages for symbol processing and artificial intelligence and computer education.

Hiroshi Nitta was born in Kanagawa, Japan on November 15, 1971. He received the B.E. degree in systems engineering from Ibaraki University, Ibaraki, Japan, in 1995. He received the M.E. degree in computer science from the University of Electro-Communications, Tokyo, Japan, in 1997. He is now a doctoral student in computer science at the University of Electro-Communications. His current research interests include storage management.

Hiroshi G. Okuno received his B.A. in Pure and Applied Sciences in 1972, and his Ph.D in Computer Science in 1996, both from the University of Tokyo . He worked for Nippon Telegraph and Telephone Corporation for more than 26 years, and has joined Kitano Symbiotic Systems Project, Japan Science and Technology Corporation in 1998. From 1999 to 2001, he was a Professor of Information Sciences, Science University of Tokyo. He is currently a Professor at the Graduate School of Informatics, Kyoto University.

Toshiharu Ono received his B.E. in Mathematics in 1950 from the University of Rikkyou and his M.E. degree in Information Engineering in 1990 from the University of Yamanashi. He is instructor of Electrical and Computer at Nishi Tokyo Science University. His research is in distributed systems, and computer languages. Since 1971 he has worked as an engineer at "NEC" and has been involved in the design and implementation of the Fortran compiler.

Satoshi Sekiguchi received his B.S. degree in information science from the University of Tokyo in 1982 and the M.E. degree in information engineering from the University of Tsukuba in 1984 respectively. He joined with Electrotechnical Laboratory in 1984, and conducted research on parallel computing systems for scientific computing. He was a visit scholar of National Center for Atmospheric Research in 1996, and a visiting scientist in ETH Zurich in 1998. He received Ichimura Academic Award in 1989, Best-Paper Award from Information Processing Society Japan (IPSJ) in 1995, etc. He is now Senior Research Scientist of ETL and leading a research group on the high performance computing group. His research interests include parallel algorithms for scientific computations, global computing and cluster computing systems.

Satoko Takahashi received her B.E. degree in mathematics in 1994 and her M.E. degree in computer science in 1996 both from Keio University. She works at Media Technology Development Center, NTT Communications Corporation Her research interests include development of CTI systems.

Ikuo Takeuchi received his B.S. degrees in mathematics in 1969 and his M.S. degrees in mathematics in 1971, all from the University of Tokyo. He had been working for

Nippon Telegraph and Telephone Corporation since 1971 till 1997, and now is a Professor of the University of Electro-Communications.

Tetsurou Tanaka received his B.E. in mathematical engineering in 1987 and his M.E. and Dr.Eng. degrees in information engineering in 1989 and 1992, respectively, all from the University of Tokyo. He is now an Associate Professor at Information Technology Center, the University of Tokyo.

Yoshio Tanaka received his B.E. in 1987, his M.E. in 1989 and his Ph.D.(Eng.) degree in 1995 all in mathematics from Keio University. He was working at Real World Computing Partnership from 1996 to 1999. He is currently the team leader of Grid Infraware Team at Grid Technology Research Center, National Institute of Advanced Industrial Science and Technology. His current research interests include Grid computing, performance evaluation of parallel systems, and memory management.

Motoaki Terashima was born in Shizuoka, Japan in June 8, 1948. He received the degrees of B.Sc. (1973), M.Sc. (1975) and D.Sc. (1978) in Physics from the University of Tokyo for his work on computer science. Since 1978, he has been a research associate of the Department of Computer Science, University of Electro-Communications, and is currently an Associate Professor of Graduate School of Information Systems. He was a visiting scholar at the Computer Laboratory of the Cambridge University in 1992. His current research interests include programming language design and implementations, memory management, and symbolic and algebraic manipulation systems. He is a member of IPSJ, ACM and AAAI.

Masayoshi Umehara received his B.E. and M.E. in information engineering in 1994 and 1996, respectively, from Tohoku University. He worked on a PaiLisp complier for his M.E. thesis. Since 1996 he has been with NEC Communications Division.

Eiiti Wada received his B.S. degree from the University of Tokyo. Then he joined Professor Hidetosi Takahasi's Laboratory of the Physics Department, University of Tokyo, as a graduate student. In 1958, when the parametron computer, PC-1 was completed, he spent many hours for preparing software library. In 1964, he moved to the Faculty of Engineering of the University of Tokyo, as an Associate Professor. From 1973 he spent one year at MIT, Project MAC. In 1990's, with his graduate students, he worked for developing the Chinese character fonts generation system, in which character shapes were composed from the definition of the elementary parts based on the synthesis algorithms. He has been the member of the IFIP WG2.1. Presently he is a Professor Emeritus of the University of Tokyo and the Executive Advisor of Fujitsu Laboratories.

Haruaki Yamazaki received the B.S. degree in Mathematics in 1970 from Nagoya University, Japan. He subsequently joined OKI electric Industry Co.,Ltd and engaged in research and development on distributed system. He received the M.S. degree in computer science in 1977, from University of Illinois at Urbana-Champaign. He received his doctorial degree in Engineering from Nagoya University in 1986. Since 1992, he has been a Professor at Department of Computer Science, Yamanashi university, kofu, Japan. His current interests are in distributed systems, distributed artificial intelligence. He is a member of Institution of Electronics and Communication Engineers of Japan, Information Processing Society of Japan, Artificial Intelligence Society of Japan and American Association for Artificial Intelligence.

Kenichi Yamazaki received his B.E. degrees in communication engineering in 1984 and his M.E. degrees in information engineering in 1986, all from Tohoku University, and received his Ph.D. degrees in 2001 from the University of Electro-Communications. He had been in Nippon Telegraph and Telephone Corporation from 1986, and is currently working for NTT DoCoMo Network Laboratories.

Taichi Yasumoto was born in 1966. He received his M.E. degree from Toyohashi University of Technology in 1990. He is currently an Associate Professor at Department of Mathematical Science, Aichi University of Education. His research interests are symbolic processing languages and parallel processing. He is a member of IPSJ, IEICE and JSSST.

Masaharu Yoshida received his B.E. degrees in electrical engineering in 1976 and his M.E. degrees in electrical engineering in 1978, all from Chiba University. He has been in Nippon Telegraph and Telephone Corporation from 1978, and is currently working for NTT-IT CORPORATION.

Taiichi Yuasa was born in Kobe, in 1952. He received the Bachelor of Mathematics degree in 1977, the Master of Mathematical Sciences degree in 1979, and the Doctor of Science degree in 1987, all from Kyoto University. He joined the faculty of the Research Institute for Mathematical Sciences, Kyoto University, in 1982. He is currently a Professor at the Graduate School of Informatics, Kyoto University. His current area of interest include symbolic computation, programming language systems, and massively parallel computation. He received an IPSJ best paper award in 1997. Dr. Yuasa is a member of ACM, IEEE, Information Processing Society of Japan, the Institute of Electronics, Information and Communication Engineers, and Japan Society for Software Science and Technology.

A Multi-Threaded Implementation of PaiLisp Interpreter and Compiler Using the Steal-Help Evaluation Strategy

Takayasu Ito

Shin-ichi Kawamoto

Masayoshi Umehara

Department of Computer and Mathematical Sciences
Graduate School of Information Sciences
Tohoku University, Sendai, Japan

ABSTRACT

PaiLisp is a parallel Lisp language with a rich set of concurrency constructs like **pcall**, **pbegin**, **plet**, **pletrec**, **par-and**, **pcond** and **future**, and an extended **call/cc** is introduced to support $\mathcal{P}$-continuation. The Eager Task Creation (ETC, for short) is a commonly-used implementation strategy for concurrency constructs. But ETC incurs excessive process creation which causes degradation of performance in parallel evaluation of a program parallelized using concurrency constructs. The Steal-Help Evaluation (SHE, for short) is introduced as an efficient parallel evaluation strategy which enables to suppress excessive process creation. This paper explains a multi-threaded implementation of PaiLisp interpreter and compiler, in which the ETC and SHE strategies for PaiLisp concurrency constructs are realized. Some experimental results of using a set of benchmark programs show that the SHE strategy is more efficient than the ETC strategy.

1 Introduction

There are several parallel Scheme languages like Multilisp[3] and PaiLisp[8], designed for shared memory architectures. Multilisp may be considered to be a minimal extension of Scheme into concurrency, introducing an interesting concurrency construct **future**. PaiLisp is an extension of Scheme with a rich set of concurrency constructs like **pcall**, **pbegin**, **plet**, **pletrec**, **pif**, **par-and**, **par-or**, **pcond** and **future**. PaiLisp may be considered to be a superset of Multilisp as a parallel Scheme language. A PaiLisp interpreter was implemented using the *Eager Task Creation* (ETC, for short) as reported in the reference 10). ETC is a commonly-used technique in implementing various parallel programming languages, but it usually incurs a serious problem of excessive process creation, in particular, in evaluating a recursively-defined parallel program. Under the ETC strategy it often occurs that for a given sequential program its parallelized version runs slower than the original sequential one. This is because when a concurrency construct is encountered the ETC strategy creates processes specifiied by it without any concern of availability of processors. The *Steal-Help Evaluation* (SHE, for short) is proposed as an efficient evaluation strategy of concurrency constructs in parallel Scheme systems[15, 16]. SHE enables to suppress excessive process creation, since it creates processes only when an idle processor is available in evaluating an expression annotated by a concurrency construct. A multi-threaded implementation of PaiLisp interpreter and compiler using the SHE strategy is implemented on a DEC7000 with six Alpha processors under OSF/1 OS. This paper explains a multi-threaded implementation of PaiLisp interpreter and compiler, called PaiLisp/MT, in which the ETC and SHE strategies are realized. Some experimental results of PaiLisp/MT are also given, using a set of benchmark programs, and they show that the SHE strategy is actually effective and efficient as a parallel evaluation strategy.

2 PaiLisp

PaiLisp is designed as a parallel Scheme language with a rich set of concurrency constructs as follows.

The meanings of sequential constructs are same with those of Scheme[1], and the meanings of concurrency constructs are given so as to preserve meanings of their corresponding sequential ones[15, 16]. For example, the meanings of **pcall**, **pbegin**, **plet**, **pif**, **par-and** and **future** are as follows.

(**pcall** f e_1 $\cdots$ e_n): After evaluating $e_1, \cdots, e_n$ in parallel, f is evaluated, and its resultant value is applied to the values of $e_1, \cdots, e_n$.

(**pbegin** e_1 $\cdots$ e_n): $e_1, \cdots, e_n$ are evaluated in parallel, and after their termination the value of e_n are returned as the value of this **pbegin** expression.

(**plet** ((x_1 e_1) $\cdots$ (x_n e_n)) E_1 $\cdots$ E_m): After evaluating $e_1, \cdots, e_n$ in parallel and binding their values to the corresponding variables, the environment is extended with these bindings. Then under the extended environment $E_1, \cdots, E_m$ are evaluated in parallel, and after their termination the value of E_m is returned as the value of this **plet** expression.

(**pif** e_1 e_2 e_3): The expressions e_1, e_2 and e_3 are evaluated in parallel, and when the value of e_1 becomes *true* the value of e_2 is returned, killing (that is, forcing termination of) evaluation of e_3, and when the value of e_1 becomes *false* the value of e_3 is returned, killing evaluation of e_2.

$$D \quad ::= (\textbf{define } x \; E) \; |(\textbf{define } f \; (\textbf{lambda } (x_1 \cdots x_n) \; E_1 \cdots E_m))$$

$$\begin{aligned}
E \quad ::= \; & V \\
| \; & (F \; E_1 \cdots E_n) \; | \; (\textbf{begin } E_1 \cdots E_n) \\
| \; & (\textbf{if } E_1 \; E_2 \; E_3) \; | \; (\textbf{cond } (E_{11} \; E_{12}) \cdots (E_{n1} \; E_{n2})) \\
| \; & (\textbf{let } ((x_1 \; E_1) \cdots (x_m \; E_m)) \; E_{m+1} \cdots E_n) \\
| \; & (\textbf{let* } ((x_1 \; E_1) \cdots (x_m \; E_m)) \; E_{m+1} \cdots E_n) \\
| \; & (\textbf{letrec } ((x_1 \; E_1) \cdots (x_m \; E_m)) \; E_{m+1} \cdots E_n) \\
| \; & (\textbf{and } E_1 \cdots E_n) \; | \; (\textbf{or } E_1 \cdots E_n) \\
| \; & (\textbf{set! } x \; E) \; | \; (\textbf{call/cc } E) \; | \; (\textbf{call/ep } E) \\
| \; & (\textbf{delay } E) \; | \; (\textbf{force } E) \\
| \; & (\textbf{pcall } F \; E_1 \cdots E_n) \; | \; (\textbf{par } E_1 \cdots E_n) \; | \; (\textbf{pbegin } E_1 \cdots E_n) \\
| \; & (\textbf{plet } ((x_1 \; E_1) \cdots (x_m \; E_m)) \; E_{m+1} \cdots E_n) \\
| \; & (\textbf{pletrec } ((x_1 \; E_1) \cdots (x_m \; E_m)) \; E_{m+1} \cdots E_n) \\
| \; & (\textbf{pif } E_1 \; E_2 \; E_3) \\
| \; & (\textbf{pcond } (E_{11} \; E_{12}) \cdots (E_{n1} \; E_{n2})) \; | \; (\textbf{pcond\# } (E_{11} \; E_{12}) \cdots (E_{n1} \; E_{n2})) \\
| \; & (\textbf{par-and } E_1 \cdots E_n) \; | \; (\textbf{par-or } E_1 \cdots E_n) \\
| \; & (\textbf{future } E) \; | \; (\textbf{call/pcc } E) \; | \; (\textbf{call/pep } E)
\end{aligned}$$

$$\begin{aligned}
V \quad ::= \; & Constant \; | \; Variable \\
| \; & (\textbf{lambda } (x_1 \cdots x_n) \; E_1 \cdots E_m) \; | \; (\textbf{exlambda } (x_1 \cdots x_n) \; E_1 \cdots E_m)
\end{aligned}$$

$$\begin{aligned}
F \quad ::= \; & Primitive\text{-}function \; | \; User\text{-}defined\text{-}function \; | \; System\text{-}function \\
| \; & (\textbf{lambda } (x_1 \cdots x_n) \; E_1 \cdots E_m)
\end{aligned}$$

Figure 1: Syntax of PaiLisp

(**par-and** $e_1 \cdots e_n$): $e_1, \cdots, e_n$ are evaluated in parallel, and if one of them yields *false* then *false* is returned, killing all the remaining processes created in evaluating $e_1, \cdots, e_n$. If none of $e_1, \cdots, e_n$ yields *false* then the value of e_n is returned.

(**future** e): When this expression is encountered the future-value for e is returned, and a new child process of evaluating e is created. The evaluation on the parent process is continued, using the future-value for e. When the true value of the future-value for e is required, the **force** operation is performed to obtain it.

PaiLisp is featured in introducing a parallel construct corresponding to each sequential Scheme construct, and in addition, PaiLisp-Kernel is extracted. PaiLisp-Kernel = Scheme + {**spawn, suspend, exlambda, call/pcc**} is a small subset of PaiLisp, in which the meanings of other PaiLisp constructs can be expressed[8].

3   Outline of PaiLisp Interpreter and Compiler

In this section we outline PaiLisp/MT, a multi-threaded implementation of PaiLisp interpreter and compiler realized on a DEC7000 with six Alpha processors using the P-thread library of OSF/1 OS. PaiLisp/MT is implemented using the *Register Machine* (RM) model of Abelson and Sussman[1], and the ETC and SHE strategies are used in evaluating concurrency constructs of PaiLisp. The PaiLisp interpreter is a parallel evaluator which consists of six sequential Scheme interpreters under a shared memory, and the PaiLisp compiler is a compiler to translate a PaiLisp program into the corresponding concurrent RM program, which is eventually translated into the corresponding C program. The resultant compiled C program is executed under the run-time mechanism equipped to PaiLisp/MT. Thus, PaiLisp/MT consists of the following.

(1) PaiLisp/MT is implemented on a DEC7000 with six Alpha processors using the P-thread library of OSF/1 OS.

(2) PaiLisp/MT is realized, using the RM model, in which an evaluator (**Evaluator**) resides, and each RM is realized as a thread of P-thread library of OSF/1 OS. Note that the RM used in PaiLisp/MT is extended to include several registers and their related commands to handle concurrency constructs.

(3) PaiLisp/MT is organized as Figure 2 (a), and its interpreter is a parallel Scheme interpreter, whose evaluator (**Evaluator**) resides in each RM. The **Evaluator** consists of five modules as shown in Figure 2 (b).

(4) In the **Evaluator** of PaiLisp/MT three parallel evaluation strategies are implemented in the **parallel construct** module to support the ETC, SHE and LTC strategies. Note that the LTC submodule is applicable only to an expression annotated by **future**.

(5) The SST (Stealable Stack) is introduced to implement and support the SHE strategy; that is, the SST is equipped into each RM as shown in Figure 2 (a).

(6) The PaiLisp/MT compiler is designed to be a compiler linked to the PaiLisp interpreter to support its run-time routine; that is, compiled codes of a PaiLisp program are executed, linking to the PaiLisp/MT interpreter.

(7) The PaiLisp compiler translates a PaiLisp program into a RM program, which will be eventually translated into the corresponding C program for evalation.

(8) Parallel evaluation strategies equipped in PaiLisp/MT are ETC and SHE, and in addition the LTC (Lazy Task Creation) strategy is realized for the **future** construct to compare the SHE-based **future** and the LTC-based **future**.

3.1   Register Machine Model and Behaviors of PaiLisp/MT

Each RM is an extended version of the Abelson-Sussman Register Machine[1], consisting of registers, stacks and an evaluator, as shown in Figure 2. In addition to the val, fun, env, argl, cont, exp and unev registers, two registers for the compiler are introduced; the process register, which is an internal register to keep record of the current process-id, and the argcount register to record the number of argument expressions. The environment in each RM will be updated in *deep-binding*. The set of RM commands is given in Appendix; they are extended from that of Abelson-Sussman's RM model so as to accommodate PaiLisp's facilities in compilation.

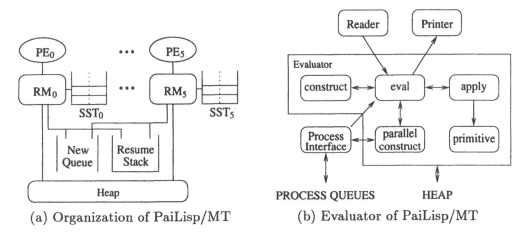

(a) Organization of PaiLisp/MT   (b) Evaluator of PaiLisp/MT

Figure 2: Organization of PaiLisp/MT

Under the ETC strategy the PaiLisp/MT interpreter works as follows. Six RMs will be executed in parallel, running each RM on the corresponding processing element (PE). When an expression containing a concurrency construct is evaluated new concurrent processes will be created. The newly created processes will be stored into the New Queue. If an idle processor is available a process in the New Queue will be executed. When a suspended process is resumed for execution, it will be stored into the Resume Stack. An idle RM checks the Resume Stack, and if there is any PaiLisp process the RM gets a process from the Resume Stack for evaluation. If there is no process in the Resume Stack then the RM checks the content of the New Queue, and if there exist any PaiLisp processes the RM gets a process from the New Queue for evaluation. The RMs share a heap area for their evaluation. In the case of the SHE strategy the SST will be used instead of the New Queue in process creation, as is explained below.

The PaiLisp/MT compiler translates a source PaiLisp program into the corresponding RM program, which will be translated into the C program. The compiled object code of the resultant C program will be executed under the run-time routines equipped to the PaiLisp/MT interpreter. The run-time routines consist of the codes for primitive functions, function application, process management and code-loading.

3.2   Evaluator of the PaiLisp/MT interpreter

The **Evaluator** that resides in each RM is a Scheme interpreter, consisting of five modules; **eval**, **apply**, **primitive**, **construct**, and **parallel construct**. Note that the **parallel construct** module consists of three modules, the ETC, SHE and LTC modules to realize parallel evaluation of PaiLisp expressions. Among six RMs there is one RM, called the *Master Processor*, equipped with **Reader** and **Printer**. Other processors, called the *Slave Processor*, are those obtained from the *Master Processor*, removing **Reader** and **Printer**.

The PaiLisp/MT interpreter is realized as a system with multiple evaluation strategies; the sequential evaluation, ETC and SHE. Similarly, the PaiLisp/MT compiler is realized as a system with the multiple evaluation strategies.

4   The Steal-Help Evaluation Strategy and Its Implementation in the PaiLisp/MT Interpreter

The Steal-Help Evaluation (SHE) strategy[15, 16] is an efficient parallel evaluation strategy that can suppress excessive process creation. In the SHE strategy a processor called the home processor starts evaluating a parallel expression in a sequential evaluation mode, obtaining an expression from the top of the Stealable Stack (SST), while an idle processor steals and evaluates an expression, obtaining it from the bottom of the SST. The SHE strategy for (**pcall** f $e_1 \cdots e_n$) works as follows.

A processor called the home processor that invoked (**pcall** f $e_1 \cdots e_n$) starts evaluating e_1, and after evaluating e_1 the home processor proceeds to evaluating an expression obtaining a pair of an expression and its shared object from the top of the SST sequentially, while an idle processor called the helper steals a pair of an expression and its shared object from the bottom of the SST, and the stolen expression will be evaluated under the environment contained in the shared object. Note that when a parallel expression like (**pcall** f $e_1 \cdots e_n$) is nested in anothor parallel expression it may be stolen by an idle processor, which will become a home processor of the stolen expression.

The SHE strategy for a parallel expression consists of the sequential evaluation mode and the steal-help evaluation mode[15, 16]. Before explaining these two modes we explain about the stealable stack and the shared object, required in correct implementation of the SHE strategy.

Stealable Stack

The *Stealable Stack* (SST, for short) with the pointers *top* and *bottom* is equipped in each RM, and a slot of the SST is formed from a pointer to an expression and a pointer to a shared object. An idle processor (a helper) will obtain a pair of an expression and a shared object from the bottom of the SST of the home processor. The helper's action of obtaining the pair is called a stealing action.

Shared Object

A *shared object* (SO, for short) is necessary for correct evaluation of an expression stolen from the SST by a helper. A shared object is formed from (a pointer to) the environment, together the name of the current concurrency construct, the name of the process that invoked the current parallel expression, the counter of counting the number of unevaluated expressions, and a mutex variable of a thread for exclusive access to the counter.

4.1 SHE-based Implementation of pcall

The SHE strategy consists of two evaluation modes, the sequential evaluation mode and the steal-help evaluation mode. We explain here how the SHE strategy for **pcall** is implemented in the PaiLisp/MT interpreter.

(1) Sequential evaluation mode for (pcall f e_1 $\cdots$ e_n)

When RM_i encounters (**pcall** f e_1 $\cdots$ e_n) for evaluation, the RM_i becomes the home processor for this **pcall** expression, and its evaluation is performed in the sequential evaluation mode as follows.

1: create a shared object SO;
2: store the expressions $e_2, \cdots, e_n$ together with their shared object SO into the SST_i in the order of placing $(e_n$. SO) at the bottom towards $(e_2$. SO) at the top;
3: evaluate e_1 with the SO on the home processor, and store the resultant value into the first place of the arg list;
4: counter := counter $-$ 1;
5: while (counter > 0)
6:     if (SST_i is not empty)
7:     then get an argument expression from the SST_i pointed by top_i;
           evaluate it;
           save the resultant value into the corresponding arg list;
           counter := counter $-$ 1;
8:     else wait until completion of handling all the argument expressions;
9: evaluate f, and apply its resultant value to the values of the argument expressions stored in the arg list;
10: return the resultant value to the val register of RM_i.

(2) Steal-help evaluation mode for (pcall f e_1 $\cdots$ e_n)

A processor RM_j would become idle after completion of evaluating expressions, and also it would become idle by suspension of evaluation. Such an idle processor RM_j can perform the following actions in evaluating an expression.

(a) if there exist any processes in the Resume Stack (RS) then a process in the RS is evaluated on the RM_j until no process becomes available from the RS; otherwise, the following *steal-help* evaluation mode is performed.

(b) the idle processor RM_j will find a processor RM_i whose SST_i is not empty, and the RM_j performs the following actions in the steal-help evaluation mode for the SST_i.

1: RM_j will steal an expression and its shared object SO from the SST_i in RM_i;

2: RM_j creates the process object for evaluating the expression stolen from SST_i;

3: RM_j will evaluate the stolen expression, and the resultant value will be saved into the corresponding place of the arg list in the RM_i;

4: counter := counter − 1;

5: if (counter = 0)

6: then resume the evaluation on RM_i;

7: terminate the process of evaluating the stolen expression;

The SST and its pointer organization is shown in Figure 3. The scheduling strategy in stealing an expression from the RMs is the one like Round-Robin scheduling, designed so as to reduce access competition among the RMs.

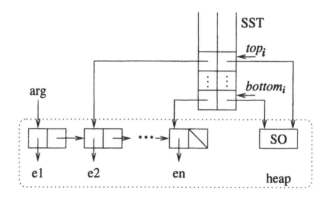

Figure 3: SST and its pointer organization

4.2   On SHE-based implementations of other concurrency constructs

Other PaiLisp concurrency constructs can be implemented, following the method explained in the references 6) and 7), but some implementational considerations must be taken into account as in the case of **pcall**. In this paragraph we give only some short comments on such implementations.

(1) par and pbegin

These constructs can be easily implemented by modifying the SHE-based implementation of **pcall**. Their implementations are slightly simpler than that of **pcall**, since there is no need of implementing function application.

(2) plet and pletrec

Note that local bindings in these constructs are performed sequentially, because the cost of local binding is much smaller than the cost of a stealing action, which is the cost of process creation in the ETC strategy. See below for the cost in the PaiLisp/MT interpreter.

(3) par-and, par-or and pif

The argument expressions in these concurrency constructs are evaluated in parallel. In the case of the **par-and** expression, when the value of one of the argument expressions becomes *false*, the value of the entire expression will become *false*, and the rest of computation at the point is killed by a **kill** signal sent from the RM which evaluated the corresponding argument expression. An actual *killing* action is realized by sending/receiving a **kill** signal. The similar arguments hold for the **par-or** expression, replacing *false* into *true*. The costs of sending and receiving a **kill** signal are 11 [μsec] and 16 [μsec], respectively, in the PaiLisp/MT interpreter. **pif** is a parallelization of **if** that the argument expressions e_1, e_2, e_3 are evaluated in parallel; they are evaluated as if (**pbegin** e_1 e_2 e_3) is evaluated in the SHE strategy with the following modification. e_2 and e_3 are stored into the SST_i of RM_i together with their shared object SO, and then the RM_i starts evaluating the expression e_1. If the value of e_1 is *false* then the following actions are taken. If the values of e_2 and e_3 are obtained then the value of e_3 is returned else if e_2 is stolen and evaluated by an idle processor then a **kill** signal is sent to the processor of evaluating e_2. After evaluating e_3 its resultant value is returned as the value of the **pif** expression. If the value of e_1 is not *false* then the similar actions are taken for the expressions e_2 and e_3.

(4) On other PaiLisp concurrency constructs

Other PaiLisp concurrency constructs are also realized. **pcond** and **pcond#** are implemented in a similar manner with **pif** and **par-and**. Following the SHE-based implementation strategy of **future** given in the reference 7), the SHE-based **future** is realized in the PaiLisp/MT interpreter. **call/pcc** and **call/pep** are the extensions of the sequential **call/cc** and **call/ep** to support $\mathcal{P}$-continuation, and they are implemented in the manner explained in the reference 9) and 10).

4.3   Experimental Results of the PaiLisp/MT Interpreter

The PaiLisp/MT interpreter is a parallel Scheme system equipped with multiple evaluation strategies (ETC, SHE, LTC, Sequential Evaluation), implemented on a DEC7000 system with six Alpha Processors under OSF/1 OS. In this section we give some basic costs in the evaluation strategies implemented in the PaiLisp/MT interpreter, and then we give some results of running several programs on the PaiLisp/MT interpreter.

4.3.1   Basic costs in the PaiLisp/MT interpreter

- The cost of a Scheme primitive (a constant, a variable, and a quote expression) is smaller than 2 [μsec].

- The cost of applying a primitive Scheme function (like **cons**, **car**, **cdr**, $+$, $-$, $=$, **null?**, **eq?**, etc.) is about 5 [μsec].

- The cost of binding a value to a variable is about 2 [μsec], and the cost of forming a lambda closure is about 2.2 [μsec].

- The cost of function application is about 5 [μsec].

- The cost of creating a shared object is 9 [μsec].

- The cost of stealing a pair of an expression and its shared object from SST is 70 [μsec], while the cost of process creation in the ETC strategy is 60 [μsec].

- The cost of exclusive access to SST by the home processor is 11 [μsec], and the costs that a helper accesses to the Resume Stack and to the SST of the home processor are about 4 [μsec].

- The cost of sending a **kill** signal is about 11 [μsec], and the cost of receiving a **kill** signal is about 16 [μsec].

- The cost of creating a future-value is 15 [μsec], and the cost of the **force** operation to obtain an actual value for a future-value is about 14 [μsec].

4.3.2   Running several programs on the PaiLisp/MT interpreter

The following programs[1] were used for an experimental evaluation of the PaiLisp/MT interpreter.

Fibonacci	(fib n), (pfib n), (ffib1 n), (ffib2 n), (ffib3 n)
Tarai	(tarai x y z), (ptarai x y z), (ftarai100 x y z), (ftarai010 x y z), (ftarai001 x y z), (ftarai110 x y z), (ftarai101 x y z), (ftarai011 x y z), (ftarai111 x y z)
Merge sort	(msort d), (pmsort d), (fmsort d)
N Queen	(queen 8), (pqueen 8), (fqueen 8)

Figure 4 shows the results of running these programs on the PaiLisp/MT interpreter, using six processors in the SEQ, ETC, SHE and LTC strategies, where SEQ means *Sequential Evaluation*. In the above benchmark programs **fib**, **tarai**, **msort** and **queen** are sequential programs of evaluating the Fibonacci function, the tarai function, the merge sorting of data and the N Queen problem, respectively. **pfib**, **ptarai**, **pmsort** and **pqueen** are their parallelized versions, using the **pcall** construct,

---

[1]These programs are available by anonymous ftp through
    ftp://ftp.ito.ecei.tohoku.ac.jp/pub/pailisp/benchmarks.tar.gz

while **ffib***i*, **ftarai***ijk*, **fmsort** and **fqueen** are their parallelized versions, using the **future** construct. Note that the suffices in **ffib***i* and **ftarai***ijk* indicate the places where **future** is inserted.

From the results of Figure 4 we can observe the following:

- The SHE strategy always runs faster than the ETC strategy.

- The LTC strategy sometimes runs slower than the ETC strategy, and the effectiveness of the LTC strategy depends upon the places where **future** is inserted for parallelization.

- The SHE strategy sometimes runs slower than the LTC strategy, although their differences are small. But the SHE strategy for a program runs faster and more stable than the LTC strategy for the corresponding program.

Thus, we would be able to say that the SHE strategy is a more stable and sound parallel evaluation strategy than the ETC and LTC strategies.

5 PaiLisp/MT Compiler

The PaiLisp/MT compiler is a compiler of translating a PaiLisp program into a RM program, and the resultant RM program is translated into the C language program. Then the resultant C program is executed under the PaiLisp/MT interpreter. The input/output routines, the heap area and the garbage collector of the PaiLisp/MT interpreter is commonly used in the compiler. The PaiLisp/MT compiler consists of two parts:

(1) Compiler for Scheme expressions.

(2) Compiler for PaiLisp concurrency constructs.

Compiled codes are dynamically linked under the interpreter. Separate compiling of procedures is possible, even if they mutually invoke and reference each other, and also compiled procedures and interpreted procedures can invoke and reference each other. Note that for PaiLisp concurrency constructs two code generation rules based on the ETC and SHE strategies are available.

On implementing call/cc and call/ep

Besides the above considerations we have to consider how to implement *continuations*. In case of Scheme it is enough to support *sequential continuation*, captured by **call/cc**. However, in implementations of PaiLisp we have to consider two aspects in supporting *continuations*. One is in introducing **call/pcc** to support $\mathcal{P}$-continuation, which is an extension of Scheme continuation ($\mathcal{S}$-continuation) into concurrency. Another is a restricted version of **call/cc**, written as **call/ep**, to support only a single-use continuation, and similarly a restricted version of **call/pcc**, written as **call/pep**,

program	SEQ [sec]	ETC [sec]	SHE [sec]	LTC [sec]
(fib 20)	0.655 (0)	–	–	–
(pfib 20)	–	0.767 (21890)	0.167 (50)	–
(ffib1 20)	–	0.519 (10945)	0.187 (51)	0.162 (66)
(ffib2 20)	–	2.011 (10945)	1.121 (531)	1.867 (10945)
(ffib3 20)	–	0.922 (21890)	0.251 (92)	0.210 (173)
(tarai 8 4 0)	0.424 (0)	–	–	–
(ptarai 8 4 0)	–	0.321 (9453)	0.097 (140)	–
(ftarai100 8 4 0)	–	0.231 (3151)	0.152 (137)	0.143 (84)
(ftarai010 8 4 0)	–	0.822 (3151)	0.829 (3151)	0.860 (3151)
(ftarai001 8 4 0)	–	0.003 (73)	0.003 (22)	0.034 (32)
(ftarai110 8 4 0)	–	0.353 (6302)	0.197 (190)	0.191 (156)
(ftarai101 8 4 0)	–	0.078 (246)	0.004 (7)	0.094 (74)
(ftarai011 8 4 0)	–	0.352 (4323)	0.004 (22)	0.063 (59)
(ftarai111 8 4 0)	–	0.151 (2910)	0.004 (30)	0.312 (60)
(queen 8)	2.144 (0)	–	–	–
(pqueen 8)	–	0.613 (11016)	0.389 (194)	–
(fqueen 8)	–	0.522 (5508)	0.411 (75)	0.394 (191)
(msort d)	0.535 (0)	–	–	–
(pmsort d)	–	0.182 (1000)	0.148 (17)	–
(fmsort d)	–	0.166 (500)	0.149 (18)	0.158 (22)

Figure 4: Results of running several benchmark programs on the PaiLisp/MT interpreter

to support a single-use $\mathcal{P}$-continuation[8, 10]. There are a number of strategies of implementing *continuations*[2]. The stack strategy is a commnonly-used technique of implementing continuations, and it is efficient for a program which does not contain any **call/cc** construct. However, **call/cc** implemented in the stack strategy is slow and heavy, since it requires the actions of copying contents of the control stack in capturing and throwing continuations. **call/ep** and **call/pep** are introduced, since **call/cc** and **call/pcc** are usually used in a single-use style of continuations in practical programs. They can be efficiently implemented only in handling tag-objects stored in the control stack without copying contents of the stack[10, 11]. Note that the stack/heap strategy[2] is efficient in implementing **call/cc** and **call/pcc**, since it does not require copying contents of the stack in throwing continuations. But it is not applicable in implementing **call/ep** and **call/pep**, because the tag information will be sometimes lost under the stack/heap strategy.

5.1 Compiler for Scheme Expressions

A Scheme compiler is implemented, slightly extending the Abelson-Sussman's compiler[1]. Let $C[E,\texttt{ctenv},\texttt{cont}]$ be the compiler of a Scheme expression E to generate the corresponding RM code program under **ctenv** and **cont**, where **ctenv** means the *compile-time-environment*, and **cont** is a keyword to be used during compilation. **cont** will be one of **return**, **next** and **LABEL**, as explained below. The compilation rules for major Scheme constructs can be given as follows.

(1) Compilation rules for quote and a constant

```
C[(quote number), ctenv, any] ==> C[number, ctenv, any]
C[(quote boolean), ctenv, any] ==> C[boolean, ctenv, any]
C[(quote TextOfQuotation), ctenv, return]
                      ==>  (assign val 'TextOfQuotation)
                           (restore cont)
                           (goto cont)
C[(quote TextOfQuotation), ctenv, next]
                      ==>  (assign val 'TextOfQuotation)
C[(quote TextOfQuotation), ctenv, LABEL]
                      ==>  (assign val 'TextOfQuotation)
                           (goto LABEL)
```

Remark: return, next, LABEL, and any

1. **return** means that after evaluating E the **cont** is restored, and then the evaluation is resumed at the point of the **cont**.

2. **next** means that there is some other expressions that is evaluated under the same environment.

3. **LABEL** means that after evaluating E the evaluation moves to the point denoted by the label **LABEL**.

4. **any** means any of **return**, **next** and **LABEL**.

Note that the compilation rules for a constant can be given similarly, replacing *TextOfQuotation* to (*identifier const*), where the *identifier* is **number** if *const* is a number, and it is **boolean** if *const* is a boolean value.

(2) Compilation rules for a variable

The rules for a global variable *var* which does not exist in **ctenv** are as follows.

```
C[var, ctenv, return]   ==> (assign val (lookup-variable-value 'var env)
                             (restore cont)
                             (goto cont)
C[var, ctenv, next]     ==> (assign val (lookup-variable-value 'var env))
C[var, ctenv, LABEL]    ==> (assign val (lookup-variable-value 'var env))
                             (goto LABEL)
```

The rules for a local variable *var* in **ctenv** can be given, replacing (**lookup-variable-value** *var* **env**) to (**lexical-address-lookup env** m n) in the above rules for a global variable, where m and n are the frame location and the value location in the environmnt, respectively.

(3) Compilation rules for function application (f e_1 $\cdots$ e_n)

We give the compilation rules that the argument expressions $e_1, \cdots, e_n$ are evaluated in the *left-to-right* rule and then f is evaluated. In the PaiLisp/MT interpreter the **apply-dispatch** is used in function application, but it is modified for the compiler so as to push argument expressions into the stack. We use **cp-apply-dispatch**, modifying **apply-dispatch**. Using **cp-apply-dispatch** we can give the compilation rules for function application as follows.

```
C[(f e1 ··· en), ctenv, return]
              ==> <(save env)> C[e1, ctenv, next] <(restore env)>
                  (save val)

                  <(save env)> C[en, ctenv, next] <(restore env)>
                  (save val)
                  C[f, ctenv, next]
                  (assign fun val)
                  (assign argcount (number n))
                  (goto cp-apply-dispatch)
C[(f e1 ··· en), ctenv, next] ==> (assign cont NEWLABEL)
                                  (save cont)
                                  C[(f e1 ··· en), ctenv, return]
                              NEWLABEL
C[(f e1 ··· en), ctenv, LABEL] ==> (assign cont LABEL)
                                   (save cont)
                                   C[(f e1 ··· en), ctenv, return]
```

where **NEWLABEL** is a newly-created label at the point of function application.
Remark: Note that <(**save env**)> C[e_j, **ctenv**, **next**] <(**restore env**)> means the following:

1. the **save** and **restore** commands will be inserted, if the expression e_j is an expression which destroys (or alters) the environment and if the succeeding evaluation requires the new environment destroyed by evaluating e_j.

2. otherwise, they are not used. This check on side-effects to the environment must be installed into the compiler.

The primitive functions in Scheme can be directly and efficiently treated by the command (**primitive** p n), reducing a considerable overhead incurred using **cp-apply-dispatch**. The compilation rules for a primitive function *prim* with n-ary arguments can be given as follows, assuming that *prim* is not a function of destroying an environment.

$C[(prim\ e_1\ \cdots\ e_n)$, ctenv, return] ==> $C[(prim\ e_1\ \cdots\ e_n)$, ctenv, next]
(restore cont)
(goto cont)

$C[(prim\ e_1\ \cdots\ e_n)$, ctenv, next]
    ==> <(save env)> $C[e_1$, ctenv, next] <(restore env)>
        (save val)
        . . . . . .
        <(save env)> $C[e_n$, ctenv, next] <(restore env)>
        (save val)
        (assign val (primitive *prim* n))

$C[(prim\ e_1\ \cdots\ e_n)$, ctenv, LABEL] ==> $C[(prim\ e_1\ \cdots\ e_n)$, ctenv, next]
        (goto LABEL)

When *prim* is a primitive function with a single argument, the second rule above may be replaced by the following rule that the result of evaluating the argument is saved into the register.

$C[(prim\ e)$, ctenv, next] ==> <(save env)> $C[e$, ctenv, next] <(restore env)>
        (assign val (primitive *prim* val))

But any primitive function of destroying an environment should be handled by the compilation rules for function application, using **cp-apply-dispatch**, mentioned above.

(4) Compilation rules for define and begin

define will be used to define a function globally or locally. We assume that the function definition is written in a lambda form, but if it is not in a lambda form it is transformed into the lambda form as follows.

(**define** ($f\ x_1\ \cdots\ x_n$) *body*) ==> (**define** f (**lambda** ($x_1\ \cdots\ x_n$) *body*))

The compilation rules for a global definition are as follows.

$C[(\text{define}\ f\ e)$,ctenv,return] ==> $C[(\text{define}\ f\ e)$,ctenv,next]
        (restore cont)
        (goto cont)
$C[(\text{define}\ f\ e)$,ctenv,next]

```
                    ==> <(save env)> C[e,ctenv,next] <(restore env)>
                        (perform (define-variable 'f val env))
                        (assign val 'f)
C[(define f e),ctenv,LABEL] ==> C[(define f e),ctenv,next]
                        (goto LABEL)
```

When **define** is used to define a function locally and internally within a **begin** expression, its definition is transformed into a form with correct local bindings, using **let**, and then the definition body is bound to the local variable, using **set!**, in the following way.

```
(begin (define x expl)...)
                ==> (begin (let ((x 'dummy)...) (set! x expl)...)
```

After this transformation the compilation rule for **begin** will be applied.

$$C[(\text{begin } e_1 \cdots e_n),\text{ctenv,any}] ==> C[(\text{begin-2 Dtrans}[e_1 \cdots e_n]),\text{ctenv,any}]$$

where $\text{Dtrans}[e_1 \cdots e_n]$ is the result obtained by transforming the expressions $e_1 \cdots e_n$ in the **begin** expression, applying the above kind of transformation for local function definitions.

```
C[(begin-2 E₁ ··· Eₘ),ctenv,any]
        ==> <(save env)> C[E₁,ctenv,next] <(restore env)>
            ......
            <(save env)> C[Eₘ₋₁,ctenv,next] <(restore env)>
            C[Eₘ,ctenv,any]
```

(5) Compilation rules for lambda and let

The compilation rules for a lambda form consist of the codes for a closure object and the codes for the lambda-body. A lambda closure will be formed from the current environment, the label to the compiled codes of the lambda-body, the number of argumemts, and a flag to indicate if an argument is a dotted list or not. Note that the compilation of the lambda-body must be done, using an environment extended with variables in the lambda-bindings.

```
C[(lambda (x₁ ··· xₙ) e₁ ··· eₘ), ctenv, return]
        ==> (assign val (make-compiled-procedure NEWLABEL1 n flag env))
            (restore cont)
            (goto cont)
            NEWLABEL1
            (assign env (compiled-procedure-env fun))
            (assign env (extend-binding-environment '(x₁ ··· xₙ) env))
            C[(begin e₁ ··· eₘ), (cons '(x₁ ··· xₙ) ctenv), return]
```

where (cons '$(x_1 \cdots x_n)$ ctenv) is the environment extended from **ctenv**. If the third argument in $C[*, *, *]$ is **next** or **LABEL**, the compilation rules can be give from the above, replacing

```
(restore cont)
(goto cont)
```

into (goto NEWLABEL2) for **next** and (goto LABEL) for LABEL, respectively.

The compilation rules for **let** and **letrec** can be given as follows.

C[(let $(((x_1\ e_1)\ \cdots\ (x_n\ e_n)))\ E_1\ \cdots\ E_m)$,ctenv,any]
$\quad$ ==> <(save env)> C[e_1,ctenv,next] <(restore env)>
$\qquad$ (save val)
$\qquad \cdots\cdots\cdots$
$\qquad$ <(save env)> C[e_n, ctenv, next] <(restore env)>
$\qquad$ (save val)
$\qquad$ (assign env (extend-binding-environment '(x1 ... xn) env))
$\qquad$ C[(begin E1 ... Em),(cons '(x1 ... xn) ctenv),any]
C[(letrec $(((x_1\ e_1)\ \cdots\ (x_n\ e_n)))\ E_1\ \cdots\ E_m)$,ctenv,any]
$\quad$ ==> C[(let ((x1 'dummy) ... (xn 'dummy))
$\qquad$ (set! x1 e1) ... (set! xn en) E1 ... Em), ctenv, any]

(6) Compilation of other Scheme expressions

(**set!** $x\ v$) will be compiled as follows, when x is a global variable.

C[(set! $x\ v$), ctenv, return] ==> C[(set! $x\ v$), ctenv, next]
$\qquad$ (restore cont)
$\qquad$ (goto cont)
C[(set! $x\ v$), ctenv, next]
$\quad$ ==> <(save env)> C[v, ctenv, next] <(restore env)>
$\qquad$ (perform (set-variable-value 'x val env))
C[(set! $x\ v$), ctenv, LABEL] ==> C[(set! $x\ v$), ctenv, next]
$\qquad$ (goto LABEL)

When the variable x in (**set!** $x\ v$) is a local variable, the second rule should be as follows.

C[(set! $x\ v$),ctenv,next] ==> <(save env)> C[v, ctenv, next] <(restore env)>
$\qquad$ (perform (lexical-address-set env m n val))

The compilation rules for other Scheme constructs can be given in a similar fashion, taking into account their meanings.

5.2 Compiler for PaiLisp Concurrency Constructs

In this section we give the compilation rules for the PaiLisp concurrency constructs.

5.2.1 Compilation rules for spawn, suspend and exlambda

(**spawn** e) is realized in the way that a label of initiating execution of the expression e and its environment is entered into the process queue.

C[(spawn e), ctenv, return] ==> C[(spawn e), ctenv, next]
$\qquad$ (restore cont)
$\qquad$ (goto cont)
C[(spawn e), ctenv, next] ==> (goto NEWLABEL1)
$\qquad$ NEWLABEL2
$\qquad$ C[e, ctenv, terminate-process]
$\qquad$ NEWLABEL1
$\qquad$ (assign cont NEWLABEL2)
$\qquad$ (save cont)
$\qquad$ (parallel alloc-spawn-process 1)
C[(spawn e), ctenv, LABEL] ==> C[(spawn e), ctenv, next]
$\qquad$ (goto LABEL)

(**suspend**) is realized by the extended RM command **parallel suspend** as follows.

```
C[(suspend), ctenv, any] ==> (parallel suspend)
```

exlambda is similar to **lambda** except creating an exclusive closure, and it is realized using `make-cpl-exclusive-procedure` for `make-compiled-procedure` in the compiled codes of **lambda**, and `cp-ex-apply-end` will be used to unlock the queue for the place of **return** in the compiled codes of **lambda**. For example,

```
C[(exlambda (x1 ... xn) e1 ... em), ctenv, return]
        ==> (assign val (make-cpl-exclusive-procedure NEWLABEL1 n flag env))
            (restore cont)
            (goto cont)
          NEWLABEL1
            (assign env (compiled-procedure-env fun))
            (assign env (extend-binding-environment '(x1 ... xn) env))
            C[(begin e1 ... em),(cons '(x1 ... xn) ctenv),cp-ex-apply-end]
```

5.2.2   Compilation Rules for pcall

There are two compilation strategies for **pcall**, depending upon use of the ETC strategy and the SHE strategy.

[1] ETC-based compilation of (pcall f $e_1 \cdots e_n$)

We consider the following cases:

(1) f is a user-defined function.

(2) f is a primitive function.

Assuming that `alloc-pcall-process` is a command to enter a process into the process queue and `determine-pcall` is a synchronization command for **pcall**, the compilation rules of (**pcall** f $e_1 \cdots e_n$) can be given as follows.

(1) f is a user-defined function.

```
C[(pcall f e1 ... en),ctenv,return]
        ==> (goto NEWLABEL0)
          NEWLABEL1
            C[en,(cons '() ctenv),determine-pcall]
              ....
          NEWLABELn
            C[e1,(cons '() ctenv),determine-pcall]
          NEWLABEL0
            (save env)
            (assign cont NEWLABELa)
            (save cont)
            (assign cont NEWLABELn)
            (save cont)
              ....
            (assign cont NEWLABEL1)
            (save cont)
            (parallel alloc-pcall-process n)
```

```
                    (parallel suspend)
                  NEWLABELa
                    C[f,ctenv,next]
                    (assign argcount (number n))
                    (goto cp-apply-dispatch)
   C[(pcall f e1 ... en),ctenv,next]
          ==> (assign cont NEWLABELb)
                    (save cont)
                    C[(pcall f e1 ... en),ctenv,return]
                  NEWLABELb
   C[(pcall f e1 ... en),ctenv,LABEL]
          ==> (assign cont LABEL)
                    (save cont)
                    C[(pcall f e1 ... en),ctenv,return]
```

(2) f is a primitive function.

When f is a primitive function *prim* it is possible to give the following compilation rules to create better codes than the above (1).

```
   C[(pcall prim e1 ... en),ctenv,return]
          ==> C[(pcall prim e1 ... en), ctenv, next]
                    (restore cont)
                    (goto cont)
   C[(pcall prim e1 ... en),ctenv,next]
          ==> (goto NEWLABEL0)
                  NEWLABEL1
                    C[en,(cons '() ctenv),determine-pcall]
                    . . . . . . . . .
                  NEWLABELn
                    C[e1,(cons '() ctenv),determine-pcall]
                  NEWLABEL0
                    (save env)
                    (assign cont NEWLABELa)
                    (save cont)
                    (assign cont NEWLABEL1)
                    (save cont)
                    . . . . . .
                    (assign cont NEWLABELn)
                    (save cont)
                    (parallel alloc-pcall-process n)
                    (parallel suspend)
                  NEWLABELa
                    (assign val (primitive prim n))
   C[(pcall prim e1 ... en),ctenv,LABEL]
          ==> C[(pcall prim e1 ... en),ctenv,next]
                    (goto LABEL)
```

[2] SHE-based compilation of (pcall f $e_1 \cdots e_n$)

We assume that `determine-pcall-she` is an run-time routine of initiating the SHE-based evaluation of the next argument expression after checking the value of the counter of counting the number of argument expressions, and `alloc-she-pcall-process` is a RM command of pushing NEWLABELn-1, $\cdots$, NEWLABEL1 into the SST. Using these RM commands we can give the following compilation rules for SHE-based evaluation of (**pcall** f $e_1 \cdots e_n$).

(1) f is a user-defined function.

```
C[(pcall f e1 ... en),ctenv,return]
            ==> (goto NEWLABEL0)
                NEWLABEL1
                  C[e2,(cons '() ctenv),determine-pcall-she]
                    ....
                NEWLABELn-1
                  C[en,(cons '() ctenv),determine-pcall-she]
                NEWLABEL0
                  (save env)
                  (assign cont NEWLABELa)
                  (save cont)
                  (assign cont NEWLABEL1)
                  (save cont)
                    ....
                  (assign cont NEWLABELn-1)
                  (save cont)
                  (parallel alloc-she-pcall-process n-1)
                  C[e1,ctenv,determine-pcall-she]
                NEWLABELa
                  C[f, ctenv, next]
                  (assign argcount (number n))
                  (goto cp-apply-dispatch)
C[(pcall f e1 ... en),ctenv,next]
            ==> (assign cont NEWLABELb)
                (save cont)
                C[(pcall f e1 ... en),ctenv,return]
                NEWLABELb
C[(pcall f e1 ... en),ctenv,LABEL]
            ==> (assign cont LABEL)
                (save cont)
                C[(pcall f e1 ... en),ctenv,return]
```

(2) *f* is a primitive function.

It is possible to give the following rule to generate better object codes, when *f*
is a primitive function *prim*.

```
C[(pcall prim e1 ... en),ctenv,return]
            ==> C[(pcall prim e1 ... en),ctenv,next]
                (restore cont)
                (goto cont)
C[(pcall prim e1 ... en),ctenv,next]
            ==> (goto NEWLABEL0)
                NEWLABEL1
                  C[e2,ctenv,determine-pcall-she]
                    ....
                NEWLABELn-1
                  C[en,ctenv,determine-pcall-she]
                NEWLABEL0
                  (save env)
                  (assign cont NEWLABELa)
                  (save cont)
                  (assign cont NEWLABEL1)
                  (save cont)
                    ....
                  (assign cont NEWLABELn-1)
                  (save cont)
                  (parallel alloc-she-pcall-process n-1)
                  C[e1,ctenv,determine-pcall-she]
                NEWLABELa
                  (assign val (primitive prim n))
C[(pcall prim e1 ... en),ctenv,LABEL]
            ==> C[(pcall prim e1 ... en),ctenv,next]
                (goto LABEL)
```

[3] Compilation of other PaiLisp concurrency constructs

Other PaiLisp concurrency constructs can be compiled by extending and modifying the above compilation strategy for **pcall**, taking into account the ETC and SHE evaluation strategies to reflect their meanings. Note that variable-bindings in the **lambda** form and the **let** and **letrec** expressions will done sequentially as in the PaiLisp/MT interpreter.

5.3   Transforming RM Programs into C Programs

A PaiLisp program will be compiled into the corresopnding RM program according to the compilation rules explained above. The resultant RM program is transformed to the corresponding C program. The resultant C program is executed, compiling it by the C compiler and linking to the interpreter. Thus a PaiLisp program is compiled and transformed as follows.

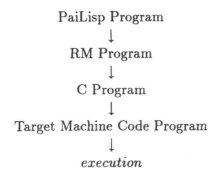

The correspondences between RM commands and their C code routines are given in Appendix. The resultant C program obtained by compiling a PaiLisp program is executed, linking it to the PaiLisp interpreter. For this purpose, a linking primitive **cload** is implemented, using the dynamic linking mechanism of the system. In order to handle compiled codes the following modifications to the interpreter are done for process management.

```
if (oid(fun) == COMPILED) {
    env = cp_env(fun);  pushobj(env);
    p_val(process) = Nil;  jump = cp_entry(fun);
    jump_loop(RM);  goto loop;
} else {
    exp = cl_exp(fun);  env = cl_env(fun);
    p_val(process) = Nil;  jump = eval_dispatch;
    jump_loop(RM);  goto loop;
}
```

The first part handles compiled processes, and the second part is for execution in the interpreter. **cp_apply_dispatch** must be prepared for function application in the compiler, and **apply_dispatch** for the interpreter must be modified to allow invocation of compiled codes from a program of the interpreter. Evaluation of an expression in the compilation mode is usually much faster than that of the interpreter, so that it is desirable to tune up the system so as to reduce the overhead in using the interpreter as a run-time system. Some considerations from this standpoint are also taken into the modifications of the interpreter.

5.4   Running several programs on the PaiLisp/MT compiler

Figure 5 shows the results of running several benchmark programs on the PaiLisp/MT compiler, comparing to their executions on the PaiLisp/MT interpreter. The environment for benchmarking is same with the interpreter; that is, a DEC7000 with six Alpha processors under OSF/1 OS is used.

- For a sequential Scheme program the compiled evaluation runs about 5 ~ 6 times faster than the interpreted evaluation.

- The ETC-based compiled evaluation is sometimes slower than the sequential evaluation.

- In the case of the SHE strategy the compiled evaluation runs about 2 ~ 5 times faster than the interpreted evaluation, and the complied evaluation in the SHE strategy is always faster than the compiled evaluation in the sequential compiler.

- The SHE-based compiled evaluation runs 1.5 ~ 4.5 times faster than the ETC-based compiled evaluation.

Programs	Sequential Interpreter [sec]	Sequential Compiler [sec]	ETC-based Compiler [sec]	SHE-based Compiler [sec]	SHE-based interpreter [sec]
(pfib 20)	0.655	0.086	0.307	0.073	0.167
(ptarai 8 4 0)	0.424	0.090	0.195	0.053	0.097
(pqueen 8)	2.473	0.278	0.272	0.090	0.389
(pmsort 11)	0.535	0.063	0.051	0.035	0.148

Figure 5: Results of running several programs on the PaiLisp/MT compiler

6   Conclusion

In this paper we explained how the multi-threaded PaiLisp/MT interpreter and compiler are implemented. The PaiLisp/MT system is a system with multiple evaluation strategies, consisting of the following:

(1) the sequential interpreter and compiler for Scheme programs.

(2) the parallel interpreter and compiler based on the ETC and SHE strategies for PaiLisp concurrency constructs.

The experimental results show that

(1) the SHE-based interpreted evaluation runs faster than the sequential interpreted evaluation and the ETC-based interpreted evaluation.

(2) the SHE-based compiled evaluation runs faster than the sequential compiled evaluation and the ETC-based compiled evaluation.

(3) the SHE-based compiled evaluation runs $2 \sim 5$ times faster than the SHE-based interpreted evaluation.

The current PaiLisp/MT compiler is a simple compiler easy to implement, since it uses the Register Machine model and the interpreter is used as its run-time routine of compiled codes. However, for implementation of a more efficient complier, it will be bettter to realize a stack-based compiler with an efficient run-time routine in running compiled codes.

Bibliography

1) Abelson, H. and Sussman, G.: *Structure and Interpretation of Computer Programs*, MIT Press (1985).

2) Clinger, W. D., Hartheimer, A. H. and Ost, E. M.: Implementation Strategies for Continuations, *ACM Conference on Lisp and Functional Programming*, pp.124-131 (1988).

3) Halstead, Jr., R.: Multilisp: A Language for Concurrent Symbolic Computation, *ACM Trans. on Programming Languages and Systems*, Vol.4, No.7, pp.501-538 (1985).

4) Halstead, Jr., R.: New Ideas in Parallel Lisp: Language Design, Implementation, and Programming Tools, *Lecture Notes in Computer Science*, Vol.441, pp.2-57, Springer (1990).

5) IEEE Computer Society: *IEEE Standard for the Scheme Programming Language* (1991).

6) Ito, T.: Efficient Evaluation Strategies for Structured Concurrency Constructs in Parallel Scheme Systems, *Lecture Notes in Computer Science*, Vol.1068, pp.22-52, Springer (1995).

7) Ito, T.: An Efficient Evaluation Strategy for Concurrency Constructs in Parallel Scheme Systems, *this volume*.

8) Ito, T. and Matsui, M.: A Parallel Lisp Language PaiLisp and Its Kernel Specification, *Lecture Notes in Computer Science*, Vol.441, pp.58-100, Springer (1990).

9) Ito, T. and Seino, T.: On PaiLisp Continuation and Its Implementation, *Proceedings of ACM Workshop on Continuations (Eds. O. Danvy, C. Talcott)*, pp.73-90 (1992).

10) Ito, T. and Seino, T.: P-Continuation Based Implementation of PaiLisp Interpreter, *Lecture Notes in Computer Science*, Vol.748, pp.108-154, Springer (1993).

[**N.B.**] Alpha is a trademark of Digital Equipment Corporation, and OSF/1 is a trademark of Open Software Foundation.

$$\left[\begin{array}{l} \text{This work was partially supported by Grant-in-Aid for Scientific Research} \\ \text{09245102 under the Ministry of Education, Science and Culture, Japan.} \end{array}\right]$$

APPENDIX: Extended Register Machine Commands

The extended RM commands and the run-time routines are all implemented in the
C language, and their major ones are as follows.

Major RM commands and their corresponding C code routines.

RM command	Meanings and the corresponding C code routines
(**assign** *reg value*)	The value *value* will be assigned into the register *reg* **reg** = *c_value* (where *c_value* is *value* expressed in the C language)
(**perform** *action*)	execute *action* of the RM *c_action* (where *c_action* is *action* expressed in the C language)
(**parallel** *p-action*)	execute a parallel action *p-action* of the RM *p-c_action* (where *p-c_action* is *p-action* expressed in the C language)
(**save** *reg*)	push the content of the register *reg* into the stack **push**(*reg*)
(**restore** *reg*)	pop a value from the stack into the register *reg* **pop**(*reg*)
(**goto** *label*)	jump to the label *label* **go**(*label*)
(**car** *obj*)	return the car part of a cons pair *obj* **car**(*obj*)
(**cdr** *obj*)	return the cdr part of a cons pair *obj* **cdr**(*obj*)
(**cons** *reg obj1 obj2*)	allocate a new cell to the register *reg* and set its car part to *obj1* and its cdr part to *obj2* **cons**(*reg*, *obj1*, *obj2*)
(**number** *int*)	allocate a integer object with the value *int* **make_num_data**(*int*)
'*var*	**create_symbol**("*var*", **strlen**("*var*")) (where *var* is a symbol)
'*list*	**cp_reader**(**RM**, "*list*") (where *list* is a list, a character or a string)
(**primitive** *prim n*)	apply the primitive function *prim* to *n* elements of the stack
(**primitive** *prim reg*)	apply the one argument primitive function *prim* to the register *reg*
(**define-variable** *var reg env*)	The value of *var* in the environment *env* will be replaced by the value of the register *reg* **define_variable**(**RM**,*env*,*c_var*,*reg*)
(**lookup-varaible-value** *var env*)	get the value of the variable *var* from the environment **sym_val**(*c_var*)
(**set-variable-value** *var reg env*)	The value of *var* in the environment *env* will be replaced by the value bound to the register *reg* **set_variable_value**(*c_var*,*val*,*env*)

(lexical-address-lookup *env f n*)	obtain the value at the n-th point in the f-th frame in the environment. lexical_address_lookup(*env*,*f*,*n*)
(lexical-address-set *env f n obj*)	replace the value at the n-th point in the f-th frame in the environment by the value of *obj*. lexical-address-set(*env*,*f*,*n*,*obj*)
(extend-binding-environment $(x_1 \cdots x_n)$ *env*)	create a frame appended to the head of the environment pointed by the *env* register The values of stack will be bound to the variables allocate_env(*env*,*env*); cp_add_binding(*n*)
(extend-binding-environment $(x_1 \cdots x_n \cdot x_{n+1})$ *env*)	allocate_env(*env*,*env*); cp_add_dotlist_binding(*n*)
(make-compiled-procedure *entry n flag env*)	create a compiled function. make_compiled(RM, *entry*, *n*, *m*) (where if $flag = \#f$ then $m = 0$ else $m = 1$)
(compile-procedure-env *clo*)	return the environment of a closure *clo* cp_env(*clo*)
(make-cpl-exclusive-procedure *entry n flag env*)	create a compiled exclusive closure make_ex_compiled(RM, *entry*, *n*, *m*) (where if $flag = \#f$ then $m = 0$ else $m = 1$)
(alloc-promise *entry env*)	create a promise with a label to a compiled program. allocate_cp_promise(*reg*, *entry*, *env*)
(add-spawn-process 1)	get a label from the stack, and enter a process corresponding to the label into the New Queue to initiate its execution add_spawn_process_to_queue(RM, 1)
(add-pcall-process-to-queue *n*)	get n labels from the stack, and enter n processes corresponding to their labels into the New Queue to initiate their executions add_pcall_processes_to_queue(RM, *n*)
(add-she-pcall-process *n*)	get n labels from the stack, and enter n processes corresponding to their lables into the SST to initiate their executions add_she_pcall_processes_to_queue(RM, *n*)

The run-time routines for **spawn, exlambda** and **pcall**.

Routine name	Meaning
terminate_process	terminate the execution of a process created by the **spawn** construct
cp_ex_apply_end	resume the execution of a process waiting for the application of an exclusive closure
determine_pcall	check whether the evaluation of all the arguments expressions of **pcall** construct is completed, and after its completion the execution of the parent process will be resumed

Design and Implementation of a Distributed Lisp and its Evaluation

Toshiharu Ono

Department of Computer Science
Yamanashi University

Haruaki Yamazaki

Department of Computer Science
Yamanashi University

ABSTRACT

To date, a number of parallel Lisp languages on shared-memory multiprocessors(e.g., Qlisp[17], Multilisp[12], mUtilisp[10]) have been proposed and implemented. , However, the current environments for existing Lisp language systems are mostly general purpose workstations(WS's) without shared-memory. We have designed a distributed Lisp system that runs on commonly used environments such as UNIX, X-Window and WS's connected via networks. The implementation of the prototype system has been successful and the performance of the system is promising for future exploration of distributed cooperative processing systems.

1 Introduction

In recent years, distributed organization of computer systems has been more commonly used than that of centralized ones. However, in a centralized system, a job without strict time constraints could be treated as a background job, but so far, in a distributed system, no established nor effective method to treat such a job has been discussed.

The easiest solution for this problem is to organize the system heterogeneously. That is, the jobs which perform time consuming computing or large file operations are executed by dedicated servers in a distributed system. However, in such a heterogeneous system, the load balancing of the processing element has been a new problem.

This paper firstly focuses on this problem and describes an experiment to execute background jobs on a workstation-based distributed system.

Secondly, since parallel execution of a program is possible in a distributed system, the execution times of these background jobs can be dramatically improved compared to single-processor execution. Our experimental results are included also in this paper.

Since the distributed system at our site is already running, which source codes are written in high level language. Therfore, one of the commonly used high level languages is desirable to write algorithms for such background jobs. We adopted, with a few modifications Lisp, since our statistical survey says that most of the jobs, which consume large CPU time and cause unbalanced CPU loads, are written in Lisp in our site. So we have designed a background job description language which is based on Lisp with extra functions added.

So far, research on parallel processing of Lisp programs such as, Multilisp, Qlisp, mUtilisp, PaiLisp, and Concurrent LISP is underway. In this research, the required architecture for the target machines, which execute the program in a parallel manner are tightly coupled multi-processors with shared memory. However, since our research objective is to implement a background job as well as the parallel Lisp processing, our target machine must be more commonly used a loosely coupled distributed system. Our prototype system runs on a typical current organizations of which system components are such as UNIX-workstations, X-windows, ether-net and so on.

The behavior of our prototype system is extremely promising. In this paper,we discuss the design and implementation of the system and also describe the evaluations of the experiments.

2   An overview of Distributed Lisp

The interpreter for our prototype Distributed Lisp system(hereinafter called DLisp) is designed and implemented based on Common Lisp. In addition to the Common Lisp language specification some distributed processing functions have been added. The execution environment for DLisp is a commonly used distributed system such as workstations, local networks or message passing facilities.

The user or the application program in the system firstly selects lightly loaded host workstations, with particular resources such as the initiation software or the data needed to start a job. This host is called 'root host' and the rest of the hosts in the system are called 'remote hosts'. Figure 1 shows the relationship between the root host and the remote hosts.

2.1   Communication Form

To initialize the system, we firstly form a logical network as the subset of a physical network. The configuration of the logical subnetwork is completely independent of the physical topology of the original network. In our prototype system, the configuration of this subnetwork is a ring where each host has two adjacent hosts, which are connected to each other via UNIX stream sockets. This logical ring network is

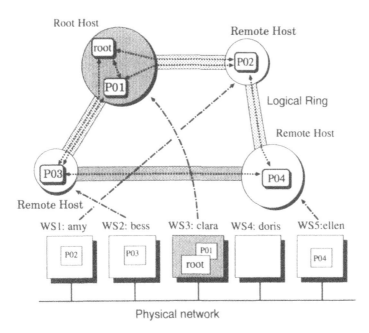

Figure 1: The relation between the logical ring and the physical network

formed statically at system initiation. Although there are a number of configurations for logical subnetworks such as a star, tree, shared bus and loop, we selected the ring configuration after considering such things as system performance, flexibility and the ease of fault detection.

2.2   Process Model

Each DLisp program which is executed sequentially is called a process. Since the system forms a logical ring, each host has two adjacent hosts (provided that the number of hosts in the system is more than two). For convenience, these two adjacent hosts are called the right host and the left host. This does not necessarily mean that these hosts are physically adjacent, but a socket pair exists between the processes of these hosts.

Although any process can dynamically create its adjacent processes on right or left hosts as well as its own (current) host, there is no shared data or program code among them. Each process can communicate with its adjacent processes via its communication channels. To execute the whole distributed Lisp program, the initial Lisp process must be executed first. This Lisp process is called the root process, and must reside in the root host. A Lisp process can dynamically create its successor process in the current, right or left host. Each Lisp process can not kill other Lisp processes, but can quit itself.

Figure 2 shows the initiation of the DLisp program at the root host. The root

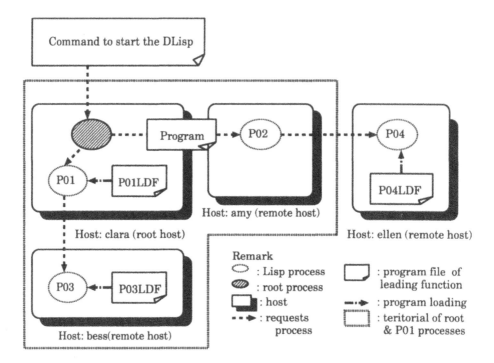

Figure 2: Root process and root host

process is invoked at the root host by the user's command. The root process loads the program from the root host's secondary storage and executes it. The root process creates the process P01 on the current host, and P02, P03 on the adjacent hosts (remote hosts). The process P04 can not be created directly since the host is not an adjacent one. The Lisp processes' scope is only within the current and two adjacent (right and left) hosts.

2.3   Inter-process Communication and Synchronization

DLisp provides the following facilities for communication and synchronization among processes. These facilities are implemented with newly added Lisp functions.

(1) 1 to 1 message passing

This facility establishes a one way stream communication channel between two processes. The initiating process issues SEND command (calls the function SEND) and the receiving process issues RECEIVE. The calling process of the function SEND, may select blocking or nonblocking calls in order to implement both the synchronized and asynchronized communications. But the function RECEIVE always blocks the caller.

(2) ring communication

DLisp provides the facility for location transparent multicast messages. The system creates two ring type communication channels which are implemented with chains of socket pairs, for all hosts at initialization. These rings are called the IN-ring and OUT-ring. The process in an arbitrary host can connect to these rings and can operate on the ring so as to realize process cooperation, load balancing, reliable or atomic multicast etc. Since the messages are passed along by the ring, the ordering of the messages is always maintained. The major operations provided on the ring are as follows:

(a) Obtaining a message from the ring.

The process may read (or if necessary modify) the message from the ring, and forward it.

(b) Transmitting messages to the ring.

The process may transmit its own message to the ring. The process may also add information to the fowarding messages.

2.4   The Distribution of Processes

A process may transmit or receive messages which consists of the functions and/or data defined as S-expressions. A receiving host evaluates these S-expressions so as to obtain the data and to execute the program. This means that the system allows explicit process migrations, since the message may contain the functions for process creation and initialization.

The assignment of the process to the host depends on the application. The typical example for the assignment is to distribute identical procedures to all hosts. In this case, the initiating host sends the messages (S-expression) with its host-id and the procedure definition. If the host receiving this message confirms that the host-ID in the message is not equal to the host-ID of adjacent hosts, then it forwards the message to the ring. The initiating host terminates the message rotation if the host id is equal to its own in order to avoid duplication. Since the system forms a logical ring network, the terminal host acknowledges that message passing is normally completed. Otherwise the host which detects time-out initiates the message rotation which aborts the procedures already sent to the hosts (atomic mulicast).

A logical ring network has several advantages;

(1) Since the ring is formed logically, any host can easily be added or removed from the system.

(2) The programming and debugging can be done within the single host and the program can be distributed to the multiple hosts without any program modifications. That is, a ring can be easily simulated within a single host by means of sending messages to itself.

2.5   Extention to the Lisp Functions

We extend the set of Lisp functions with extra functions in order to support distributed and parallel processing. These functions are based on CSP(Communicating Sequential Processes)[7]. There are 15 added functions. These are briefly described as follows;

Here,{ a | b } denotes the disjunction of two elements a and b.

(create-process *process*   :position { 'current | 'left | 'right } :x-window { 'use | 'unuse}
{ :initial-file *file_name* | :initial-prog *prog_list* | :initial-non })
This function creates a process *process* in the current, right or left host according
to :position. If :x-window is 'use, then X-window is opened. If :inital-file is specified,
the created process evaluates the *file_name*. If :initial-prog is specified, the created
process evaluates the *prog_list*. Otherwise the process waits for the program to be
executed via input from the keyboard.

(existp *process*)
This function checks the existence of the process with name *process* in the current
or adjacent host.

(connect *process*)
This creates several constructs to communicate with the process *process*.

(host-name :position { 'current | 'left | 'right })
This function returns the host name to the position specified.

(cpu-status)
This function obtains the consumed CPU ratio and the number of processes waiting.

(ssend *process msg* { :blocking :time-out *time* | :nonblocking })
This function sends a evaluated S-expression message to process *process*. If :blocking
is specified, the caller is blocked until *process* receives the message or the period of
time assingned by :time-out expires. If :nonblocking is specified, it proceeds to process
without the acknowledge from *process*.

(sreceive *process*)
This function receives a message from *process*. The caller is blocked until the message
is received from *process*. The returned value of the function is the message itself.

(comsync *process msg*)
This function is for the calling process to synchrinize with process *process*. So, this
function sends the message to *process*, and waits for the message from *process*. If
process sends a message, the returned value of this function is that message. Therefore this works like a rendezvous with *process* in the adjacent host.

(ring-get {:IN | :OUT } :timeout *time*)
This function receives the message from a specified ring (IN or OUT) and locks the
ring. Therefore, except for the caller process, no message forwarding or modification
of the message is executed after this function is called. The caller process is blocked
until new message arrives from the adjacent host or the period of *time* specified :by

time-out expires. The returned value of this function is the message itself or null if timeout occurs. The lock on the ring is not released until the caller issues the ring-put or ring-clear functions.

(ring-put {:IN | :OUT } *msg*)
This function sends the message specified by *msg* to the ring (IN or OUT). If this function is called by the caller of ring-get, the lock on the ring is released and the message forwarding is restarted on the ring.

(ring-read {:IN | :OUT } :time-out *time*)
This function is the same as the function ring-get but there is no lock on the ring, i.e., the message is forwarded.

(ring-write {:IN | :OUT } *msg*)
This function inserts *msg* to the forwarded message on the ring. The caller is not blocked.

(ring-clear {:IN | :OUT })
This function is called only by the caller of ring-get, and it releases the lock on the ring.

(email *address msg*)
This function sends an e-mail to the specified address.

(quit)
This function kills the caller itself. If the calling process is using x-window, the window is closed.

2.6   Examples

Figure 3 shows the examples for the usage of send and receive functions. In this figure, the root process creates P01 on the current host and P02 on the right host. On creation of process P01, it executes P01LDF file. Similarly, P02 executes specified progbody. Thus, two processes P01 and P02 are executed on their own hosts.

3   Prototype System Design

To design the DLisp prototype system, the major issues are : How to design Lisp processes in a host and what types of interprocess communication must be supported. The following two sections discuss these issues.

root process

```
(setq  progbody '( ;;;
                   ;;; Restructured program body
                   ;;;
                       ..............
                   )  )
(create-process 'P01 :position    'current
                     :x-window 'use
                     :initial-file 'P01LDF )
(connect 'P01)
(create-process 'P02 :position 'right
                     :x-window 'unuse
                     :initial-prog  progbody )
(connect 'P02)

(ssend 'P02 progbody)
        ................
```

P01LDF file

```
(connect 'root)
(defun rstr (progbody)
       (cond ((null progbody) () )
             (t eval (car progbody))
                     (rstr (cdr progbody)))) )
(setq p01body (sreceive 'root :blocking))
(rstr p01body)
(quit)
```

Figure 3: Example of send and receive functions

3.1 Lisp Process

The design and implementation of the Lisp application process strongly affects the performance and configuration of the overall system. In particular, the relation between the Lisp application process and the UNIX process is important. We have two alternatives for designing Lisp application processes:

(1) A single Lisp interpreter that manages multiple Lisp application processes.

(2) A single Lisp interpreter that manages a single Lisp application process.

The advantage of the alternative (1) is that only one program code for the Lisp interpreter is required in a host. This means that the program storage for redundunt Lisp interpreters are saved, and the performance of the program improves if we use a light weight process or thread (e.g. SUN Microsystem Light weight) for multiple Lisp application processes. In the alternative (1), there are two ways of designing the process scheduling mechanism. One is to design this mechanism independant of the interpreter and the other is to incorporate it into the Lisp interpreter. The example for the latter is Multi-Lisp, which is implemented on UNIX based multi-processors.

To design our prototype system the following problems of alternative (1) are recognized:

(a) To port the thread library to the current environment is difficult.

(b) More than expected modifications on the existing Lisp language processors are required.

Since our initial goal is to implement a background job on a distributed system, we concluded that the improvement of the execution time by light weight process is preferable but not indispensable.

Thus, we chose alternative (2) for our prototype system. In alternative (2), the

Lisp application and Lisp interpreter form a single Lisp process which is a single UNIX process.

3.2 Interprocess Communication

In order to execute the processes concurrently and in parallel, the mechanism with which the distributed processes communicate and synchronize with each other must be provided.

3.2.1 Interprocess Communications within a Host

The original UNIX provided various types of system calls for interprocess communication within a single host. However, taking account of the flexbility for message handling, we selected the System V IPC (Interprocess Communication) mechanism.

3.2.2 Interprocess Communications among Multiple Hosts

In our system, the IN and OUT-rings are designed as a chain of UNIX socket pairs. So far, two types of sockets are supported in UNIX. These are Berkeley sockets and System V Transport Layer Interfaces (TLI). Basically, these two types are the same, so we chose the Berkeley socket simply because of the availability. On creating socket pairs for the IN or OUT-ring, INET domain and TCP are specified.

4 Implementation

The DLisp prototype system is implemented on the fourteen SUN SparcStation 2 which are connected via ethernet. The prototype system in each host consists of Lisp interpreter, process manager (PM), export communication process (ECMP), import communication process (ICMP),ring manager (RM), message manager (MM), message queues (MQPM, MQCH, MQLH, MQRH, MQRB and RRQ), ring buffer (RB) and process name table (PNT) (see figer 4). These programs and data are stored in each host's secondary storage.

4.1 The Initialization of the System

To start the system, the user issues a command to invoke PM at the root host. Then, PM loads and invokes ECPM, ICPM, RM and MM. Then, ECPM, ICPM, RM and MM in the root host invokes PMs in specified remote hosts. Each PM invokes ECPM, ICPM, RM and MM within its own host and creates sockets based on the port number assigned to the host and then establishes the connection between the adjacent nodes. Thus, PMs cooperatively complete the communication ring (the IN-ring and OUT-ring) and then the PM in each host initializes its working storage.

Then, each PM sets its process ID to 1. Finally the PM in the root host opens X-window and invokes the Lisp interpreter at the opened window.

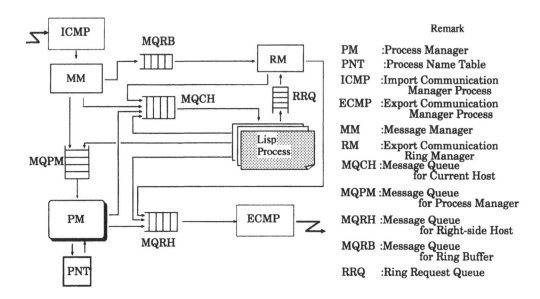

Figure 4: Messages flow in a host

4.2   Process Management

Figure 4 describes the flow of messages and controls within a host. Through MQPM (message queue for process manager), the PM receives the message and key information such as the message source process ID and the destination process ID. MQPM contains the internal message which consists of queue type code, process ID, action code, reference to the message itself, and source and destination process IDs. If the internal message is (create-process *process* :position 'current ...), then the PM examines the PNT to check whether *process* already exists. If not, the PM creates a Lisp interpreter process with process name *process* by means of the exec system call and registers it to the PNT. If the internal message is (... :position 'right (or 'left)...), the PM changes it to (... :position 'current ...) and attaches it to the queue MQRH (MQLH). Thus the PM commits this internal message to the right (left) host. The ECMP detaches the message from the MQRH or MQLH and transmits it to the right or left host. Therefore the ICPM in the adjacent host receives that message. On receiving it, the ICPM attaches the message to the MQPM and then, the adjacent PM proceeds the message handling as described above and creates a process within the host. In both cases, the source process which initially required the creation of process is notified of the created process ID by a message. The source process is blocked until the arrival of that message.

4.3   Message Management

This process manages the messages from the adjacent host. The ICMP (Import Communication Manager Process) passes the incoming message to MM, and then

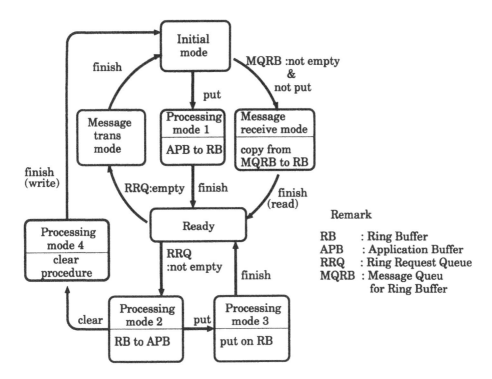

Figure 5: Transition diagram of Ring Buffer in Ring Manager

MM checks the action code of the message. If the action code is the order or query for the process, MM distributes the message to MQPM. Otherwise it sends the message to MQCH, or MQRQ, then the action code is placed in the interprocess communication within the host, or is an operation on the ring.

4.4   Ring Management

The input or output of a message to the ring is managed by the ring manager through the RB. The state transition of the RB is described in figure 5. As shown in the figure 5, if no operation is blocked on the ring within the host, the RM detaches the message from MQRB, stores it in the RB, and then attaches it to MQRH or MQLH in order to transmit it to the next host on the ring. Suppose a Lisp process A asks to obtain a message from the ring. It calls the function ring-get which makes the RM attach A's process ID to the RRQ, and to block process A until a new message arrives.

Once the new message arrives, the RM detaches the message from MQRB and stores it in the RB. It then copies the message to the memory location assigned by process A. The message forwarded to the adjacent host is blocked until A calls the function ring-put or ring-clear. While the message is blocked, the content of the RB is locked by process A. Therefore if some other process B issues ring-get while the message is blocked, the RM stores B's ID to the RRQ and blocks B until A unlocks the RB by ring-put or ring-clear. If A issues ring-put after the modification of RB, the RM does not forward the message, but instead copies the message to the memory location assigned by process B. So, the modified message is processed as if it is a newly arrived message for B.

5   Experiments

Some application programs are executed on the DLisp system. Here we discuss the results of two typical program executions: 8-queen problem and sorting. The former is a typical example of a heavy computation load job and the latter is a job with a large amount of data. Both of the programs are written in Lisp, and the execution time of each problem is observed.

5.1   8-queen Problem

The algorithm for this problem is well known tree-searching. In our experiments, the logical ring consists of k workstations (where k varies between 2 to 8), in each of which two application processes are created.

These processes are:

(1) $SDPP$: Data input process. $SDPP$ extracts a starting point for the search from the IN-ring and gives it to the IP process on every message rotation. Here, the starting point consists of a pair (X, Y), where X and Y are the row and column respectively.

(2) IP : subtree-searching process. IP begins the subtree search with the starting point given by $SDPP$.

Information about the set of starting points rotates on the IN-ring and the $SDPP$ process in the i-th host extracts a single starting point of information and forwards the remaining starting points to the IN-ring. Then, the $SDPP$ in the i-th host gives the obtained starting point to the IP to invoke the subtree search. After completing the search, the IP puts the results of the search on to the OUT-ring. Since the above procedures are repeated until all the starting points are exhausted on the IN-ring, some hosts may contain more than two starting points (if the number of starting points is greater than k).

Thus, the results on the OUT-ring can be collected by the initiator process.

We observed the following results after two trials:

(1) The $SDPP$ in each host extracts the starting point of each IN-ring rotation and queues it. Then it gives the queued starting point to the IP every time IP's completes its subtree search.

(2) The IP in each host directly extracts a starting point from the IN-ring after every completion of its subtree search. Therefore only one starting point exists at a time in each host.

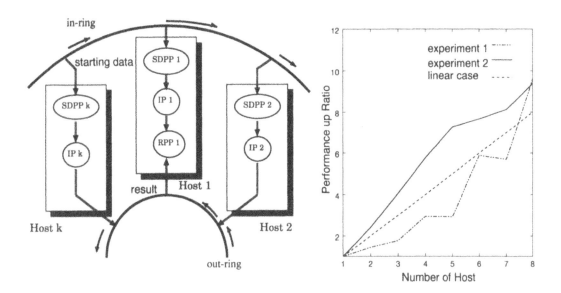

Figure 6: The outline of 8-queens problem

Figure 7: Comparison of 8-queens problem performance improvement ratio on experiment 1 and 2

5.2 Results

Figure 7 describes the experiment's results. Here, it should be noted that the execution time for experiment 2 is not only better than that of experiment 1 but that the time for a single host execution divided by the number of hosts (which is considered to be the theoretical upper bound for parallel execution)is also better. The main reasons for this are as follows:

(1) Since the problem is divided into smaller subproblems and are distributed among the hosts, the frequency of garbage collection by the Lisp interpreter is much less than in the original problem.

(2) The CPU loads are balanced better in experiment 2 than in experiment 1, since in experiment 1, the *SDPP*s in some hosts may keep multiple starting points even though some other idle hosts are waiting for starting points on the empty IN-ring but in experiment 2, the starting point is extracted every time the *IP* completes its subtree search.

5.3 Sorting

We tried two experiments concerned with sorting.

(1) Firsty, the initiater process deposits (by ring-put) a set of data items which should be sorted on the IN-ring. Then, the receiving process extracts a subset of data items from the set of data on the IN-ring and leaves the remaining data. Then,

the receiving process starts a local sort on the extracted subset. After the completion of the local sort, the process gets the data from the OUT-ring and merges it with its own sorted data. Then, the merged data is deposited on the OUT-ring so it can repeat the same procedure. The above procedure is repeated until all the data items on the IN-ring are consumed. At the final stage of execution, the initiator collects the sorted data items on the OUT-ring.

We call this **data-flow** sorting, since the data is flowing onto the ring.

(2) A large file which consists of a collection of records is divided into multiple subfiles and is distributed over multiple hosts. Each host maintains its own subfile(i.e. distributed data environment). Each record contains a key field of numerical values. The goal of processing is to obtain upper (value larger) k records ordered by a key field value from the whole file.

In our experiments k varies from 50 to 900, and the total number of records is 1000. These records are equally divided into m hosts and distributed amongst them.

The initiating process firstly multicasts the sorting program to all hosts through the IN-ring, and then the hosts evaluate the received program. The local sorting procedure at each host creates upper k records. After completion of local sorting the process in each host gets the data (which is the upper k records) from the OUT-ring, then merges it with its own k records, and puts the newly sorted k records on the OUT-ring. This procedure terminates when the initiator obtains the data from the OUT-ring. This occurs when all hosts complete their local sorting. We call this **program-flow** sorting, since the program is flowing on the ring. Both of the experiments are measured in terms of execution time. The execution time starts when the initiator deposits the data to be sorted and continues until the initiator gets the final sorted result.

5.4   Results

Figure 8 shows the execution time of **data-flow** sorting. The data to be sorted must be divided, distributed and merged. This makes load balancing more difficult than that of the 8-queen problem. Therefore, no effect of parallelism is observed in the range where the number of hosts is between 3 to 5. If the number of hosts is more than 9 and the number of data items is less than 500, the improvement of the performance is approximately proportional to the number of data items, but in the region of more than 500 data items this improvement is not observable.

Figure 9 describes the execution time of **program flow** sorting. In the case of 50 data items, the performance is better than that of the theoretical upper bound. There are two main reasons for this:

1) All data is not necessarily transmitted.

2) Good load balancing is performed compared to **data-flow** sorting.

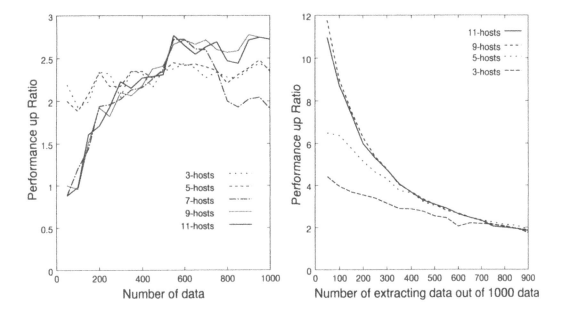

Figure 8: Distributed sort by data flow method

Figure 9: Distributed sort by program flow method

6   Conclusion

How to detect idle or lightly-loaded workstations is still a basic issue. However, if a job can be divided into equally loaded segments, then execution by DLisp is fairly effective in terms of processing time. Furthermore, in the case of the Lisp programs, the smaller the job, the less frequent the execution of garbage collection. This makes our approach more appropriate.

In addition, we can expect the advances of communication technologies. For example, within the near future, high speed networks such as ATM-based local networks may be more commonly used. This might remove the communication bottleneck, and will make DLisp more effective.

The results of sample application programs with DLisp execution are promising, and we believe that the approach can be an effective tool for the network distributed environment.

Bibliography

1)   Bach,M.J., *The Design of the UNIX Operating System*. Englewood Cliffs,NJ Prentice Hall, 1987.

2)   Benjamin Zorn, Kinson Ho, James Larus, Luigi Semenzato, Paul Hilfinger, Multiprocessing Extensions in Spur Lisp. *IEEE Software*, Vol.6, No.4, pp.41–49,1989.

3)   Chow,T.C.K., Abraham,J.A., Load Balancing in Distributed System. *IEEE Trans.on Software Engineering*, Vol. SE-8, pp.401-412, July 1982.

4) Chang, E., and Roberts, R., An improved algorithm for decentralized extrema-finding in circular configurations of process. *Communication of ACM*, Vol.22, pp.281–283, July 1979.

5) Doug Baldwin., Consul:A Parallel Constraint Language. *IEEE Software*, Vol.6, No.4, pp.62–69, 1989.

6) R.H. Halstead,Jr., Multilisp:A Language for Concurrent Symbolic Computation. *ACM Trans. Programming Languages and Systems*, Oct. 1985.

7) Hoare,C.A.R., Communicating Sequential Processes Processing. *Commun. Ass. Comput.*, Vol.21, pp.666–677,1978.

8) Harrison III,W.L., Ammarguellat,Z., The Design of Automatic Parallelizers for Symbolic and Numeric Programs, Parallel Lisp. *Languages and Systems. LNCS*, No.441, pp.235–253, 1990.

9) Henri E.Bal, Jennifer G.Steiner, Andrew S.Tanenbaum, Programming Languages for Distributed Computing System. *ACM Comp. Surveys*, Vol.21, No.3, pp.261–322, Sep. 1989.

10) Hideya Iwasaki, Programming and Implementation of a Multiprocessing Lisp. *Trans. of IPSJ*, Vol.28, pp.465–470, 1987.

11) Hideya Iwasaki, Implementation of Parallel Processing Language System on a Multiprocesor Unix Machine. *Trans. of IPSJ*, Vol.33, pp.1351–1360, 1992.

12) Korach, E., Rotem,D., and Satoro, N., A probabilistic algorithm for extrema finding in a circle of processors. Technical Report CS-81-19, University of Waterloo, Canada, 1981.

13) Isao Miyamura, Hajime Enomoto, On a Language for Parallel Processing System. *Trans. of IPSJ*, Vol.24, No.5, pp.614–621, 1983.

14) Nicholas Carriero,David Gelernter, How to Write Parallel Programs: A guide to the Perplexed. *Computing Surveys*, ACM, Vol.21, No.3, pp.323–357, 1989.

15) Osborne,R.B., Speculative Computation in Multilisp, Parallel Lisp. *Languages and System, LNCS*, No.441, pp.103–137, springer Verlag, 1990.

16) Robert H.,Halstead,JR., Multilisp: A Language for Concurrent Symbolic Computation. *ACM Trans. of Prog. Lang. Syst.*, Vol.7, No.4, pp.501–538, 1985.

17) Ron Goldman, Richard P.Gabriel, Qlisp:Parallel Processing in Lisp. *IEEE Sodtware*, Vol.6, No.4, pp.51–59, 1989.

18) Steele,G.L., *Common Lisp: The Language (2nd)*. Digital Press, 1990.

19) Stone,H.S.,Bokhari,S.H., Control of Distributed Process. *IEEE Computer*, Vol.11, pp.97–106, July, 1978.

20) Stumm,M., Zhou,S., Algorithms Implementing Distributed Shared Memory *IEEE Computer*, Vol.23, pp.54–64. May 1990.

21) Takashi Chikayama, Implementation of the Utilisp System. *Trans. of IPSJ*, Vol.24, No.5, pp.599–604, 1983.

22) Tanenbaum,A.S., Van Renesse,R., Distributed Operating Systems. *Computing Surveys*, ACM, Vol.17, Dec. 1985.

23) Tay,B.H., Ananda,A.L., A Survey of Remote Procedure Calls *Operating Systems Review,* Vol.24, pp.68–79, July 1990.

24) Tomohiro Seino,Takayama Ito, On Implementation of Parallel Constructs of PaiLisp and Their Evaluations. *Trans. of IPSJ,* Vol.34, No.12, pp.2578–2591, 1993.

25) T.,Ito, and M.,Matsui, A Parallel Lisp Language PaiLisp and Its Kernel Specification, Parallel Lisp. itl Languages and System, LNCS, No.441, pp.58–100,1990.

26) T.,Ito, Lisp and Parallelism, *Artificial Intelligence and Mathematical Theory of Computation.* Lifshitz,V.(ed.), Academic Press, 1991

3

Implementation of UtiLisp/C on AP1000

Eiiti Wada

Fujitsu Laboratories

Tetsurou Tanaka

The University of Tokyo

ABSTRACT

Implementation of UtiLisp/C, which is a newly coded version of UtiLisp for Sparc workstations, on AP1000 has been attempted. The goal is to reform UtiLisp for AP1000 with a very few lines in C language modified, and a small number of special functions added, for distributed memory machines so that the basic feeling of parallel programming will be obtained in a relatively short time. None of the new fashionable functions often implemented in parallel Lisps, e.g., future and so forth, are included yet; only a set of inter-cell streams mechanisms are added to execute top level eval loops in parallel. The set of the original UtiLisp functions proved well suited for use on MIMD machine.

1 Introduction

The Lisp Programming language has been implemented on various multiprocessors many times. Most of those multiprocessors, however, were shared memory machines [1] [2]. As the number of processors in a single machine increases, distributed memory machines become more practical. AP1000 is of such machine architecture and a number of programming language systems are currently being implemented [3] [4].

One implementation of UtiLisp, a Lisp dialect [5], is coded in C language (so, it is called UtiLisp/C) and tuned for Sparc processors, the heart of AP1000, thus it seemed relatively easy to transfer the system to AP1000 with minimal hacking time. The resultant system may serve as a test platform for developing Lisp programming style on multiprocessors and to confirm the suitability of the language for use on AP1000 beside the Lisp's original merit of its easiness of rapid prototyping stemming from the interpretive operation mode.

The general idea is as follows. The same UtiLisp interpreter is to run on each cell of AP1000. The host machine was, in the early design stage, also to have Lisp interpreter as a master of the application program. This idea was soon thrown out because the host machine is running under multiuser mode and it would be difficult to measure the total system performance. The mission of the host machine is, therefore:

1. to distribute the lisp interpreter to each cell;

2. to broadcast the lispsys.l file (start up file) to each cell;

3. to serve as the input/output channels with the user.

4. to read/write files in the file system for the interpreters on the cells.

Similar to the top level read/eval/print loop in the typical lisp interpreters, cell programs wait for an S-expression form fed from a processor, i.e., host or other cells, then evaluate it and send back the resultant S-expression to the original processor. In other words, cells work as the eval-servers. Communications between host and cell or between cells are realised by means of standard lisp stream functions, **read** and **print**, employing the AP1000 communication library functions.

Nothing special was taken into consideration for garbage collection, since every cell has a completely independent memory management system. When the pool of free cells reaches the lower limit, the garbage collector starts up autonomously.

2   Implementation

In transplanting the original UtiLisp interpreter to AP1000, the largest modification was done around the read/write (in terms of Lisp, read/print) functions, for cells on the distributed multiprocessor machine have to exchange all information by inter-cell communication using T-net (torus topology) (or sometimes B-net (broadcast type network)). The read/write functions in UtiLisp could have an additional argument to designate the stream. The default streams are those bound to standard-input for read and standard-output for write, normally being bound to terminal-input and terminal-output. A stream parameter is indeed needed when the system wishes to read/write files in the file system. In such cases, streams are first created by a function call (**stream** *filename*), and by executing **inopen** or **outopen**, file descriptors are assinged. UtiLisp/C has additional features to assign file descriptors directly by calling stream functions with an integer argument.

Unix assigns file descriptor 0 to standard read and 1 to standard write. Moreover, the AP1000 operating system assigns higher integers up to 63 to arbitrary files. Accordingly, for inter-cell communications, integer n ($256 \leq n \leq 1279$) is assigned to the file descriptors designating $(n-256)$th cell. For example, file descriptor 256 is for communicating with the cell 0, file descriptor 257 for the cell 1, and file descriptor 1279 for the cell 1023.

File descriptor 4096 is reserved for communication with the host processor, because host id is 4096 in AP1000. Descriptor 4095 is reserved for reading in from arbitrary cells and for writing in broadcasting fashion.

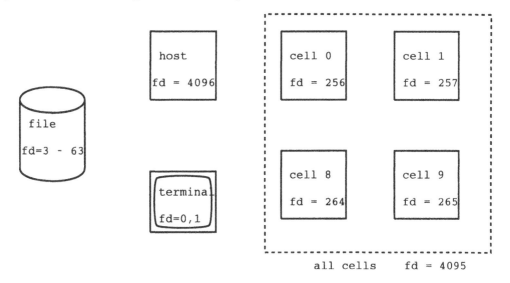

Figure 1 File descriptors of AP1000 UtiLisp/C

The top eval loop of the cell 0 normally awaits input from the host; the other cells' top eval loops expect input from the host or other cells. When an S-expression to be evaluated arrives via cell to cell or host to cell communication, the evaluated value is sent back to the originator; however, when the eval form comes by broadcast communication, the eval servers understand that the sender expects the side effect rather than the value, and values are not returned.

The most simple program to illustrate the usage of the numbered streams is to send the function (hello) to the next numbered cell (except the last cell) and append everywhere one character to the returned string:

```
(defun hello ()
  (lets ((ncel (getncel)) (cid (getcid))
         (out (outopen (stream (+ cid 257))))
         (in (inopen (stream (+ cid 257)))) (string))
    (cond ((< cid (1- ncel))
           (print (list 'hello) out)
           (setq string (read in))))
    (string-append (make-string 1 (+ cid 48)) string)))
```

The function call (getlcel) returns $\log_2 c$ where c is the total number of cells. The function call (getcid) returns the ordinal number of the current cell. The output of the above function on a 64-cells system is:

```
"0123456789:;<=>?@ABCDEFGHIJKLMNOPQRSTUVWXYZ[\]^_`abcdefghijklmnonil"
```

3   Example

The first example is the function to calculate the nth Fibonacci number.

Imagine that cell 0 needs fib(n).

- Then fib($n-1$) and fib($n-2$) are needed.

- The cell 0 calculates fib($n-1$) by itself and asks the cell 1 to calculate fib($n-2$).

- When the cell 0 calculates fib($n-1$), it calculates fib($n-2$) by itself and asks the cell 2 to calculate fib($n-3$).

- On the other hand, when the cell 1 calculates fib($n-2$), it calculates fib($n-3$) by itself and asks the cell 3 to calculate fib($n-4$).

- The difference of cell numbers, asking and being asked, is 1 in the first step, 2 in the second step, 4 in the third step ....

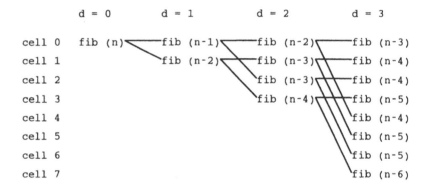

Figure 2 Process tree for calculating fib(n)

Let c be the number of total cells. The distributed calculation may be performed until $\log_2 c$ steps. (see Figure 2)

The Fibonacci program requires an additional argument d to control steps.

```
(defun fib (n (d 0))
 (cond ((lessp n 2) 1)
       ((lessp d (getlcel))
       (lets ((mycid (getcid))
              (child (+ mycid (expt 2 d))) (myret)
              (childret)
              (cstream0 (outopen (stream (+ child 256))))
              (cstream1 (inopen (stream (+ child 256))))))
        (print (list 'fib (- n 2) (1+ d)) cstream0)
        (setq myret (fib (1- n) (1+ d)))
        (setq childret (read cstream1))
```

```
        (+ myret childret)))
    (t (+ (fib (1- n) (1+ d))
          (fib (- n 2) (1+ d))))))))
```

The second argument (d 0) tells that unless the second argument is explicitly given, d will be bound to 0. The variable child is the ordinal number of the sub-processor cell. cstream0 and cstream1 are respectively input/output streams to communicate with the child cell. By issuing (print (list 'fib (- n 2) (1+ d)) cstream0), the current cell asks the child cell to calculate fib($n - 2$) and with (read cstream1), it gets back the evaluated value.

If the number of steps reaches to the upper limit, i.e (getlcel), each cell executes the calculation by itself.

Changing the number of cells from 64 to 32, 16, 8, ..., 1, execution time of fib(20) in 1/60 sec was measured. Figure 3 indicates how the execution time decreases as the total number of cells increased.

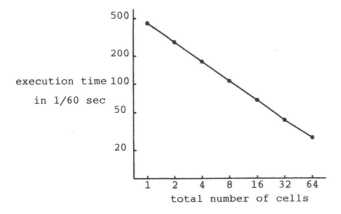

Figure 3 Speed up curve

4 Synchronization

From time to time, to guarantee the correct operations, execution of processes must be regulated; the most typical control is synchronization. Since the goal of this implementation was to minimize the necessary modification made on the original interpreter, there were no synchronization primitives in the first version. Synchronization is realized by exchanging messages between cells. However, this is not an exercise of the Firing Squad Problem; and a method to call the synchronization primitives in the cell library in the Lisp environment is provided.

In the following program, four cells, 0 to 3, are to execute a loop cid (cell number) times, i.e. 0 times for the cell 0, 1 times for the cell 1, etc. Until all cells exit the loop, those who have terminated wait in a second loop. At the end of the program, all the cells print "**end**" using the debugger function. (see Figure 4)

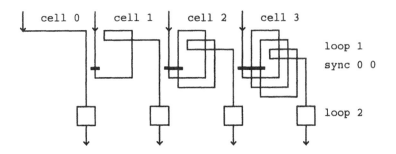

Figure 4 Synchronization test

```
(defun synctest ()
 (pstat 1)         ;set state 1
 (sync 0 0)        ;synchronization to start all simultaneously
 (setq count (getcid))
 (loop
  (cond
   ((0= count) (pstat 0)   ;when counter becomes 0,
    (exit)))               ;set state 0 and exit loop
  (debug count)
  (setq count (1- count))    ;decrease counter
  (sync 0 0))                ;loops procede synchronously
 (loop
  (debug
   (list 'c (cstat) 'g        ;check logical or of stat
    (gstat)))
  (cond
   ((0= (cstat)) (exit)))  ;wait till all cell set state 0
  (sync 0 0))
 (debug (list 'end (cstat))) ;print "end" with or-ed state
 (sync 0 0))

(cond ((0= (getcid)) (broadmessage '(synctest)) (synctest)))
                            ;driver program for cell 0
```

In the program above, (**sync 0 0**) is the barrier synchronization. Each cell keeps one status bit which is set by (**pstat 1**) and reset by (**pstat 0**). The status information is accessed by (**gstat**) or (**cstat**). (**gstat**) returns the status of the own cell, and (**cstat**) returns logical or of all cells. The structure of the program is as follows: Before entering into the first loop, each cell sets the status to 1 by (**pstat 1**). Then passing through the barrier synchronization, the individual cell decreases the counter, and when the content of the counter became 0, the cell resets the status by (**pstat 0**). In the second loop, each cell checks the status of all cells by (**cstat**).

When all cells came to the second loop, since every status bit is reset to 0, (cstat) returns 0.

The script is shown below; the host program was invoked with 4 cells.

```
> (exfile "sample/synctest.l" t)
synctest                     ;value of (defun synctest ()...
(0 c 1 g 0)                  ;cell 0 entered into the 2nd loop (1st)
(1 . 1)                      ;cell 1 in the 1st loop (1st)
(2 . 2)                      ;cell 2 in the 1st loop (1st)
(3 . 3)                      ;cell 3 in the 1st loop (1st)
(2 . 1)           ;sync 1 ;cell 2 in the 1st loop (2nd)
(0 c 1 g 0)                  ;cell 0 in the 2nd loop (2nd)
(1 c 1 g 0)                  ;cell 1 entered into the 2nd loop (1st)
(3 . 2)                      ;cell 3 in the 1st loop (2nd)
(1 c 1 g 0)       ;sync 2 ;cell 1 in the 2nd loop (2nd)
(0 c 1 g 0)                  ;cell 0 in the 2nd loop (3rd)
(2 c 1 g 0)                  ;cell 2 entered into the 2nd loop (1st)
(3 . 1)                      ;cell 3 in the 1st loop (3rd)
(1 c 1 g 0)       ;sync 3 ;cell 1 in the 2nd loop (3rd)
(0 c 1 g 0)                  ;cell 0 in the 2nd loop (4th)
(2 c 1 g 0)                  ;cell 2 in the 2nd loop (2nd)
(3 c 0 g 0)                  ;cell 3 entered into the 2nd loop (1st)
(1 end 0)                    ;cell 1 exited the 2nd loop
(0 end 0)                    ;cell 0 exited the 2nd loop
(2 end 0)                    ;cell 2 exited the 2nd loop
(3 end 0)                    ;cell 3 exited the 2nd loop
0                            ;value of (sync 0 0)
nil
> (quit)
```

The output shown above indicates that each cell, after counted down its own counter, waited for the state to be synchronized in the second loop. When the latest process, that is the cell 3, reached to the synchronization point, all the cells moved to the final debugger print function. All the cells printed "end" messages simultaneously.

5   Load Balancing

In multiprocessor system, load balancing is one of the key issues. The eight queens puzzle is used to demonstrate the load balancing strategy. The eight queens puzzle for a single processor is shown first

Three bit arrays, col, up and dn keep the information about the free columns and diagonals. (see Figure 5)

```
(defun generate (n x col up dn)
  (lets ((h))
```

```
(cond ((= n 8) (print x))
      (t (do ((h 0 (1+ h)))
             ((= h 8))
           (cond
            ((and (bref col h)
                  (bref up (+ n (- h) 7))
                  (bref dn (+ n h)))
             (generate (1+ n) (cons h x)
              (place col h) (place up (+ n (- h) 7))
              (place dn (+ n h)))))))))))

(defun place (str pos)
 (lets ((str1 (string-append str))) (bset str1 pos nil) str1))

(generate
   0
   nil
   (make-string 1 255)
   (make-string 2 255)
   (make-string 2 255))
```

((bref *bits index*) returns t if *index*-th bit of *bits* is set; otherwise it returns nil.
(bset *bits index value*) sets the *index*-th bit of *bits* if *value* is not nil; otherwise the
bit is reset.)

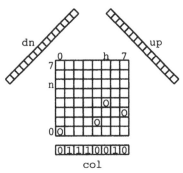

Figure 5 Eight queens puzzle

The master-slave strategy for the multiprocessor version is as follows:

The program in cell 0 keeps three lists, cell, task and answer.. In the beginning,
cell has a list of all free cells, i.e. a list from 1 to 15 (in the case of 16 cells), and
task is nil.

The cell 0 program dispatches a task to the cell 1. The cell 1 generates new tasks
and sends results back to cell 0. The message is of the form:

```
(nqueens newtask generate 1 ...)
```

Each message is received by **break** by setting a function in **my-break**. The break function for the AP1000 first reads in the incoming message in **inputdata** and then checks whether a symbol **my-break** is bound or not. If it is bound, the break function funcalls **my-break**. Accordingly, **my-break** may be programmed as in the example.

The main part of the cell 0 program is a loop where tasks in the task list are sent to any free cell; the loop is exited if it finds that the task list is null and that the cell list is full.

my-break sorts the type of the incoming messages by their second tag. (The first tag is always "nqueens".) If the tag is **newtask**, the rest is consed to the task list. If the tag is **free** it means that the cell has come to the end of its work, so it is registered in the **cell** list. If the tag is **result** the result value will be consed to the **answer** list. (see Figure 6)

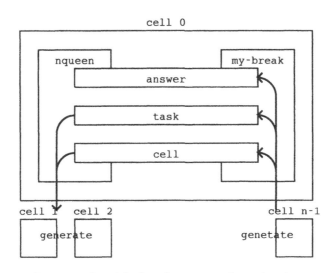

Figure 6 Load balancing control mechanism

```
(defun nqueens ()                    ;program running on cell 0
  (lets ((ncel (getncel)) (cell (genlist 1 ncel)) (task)
         (nextcell) (nexttask) (answer)
         (my-break    ;my-break is bound only inside of nqueen
           '(lambda (inputdata)
              (cond ((and (consp inputdata)
                          (eq (car inputdata) 'nqueens))
                     (selectq (cadr inputdata)
                       (newtask
                         (setq task
                           (cons (cddr inputdata) task)))
                       (result
                         (setq answer
                           (cons (caddr inputdata) answer))
                         (setq cell
```

```
                              (nconc cell
                                (list (cadddr inputdata)))))))
                            (free
                             (setq cell
                               (nconc cell
                                 (list (caddr inputdata)))))))))
                        (t nil))
                  (setq interrupt-mask 1))))
          (setq nextcell (car cell) cell (cdr cell))
          (sendto nextcell
                  (list 'generate
                        0
                        nil
                        (make-string 1 255)
                        (make-string 2 255)
                        (make-string 2 255)))
          (loop (cond ((and (null task)
                            (= (length cell) (1- ncel)))
                        (exit answer)))
                (lets ((interrupt-mask 0))
                 (cond ((and task cell)
                        (setq nexttask (car task)
                              task (cdr task)
                              nextcell (car cell)
                              cell (cdr cell))
                        (sendto nextcell nexttask)))))))))

(defun genlist (x y)            ;generate a list (x x+1 ... y-1)
  (cond ((= x y) nil) (t (cons x (genlist (1+ x) y)))))

(defun sendto (cell-to-send msg-to-send)
  (lets ((s (outopen (stream (+ cell-to-send 256)))))
    (print msg-to-send s)
    (close s)))

(defun generate (n x col up dn)
  (lets ((h) (mesg))
    (cond ((= n 8) (list 'nqueens 'result x (getcid)))
          (t (do ((h 0 (1+ h)))
                 ((= h 8) (list 'nqueens 'free (getcid)))
               (cond
                 ((and (bref col h)
                       (bref up (+ n (- h) 7))
                       (bref dn (+ n h)))
```

```
                    (setq mesg (list 'nqueens 'newtask
                                'generate (1+ n)
                                (list 'quote (cons h x))
                                (place col h)
                                (place up (+ n (- h) 7))
                                (place dn (+ n h))))
                    (sendto 0 mesg)))))))))

(defun place (str pos)
  (lets ((str1 (string-append str))) (bset str1 pos nil) str1))
```

In the case of the eight queens puzzle shown above, the work load of the cell 0 is too heavy because it is constantly managing the jobs for other cells.

To measure the load balance, the function time is used as follows. On entering to and on exiting from the main program, two functions start and stop are inserted which update the value of the running-time.

The function collect-time collects all the values of running-time.

```
(setq running-time 0)
(defun start () (setq running-time (- running-time (time))))
(defun stop () (setq running-time (+ running-time (time))))
(defun collect-time ()
 (lets ((ncel (getncel)))
  (print (list 0 running-time))
  (do ((i 1 (1+ i)))
      ((= i ncel))
      (lets ((s0 (outopen (stream (+ i 256))))
             (s1 (inopen (stream (+ i 256)))))
       (print (list 'sendback-time) s0)
       (close s0)
       (print (list i (read s1)))
       (close s1)))))
(defun sendback-time () running-time)

(putd 'generate1 (getd 'generate))

(defun generate (n x col up dn)
  (start) (prog1 (generate1 n x col up dn) (stop)))

(defun bar ()
  (start) (nqueens) (stop) (collect-time)))
```

The load balance measured by the above technique is seen as:

```
> (bar)
```

```
(0 389)
(1 30)
(2 23)
(3 28)
(4 30)
(5 27)
(6 21)
(7 26)
(8 25)
(9 17)
(10 19)
(11 21)
(12 31)
(13 30)
(14 28)
(15 24)
```

This result confirms that the cell 0 runs all the time because of its management job. The runtime of others (cells 1 to 15), seem more or less even.

6 Modification

Our porting of UtiLisp/C to AP1000 aimed to minimize the coding needed for modification. Comparing the lines in the corresponding source files, the statistics of the modification lines are shown here:

name of files	number of lines modified
host.c(host main)	134 (new file)
machdep.c(cell input/output)	259 (new file)
main.c(cell main)	39 (additional)
eval.c(interrupt)	6 (additional)
sysfnmis.c(cell functions)	94 (additional)

Functions written in Lisp are collected in a file "lispsys.l". The current length of lispsys.l is 247 lines because only necessary functions are included, but ever lengthening. Normal lispsys.l has 630 lines.

7 Conclusion

The primary goal of transplanting the UtiLisp/C system to AP1000 with minimal modification seems to be achieved. Most of necessary functions or features were programmed in Lisp itself and are included in the lispsys.l file. Accordingly, it is quite easy to debug or improve the system or to monitor the performance.

Although only a few programs were explained in this report, other programs are being tested; for instance, to examine the effectiveness of broadcasting messages, distributed Eratosthenes' sieve was coded. This program proved that broadcasting urgent messages worked satisfactorily, but the program ran slower than expected.

Through the experiment of running a small set of parallel UtiLisp programs, it became clear, that, as reported widely, linear acceleration is hard to obtain; algorithms developed for a single processor environment contain the subconsciously included regulation of execution order, which must be explicitly regulated when rewritten for multiprocessors. Lisp is still easy to run on multiprocessors; UtiLisp/C implementation was considerably modular so that the modification for AP1000 is quite simple.

Tuning up of programs may require precise time data analysis. The present `time` function is slightly underpowered for such structural analysis. An improvement of the time function must be developed.

Finally, system size is mentioned. The size of binary text area of the interperter is about 225KB. The largest work area is for the heap. The default size of heap area is 512KB. As each cell of AP1000 is equipped with 16MB memory, there still is enough memory to run bigger programs.

Bibliography

1) Halstead, R.H.: Multilisp: A Language for Concurrent Symbolic Computation, *ACM Trans. Program. Lang. Syst.*, Vol.7, No.4 501-538(1985)

2) Iwasaki, H.: Programming and Implementation of a Multi-processing Lisp, *Trans. IPS Japan*, Vol.28,No.5,465-470(1987)

3) Baily, B., Newey, M.: Implementing ML on Distributed Memory Multiprocessors, *ACM Sigplan Notices*, Vol.28,No.1,56-59(1993)

4) Taura, K., Matsuoka, S., Yonezawa, A.: An Efficient Implementation of Concurrent Object-Oriented Languages on Stock Multiprocessors, *ACM SIGPLAN Notices*, Vol.28, No.7 218-228 (1993)

5) Tanaka, T.: UtiLisp/C : An Implementation of UtiLisp Featuring SPARC Architecture, *Trans. IPS Japan*, Vol.32,No.5,684-690(1991)

4

Multithread Implementation of an Object-Oriented Lisp, EusLisp

Toshihiro Matsui

Satoshi Sekiguchi

National Institute of Advanced Industrial Science and Technology

ABSTRACT

EusLisp is an object-oriented Lisp with geometric modeling facilities for robotics applications. In order to boost the execution of robotics applications and to add asynchronous programming facilities in Lisp, EusLisp is re-implemented to make use of multithread capability of modern SMP machines. The implementation employs the thread pool to minimize the time required for the thread creation, the per-thread free lists for efficient memory allocation, and the *last-alloc* structure to enable safe garbage collection at anytime. Most Lisp primitives exhibit almost linear performance to the increase of concurrency, while reasonable performance is obtained for memory hungry benchmarks.

1   Introduction

We have developed an object-oriented Lisp system called EusLisp and have continued to extend it for years [1, 2, 3, 4]. EusLisp is a practical language aiming at high-level programming in robotics applications. EusLisp implements the 3D solid modeling that performs a great role in a robot's planning capability, on the basis of object oriented programming. As EusLisp is mostly compatible with the Common Lisp [5, 6], it can also be applied to general AI programming. It has actually been applied to many areas of robotics research, such as collision-free path planning [7], grasp planning [8], analysis of motion in contact for assembly planning [9], simulators for teleoperation [10, 11], etc. In order to extend the application fields in a more real-time oriented direction, we redesigned EusLisp to support parallel and asynchronous programming using the Solaris-2 operating system's multithread facility.

There are two reasons for the necessity of concurrent and parallel processing for the realization of intelligent systems. One is the scaleable computational power obtained from multiprocessor architectures. Parallel programming is a promising approach to improve performance of computation bound processing such as image processing and interference checking in path planning, which are often claimed as bottlenecks for many robot applications. Second is the asynchronous processing.

Asynchronous programming is required to write programs that respond to multiple external events occurring independently of the program's state. Both performance gain and asynchronism are inevitable for real-time activities of robots operating in a physical world.

Many implementations, such as Multi lisp, TAO, PaiLisp, mutilisp, vectorized Lisp, *Lisp, etc., have been presented in the field of parallel Lisp systems. One reason that none of these could take a prevailing position in AI applications was that these systems relied on special, usually expensive, multiprocessor hardware. On the other hand, recent workstations tend to adopt shared-memory multiprocessor architecture to provide higher performance without raising clock speed too much. Multiprocessor workstations with 2 to 32 processors are a commodity of most laboratories and enterprises. Use of these common machines is not only economical but also good for developing large scale applications linked with other software packages.

This paper describes the implementation of the parallel EusLisp based on multithread facilities of the Solaris-2 operating system. The multithread EusLisp succeeded in introducing concurrent computation and asynchronous programming in Lisp on stock hardware. The next section describes the outline of the sequential EusLisp with its basic functionalities. The third section describes the design criteria to extend EusLisp to a multithread language compared with other parallel Lisp. The fourth section discusses memory management, the hardest problem in parallel Lisp implementations, and the fifth section describes EusLisp's parallel programming from the programmer's view. The last section presents the performance of EusLisp evaluated on a real parallel workstation consisting of 32 processors.

2   EusLisp

The first goal of EusLisp was an efficient implementation of a solid modeler. A solid modeler is a software system that defines shapes of 3D objects and does interference checking, motion simulation, graphics display, etc. As geometric components such as vertices, edges, and facets are well defined by objects, and their topological relations are well represented by pointers, an object oriented Lisp can be the best implementation language of solid modelers.

Important factors for efficient execution of an object oriented Lisp are memory management and type discrimination. EusLisp's memory manager uses the Fibonacci buddy method to efficiently allocate and reclaim memory cells of various sizes. In order to discriminate types of objects in dynamically-changing type hierarchy, a segmented tree representation which finds the largest set of the subtype tree by two comparisons of integers is used.

Although compatibilities with the Common Lisp specification have been respected, the object-orientedness at the basis of the implementation brought in some incompatibilities. EusLisp's object oriented programming differs from CLOS in that it only supports single-inheritance and it does not allow the method combination. Functional closures cannot have the infinite extent. Multiple values are unsupported.

On the other hand, to facilitate robotics applications, EusLisp has extended Common Lisp to have built-in geometric functions with 3D drawing functions, interprocess communication, foreign language interface, Xwindow interface with a tool kit, relational database interface, etc.

EusLisp was first developed on Sun workstations and has been ported onto several architectures such as Alpha, SGI, Linux, and Windows. Although descriptions about the implementation of the multithread EusLisp hereafter may depend on Solaris-2 operating systems, the essentials are common to every operating systems that support multithreads either by the kernel or by the library.

3 Design of Multithread EusLisp

As mentioned above, multithreaded parallelism of EusLisp aims at increased computational power by parallel processing, and an improvement of real-time response by means of asynchronous programming. Moreover, in order not to sacrifice the software assets, it is important to keep the compatibility with the sequential version and to minimize the execution overhead needed for multithreading. Considering the machine architecture and the parallel computation model of the target operating system, Solaris-2, the implementation of the multithread EusLisp has to be carefully designed.

3.1 Multithread paradigm of Solaris-2

According to the literature [15], a thread is an execution context that shares resources, particularly a memory space, with other threads in a process. Thus, interdependent functions in a process that reference common memory objects can concurrently be executed by multiple threads. A thread is also an entity to which physical CPU is assigned. If there are multiple processors in a system, multiple threads in a process produces parallelism.

Multithreads are well understood when compared to processes. The classical multi process architecture of Unix is regarded as a multithread system where each process is allowed to have only one thread. When parallelism is needed, each process has to run in different address spaces. In other words, the modern multithread mechanism provides the shared-memory concurrency and parallelism. Since the address mapping is common to all threads in a process, faster creation, synchronization, and switching of threads are accomplished.

Unlike the Solaris-1 operating system which implements threads only in libraries at the application level, the Solaris-2 operating system distinguishes library threads and kernel threads. The latter are often called light weight processes (LWPs). An LWP is an entity for the kernel to allocate CPU from the multiprocessor pool, and to do the preemptive scheduling. While the LWP is the finite kernel resource, the thread is the virtual LWP defined by a thread library to provide flexibility and enhanced synchronization functions. **Fig. 1** shows the relationship between CPUs, LWPs and threads in a process.

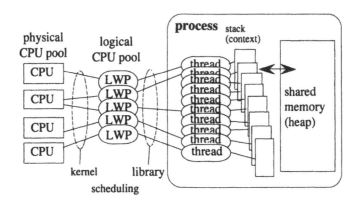

Figure 1: Threads in a process and CPU allocation scheduling

By making use of threads, programmers are allowed to write parallel programs without worrying about kernel resource limitations and number of processors. Namely, programmers just write functions running in parallel in a single address space. The thread library maps executable threads on available LWPs, and the kernel allocates physical CPUs to executable LWPs.

A thread has an independent context (a stack), and can issue a system call simultaneously with other threads. Therefore, static variables that are set by system calls, like errno, have to be allocated independently to each thread.

A bound thread which is statically assigned to an LWP can have a signal stack and timers. A thread is associated with an execution priority, which is used for time-sharing or realtime scheduling.

Since multiple threads can be put in a running state on multi-processor machines, and this scheduling may be preemptive and asynchronous, it is impossible to tell when a task switch occurs. This potential parallelism discourages a strategy to replace variable bindings at the task switch time.

The multithread model of Solaris-2 does not guarantee orders of memory access between threads. Suppose *thread-1* writes to *var-A* and *var-B* in this order, and *thread-2* is monitoring new values of *var-A* and *var-B*. However, finding a new value in *var-B* does not guarantee that the value of *var-A* is also new. Access order inversion can occur, because access speed takes precedence over synchronization in the memory controller. To avoid this inversion, a synchronization instruction must be issued. Unlike the multi process model that assumes independent address spaces, multithreads in a process share a single memory space and use global variables for communication between threads. Since memory access order is not preserved as described above, communication must carefully be serialized by synchronization primitives. As such synchronization primitives, Solaris-2 provides *mutex-lock, condition-variable, semaphore*, and *reader-writer-lock*.

Among these synchronization primitives, *mutex-lock* is most frequently used and assumed lightest. On a Sparc station-10 (SS-10), the time needed for a combination

```
/* thread context */
typedef struct {
        pointer     *stack, *vsp,*stacklimit;
        struct      callframe         *callfp;
        struct      catchframe        *catchfp;
        struct      bindframe         *bindfp;
        struct      specialbindframe  *sbindfp;
        struct      blockframe        *blkfp;
        struct      protectframe      *protfp;
        struct      fletframe         *fletfp, *newfletfp;
        pointer     lastalloc;
        pointer     errhandler;
        pointer     threadobj;
        struct      methdef           *methcache;
        struct      buddyfree         *thr_buddy;
        int         alloc_big_count, alloc_small_count;
        pointer     specials;
        int         intsig;
        } context;
```

Figure 2: Thread context structure definition

of mutex-lock and unlock was 2 micro seconds when there was no actual thread switch, and a few dozen to a few hundred micro seconds for a semaphore to switch threads depending on the number of available processors and bound/unbound LWPs.

3.2   Separation of Lisp contexts

For EusLisp to run a parallel program using multithreads, independent thread contexts must be managed. Roughly speaking, a context consists of a control stack, a bind stack, stack pointers, various frame pointers, a method cache, etc. Frame pointers indicate linked lists of value-binding, special-value-binding, block frames, catch frames, and flet/labels frames. These pointers bound to global variables in the sequential EusLisp are grouped together in a **thread context structure**, and a base pointer for a context picks up the current context frame. **Fig. 2** shows the thread context structure.

An alternative idea is to make a fork of a stack when a new thread is created and to share the root part of the stack between threads. We rejected this for simplicity. Therefore, threads communicate with each other through values bound to global symbols accessible by symbol-value, symbol-plist, etc. In other words, local variables introduced by let and lambda, or control structure defined by block, catch, throw, flet and labels, are not shared. For example, a catch tag is only valid for the thread that created it, and other threads cannot throw to the tag.

Scope of special variables is another issue. The sequential EusLisp adopted shallow binding for special variables, in which current values are always found in the value slot of a symbol and its old value is saved in a bind stack. Consequently the **symbol-value** of a symbol equals its most recent special value. This is reasonable for sequential programs, but not in a multithread environment which has multiple bind stacks. The problem arises because the value slot of a symbol is used in both ways as the global value and as the special value. We separated these usages by declarations. **Defvar** and **defparam** are used to define global variables, whereas a new directive, **deflocal**, defines special variables locally used in threads. For example, ***load-path*** introduced by **defvar** is a global variable common to all threads, whereas ***print-case*** and ***standard-output*** defined by **deflocal** are thread local special variables to control behaviours of the printer.

To realize the latter binding, a thread holds a static binding list for local special variables. When the evaluator encounters with a reference to a symbol value, it checks whether the symbol is declared as global or local, and looks in the static binding list, if local.

Reference to the context information happens very frequently as in push/pop operations of the bind stack. We added a pointer to this context information structure as another argument in every function call. This is not a big overhead because access to an argument held in a register is normally faster than to load a stack or a frame pointer from the global variable.

3.3 Thread allocation

A thread is associated to a Lisp context one to one. That is, a new stack object is allocated each time a new thread is created. Although a thread library imposes a limit to the number of threads, this limit, approximately several hundreds to several thousands, is usually large enough to accommodate a huge application in a 32-bit address space.

Though thread creation is lighter than a process creation, it is not a good idea to create a thread each time a new Lisp context is requested, because extra costs other than merely creating a thread are needed. These overheads are allocation of two big stacks for control and value binding, and setting attributes of pages at the edge of stacks to detect stack-overflow. Since typical stack size is roughly 1 MB, and the changing page attribute needs system calls, these costs are not negligible. Our measurement showed Lisp thread creation needed a time ten times as long as a simple thread creation.

Therefore, we take a strategy to prepare a thread pool before entering a heavy thread computation. Each time a function evaluation is committed to a thread, a thread is picked up from the pool and activated through the thread library. Details are discussed in sections 5.2 and 5.3.

3.4 Mutual exclusion

Access to global variables that are not accommodated in the context structure needs mutual exclusion by *mutex-lock*. The global variables most frequently accessed are the heap management database. This is discussed in the memory management section.

Mark bits in a memory object is another major shared resource. Each memory cell in the heap has three mark bits: *GC mark*, *copy-done mark* used by the `copy-object` function for deep copying, and *cycle-mark* to check recursive reference in the print and equal functions. These functions are not executed so frequently that exclusive access to these resources are controlled by the mutex-lock.

Method cache to speed up method search at message send operation needs to be updated exclusively if there is only one global cache in the system. Assuming a thread is likely to do different types of computation which collect different method entries in the cache, we allocate separate method caches to threads. This is reasonable, since mutex-lock of each method invocation would end up with significant performance degradation. Number of entries in a method cache is 256, which achieves 98% cache hits, and a cache table of 4KB is allocated to a thread.

Every thread shares memory objects such as `symbols`, `conses`, `strings`, etc., created in the single heap space. If an object is manipulated by more than one threads, unexpected effects may result. One particular example is an unexpected update of a hash table in a `package` object. If two threads are reading symbols in the same package in parallel, each read operation has a possibility to cause an extension of the hash table, resulting in a destruction of the hash table. In the extreme, every object has to have a mutex-lock, which is intolerable and unrealistic. So we left the responsibility of mutex operation of objects to programmers.

3.5 Comparison with other parallel Lisp systems

This section tries a comparison of the multithread EusLisp with other parallel Lisps, namely, *Lucid Common Lisp* and **Lisp*.

Lucid Common Lisp (abbreviated LCL hereafter) implements the full Common Lisp with many extensions [19]. LCL's multi-process facility is implemented by the Lisp system independently of the operating system's multithreads. Therefore, LCL can take full control over scheduling, process switching, prioritization, and so forth. Since everything is under LCL's control, it can correctly capture the timing to change variable bindings. On the other hand, independence from the operating system's multithread facility makes it impossible to associate a physical processor or a realtime priority, which are kernel resources, to a thread. We suppose LCL's copying GC will also be a bottleneck to a true multithread implementation, since every thread has to prepare for the changes of memory object locations caused by a GC, which may happen at any moment.

*Lisp is a parallel Lisp on CM-5, a parallel machine based on a distributed memory architecture. This memory architecture produces many differences both in implementation and in programming. For example, programmers are requested

to explicitly specify whether a memory object is allocated in the heap or in the stack. Lisp processes are running independently on physically separated processors, and 'pvar' is used to distribute immediate values. From a programmers viewpoint, lack of list, *Lisp looks like a different language from Lisp. If such inconsistency is imposed to take advantage of parallel processing, we would prefer to continue using sequential Lisp. From the above observation, we can conclude EusLisp can exhibit better functionality taking advantage of kernel and library threads, and can provide seamless compatibility with the Lisp programming paradigm.

4 Memory Management

4.1 Memory management in the sequential EusLisp

The memory management plays an important role in every Lisp system [16]. Among the many memory management schemes, EusLisp has adopted Fibonacci buddy memory management [14]. The main reasons to choose the Fibonacci buddy are that it provides high memory efficiency to variously sized memory requests, and GC runs fast because it does not copy objects. A drawback of buddy methods is an overhead needed for cell splitting at the allocation time and for merging at the reclaiming phase. Probably because this overhead has been estimated high, very few Lisp systems use the buddy method. However, in our experiment, we confirmed this drawback could be relieved by leaving certain amount of memory unmerged at the reclaiming phase.

EusLisp allocates memory objects in a uniform heap. Unlike the Big-Bag-of-Pages scheme, all objects of different types and sizes are created in a logically contiguous heap space. The single uniform heap frees programmers from parameter tuning for better allocation ratio to different types of objects. In the actual memory, many memory pages are linked to form the contiguous heap. New pages are requested whenever enough memory could not be reclaimed, enabling dynamic expansion of the heap.

Unused memory cells in the heap are moored to the buddy-base, which is the global database of free cells. The structure is depicted in **Fig. 3**. Memory allocation is handled by the **alloc** function. **Alloc** searches for the smallest free cell that satisfies a request in the buddy-base, and splits the cell according to the Fibonacci sequence if needed. Because the memory request pattern is biased to small cells, as depicted in **Fig. 4**, average length of this search does not exceed two, although the buddy-base moors free lists of 30 different sizes.

The initial numbers of the Fibonacci sequence are three and three, because the **cons**, the minimal structure, requires two words for car and cdr plus one word for the header. The logarithmic frequency of the memory requests regarding to the cell sizes is shown in **Fig. 4**.

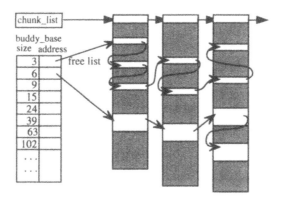

Figure 3: Fibonacci buddy cells allocated in heap pages and linked from the buddy-base

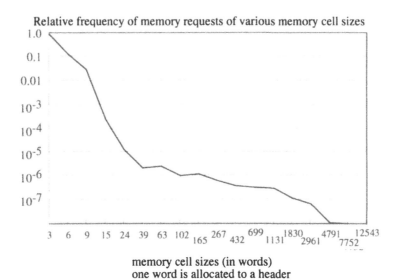

memory cell sizes (in words)
one word is allocated to a header

The frequency was observed when a typical EusLisp application for a solid modelling is run on SS20. 1,734sec was spent for the computation and totally 1.3GB of memory was allocated. Heap size of 6.2MB. GC ran 1204 times and 198 sec. spent for marking, 132 sec. for sweeping.

Figure 4: Memory request frequency pattern

4.2   Memory allocation in the multithread EusLisp

In order to apply the memory management scheme presented above to the multi-thread environment, there are two naive tactics. One is to provide many independent heaps for multiple threads, and the other is to allocate memory from one global heap, as the previous implementation.

While the former memory allocator can run independently of other threads' activity, the latter needs mutex-lock to exclusively access to the global buddy-base. It seems very costly to issue a mutex-lock every time **cons** is requested. From the viewpoint of memory efficiency, the former seems to leave more heap unused, since GC is needed to run whenerver the most memory-hungry thread exhausts its heap. This would result in worse memory usage, and frequent pause for GC as well, since every thread has to stop until the GC finishes.

There seems to be a trade-off between these two strategies. First, we did an experiment to take the latter technique. Access to the buddy-base is mutually excluded, and only one thread can call **alloc** at one time. Assuming the ratio for a thread to spend for allocation is 10% of all computation, even a 100% overhead in alloc would only bring 10% performance drop. On an SS-10, the time needed for a **cons** in the sequential EusLisp was 9 micro seconds, which was raised to 10 micro seconds in the mutex-locked alloc. Therefore, for some applications, mutex-locked alloc works fine.

4.3   Split Free List

Later, we found the estimated ratio of the time for allocation, 10%, was too optimistic for some applications. Particularly, a benchmark program that just copies lists spends more than 50% of the time for the memory management. If several threads are calling **cons** very frequently, they race for the right to enter **alloc**, having other threads being blocked. As will be demonstrated in the sixth section, a worst case benchmark exhibits very poor performance as the parallelism increases.

To improve the memory allocation performance, we took a compromising approach between the global heap and distributed heaps. The idea is to prepare a global heap and to associate a buddy-base (free list) to an individual thread, as depicted in **Fig. 5(a)**. Since each thread has a free list, the **alloc** function can handle memory allocation requests without doing mutex-lock. Each buddy-base of a thread has free lists for different sizes of cells. When a free list exhausts, mutex-lock is done, and ten to several hundred free cells are transferred from the global free list. In this way, the frequency of locking mutex is greatly decreased. For the garbage collector, cells transferred to local free-lists are treated as in use. If too many free cells are stored in the local free lists, chances to run GC increase, and memory is wasted. If the number of cells in the local free list is too few, chances of mutex-lock increase. Regarding the trade-off between these parameters, we experimentally decided the number of free cells in the free list as shown in **Fig. 5(b)**.

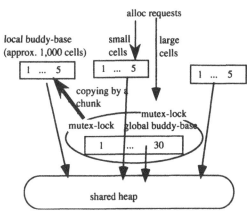

index	cell size	num cells	quantity (words)
1	3	500	1500
2	6	300	1800
3	9	20	180
4	15	15	225
5	24	10	240

(a) Split free-list heap management   (b) allocation of free memory to a thread

Figure 5: Split heap management implemented by the local and global buddy-base structures

4.4   Garbage Collection

The sequential EusLisp is not designed to allow a garbage collection to happen at arbitrary time. For example, for a short time just after a memory allocation, the pointer to the allocated object is only on the register. If GC is invoked in this period, a newly allocated object might be reclaimed as unused memory, since there is no indication in GC roots that the cell is in use.

There are two methods for solving this problem. Explicitly giving the timings when GC may run, or changing the result passing sequence to allow GC to happen at any moment. The former checks requests for a GC, for example, at the beginning of eval and alloc, lets GC run, and waits for the completion using a semaphore. The latter requests a new rule to place every living pointer on stack. In the current implementation, a function result is passed to the caller by a **return** statement in C. This should be changed to pass on stack, which would include changes and insertions of thousand of lines of code.

GC can run, if all pointers to living objects are interned in the root database, namely packages and stacks. The only case violating this rule is the dangling pointer just after **alloc** is finished. The pointer to a newly allocated object is returned to the requester, which will keep it in a register or in a local variable. It is guaranteed to write the pointer on the stack by the time **alloc** is called again for another memory allocation. This is all right for the sequential EusLisp, because GC is always run by **alloc** when it finds no free space. This is not true in a multithread execution, however, because other threads may call **alloc** interrupting the time period before the pointer is written to the stack. If the second **alloc** call invokes a GC, the last allocated cell can be recognized as a garbage (unmarkable) cell, and is reclaimed, which is wrong. In order to ensure this does not happen, we prepare the **last-alloc** slot in a thread context structure that holds a pointer to the last allocated cell, as shown in **Fig. 2**. The GC uses this pointer for marking as another root pointer.

To sum up, changes made to the memory manager are as follows:

1. Include a local buddy-base and `last-alloc` in a thread context structure

2. For small cells, `alloc` attempts to get a cell first in the local buddy-base.

3. When a local free list exhausts, a number of free cells are moved from the global free list. Mutex-lock is needed for this operation.

4. For large cells, the global buddy-base is always looked for.

5. `alloc` puts the pointer to the new memory cell in a thread's `last-alloc` slot.

6. If the global buddy-base is exhausted, all other threads are suspended, and a GC runs.

7. GC uses the list of package, stacks, and the `last-alloc` slots for marking roots.

4.5   Concurrent GC

It is only one thread that can begin GC; the thread mutex-locked for getting free cells in the global buddy-base. The marking and collecting phases can be processed by multiple threads for speed-up. Also, based on the parallel GC technique, we can run mutator and collector concurrently. This opens a path to the real-time application in Lisp. Y. Tanaka tried an implementation of concurrent GC in EusLisp and succeeded in reducing the GC pause from 300ms to 30ms [18].

5   Concurrent Programming in EusLisp

This section describes the implementation of concurrent primitives in the multithread EusLisp and concurrent programming from a programmer's viewpoint.

5.1   Thread creation

The Solaris thread library provides the `thr_create` function that creates a thread for a computation of a specified function.

```
thr_create(stackbase, stacksize, func, arg, flag)
```

As stated in 3.3, it is costly to create a thread each time commitment is made, and to destroy it when the computation finishes. Therefore, we create threads in advance of commitment. The following expression creates n threads and puts them in the global thread pool.

```
(make-thread n)
```

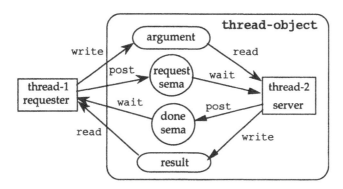

Figure 6: Threads communicating via semaphores in a thread-object for invocation and result transfer

5.2 Computation commitment to a thread

When a thread, which might be the main thread, commits a computation to another thread picked up in the thread pool, the communication depicted in **Fig. 7** is performed. Two semaphores intervene in the commitment. The requester places parameters in a fixed location and signals the *request semaphore*. The server thread is woken up by the *request semaphore*, and begins evaluation using the given parameters. When the computation is done, the server thread puts the result in a certain location and post to the *done semaphore*. While the server is evaluating the arguments, the requester thread can do other computation. The requester waits for the *done semaphore* when it wants the result.

5.3 Thread pool

In order to distribute computation to many threads and to get results, the requester must be able to identify a thread for a particular computation. Since EusLisp threads do not share contexts, any thread should produce the same result. Therefore, threads in the thread pool are treated equally. The thread pool consists of a list of free threads and a semaphore to signal existence of at least one free thread.

For Lisp programmers, a thread is represented by a **thread** object. A **thread** object has thread-id, semaphores for the commitment, and slots for parameters and a result. When a thread becomes ready to perform computation, it puts itself in the *free-thread-list*, and posts to the *free-thread-semaphore*. A requester waits for the *free-thread-semaphore*, and takes one thread out of the *free-thread-list*.

5.4 Synchronization

EusLisp provides the **mutex-lock** class and **semaphore** class which inherit the **integer-vector** class for low-level synchronization. Since lock and unlock are always paired for mutual exclusion, the following macro is defined.

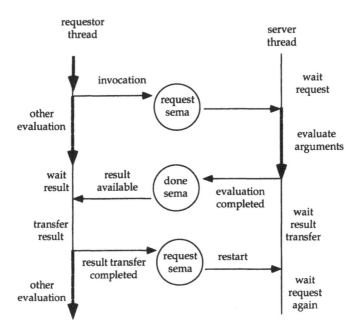

Figure 7: Control flow and communication upon a thread invocation

```
(mutex lock . forms)
```

Since this form is expanded into an **unwind-protect** special form, we can ensure
mutex-unlock even when a **throw** is executed to an upper level.

Using
this **mutex-lock** and semaphore as primitives, the **barrier-synchronization** for
more than two threads to synchronize and the **synchronized-memory-port** class for
synchronized communication in which the reader and writer are forced to wait until
the data is actually transferred are provided.

5.5   Parallel syntax

As for the representation including execution semantics, MultiLisp has proposed
the *future* syntax, and Scheme or PaiLisp has proposed the *continuation*. Though
EusLisp's parallel syntax has not yet matured, the following primitives, i.e., **thread**
and **wait-thread** are powerful enough for most applications.

```
(thread func . args) --> a thread object

(wait-thread thread)  --> result of (func . args)
```

Thread finds a free thread in the free thread pool and commits evaluation of a
function, and returns immediately without being blocked. **Wait-thread** retrieves the
result of the evaluation.

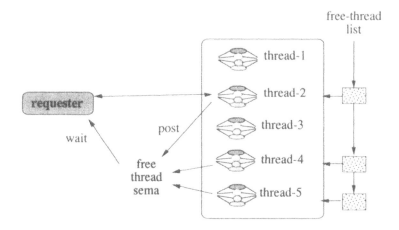

Figure 8: Thread pool

For easier description of a parallel computation, the `parlist` macro is provided. `Parlist` is expanded to evaluate every argument using the `thread` function and to wait for the completion of all threads, and list the results.

```
(parlist form1 form2 ... form-n)
```

6 Performance Evaluation

Based on the above discussions, EusLisp has been re-implemented as a multithread Lisp. Its performance has been evaluated by running benchmark programs on multiprocessor machines.

First of all, we compared the performance of the dynamically-linked multithread EusLisp with the statically-linked sequential EusLisp by running a sequential program in one thread. The performance drop was approximately 5 to 10%. We estimate this comes from overheads introduced by the multithreading and the dynamic linking to call shared library on Solaris-2.

6.1 Multiprocessor platforms

We used CS6400 of Cray Research Inc. for the performance evaluation. A processing unit (PU) of a CS6400 consists of 60MHz Super Sparc+ processor and 2MB level-2 cache memory. Four PUs are combined to form a node. Each node is connected to the shared memory through four-way interleaved XDBus, each of which transfers 64 bit words at 55MHz. We used a CS6400 of 32 PUs operated by RIPS, Agency of Industrial Science and Technology, Tsukuba, Japan.

6.2 Benchmark programs

We ran the six benchmark programs with the following names and characteristics.

benchmark	cached code	cached data	seq. access	non-shared data	no alloc.
Compfib	O	O	N/A	O	O
Intfib	X	X	N/A	O	O
Inner prod	O	O	O	X	O
List replace	O	O	X	X	O
Copy-seq	O	O	X	X	XX
Body-intcheck	X	X	X	X	X

Table 1: Characteristics of benchmark programs

(a) **compfib** This is a compiled Fibonacci function. Since the size of the compiled code is very small, the entire code can be accommodated in a local cache. Depth of the recursion is 30. Memory accesses are bound to local memory, i.e., stack, and no access to the shared memory happens. No memory allocation is requested.

(b) **intfib** This is an interpreted Fibonacci function, whose memory access spreads much greater than compfib. The interpreter reads shared data such as symbols as variable names and the program represented by lists. Interpreter does not request memory, even a cons.

(c) **inner-prod** A built-in function v. (v-dot) is repeatedly applied to single-precision floating-point vector of one thousand elements. The code of v. is small enough to run in cache. Two argument vectors in the shared heap get sequential access by many threads simultaneously. No memory allocation is requested.

(d) **list-replace** A list of one thousand elements is copied to another list using the replace function. The function code is small enough to run in cache. The list read in is shared data, and the list written is local data stored in the heap. Access pattern differs from **inner-prod**, because conses in a list are not necessarily arranged consecutively. No memory allocation is requested.

(e) **copy-seq** A list of one thousand elements is allocated and the contents are copied from a given list. The list read in is shared data, whereas the output list is only accessed locally to each thread. Copy-seq is small enough to run in cache, but requests huge number of conses. If run in the sequential EusLisp, it spends 35% time for memory allocation, 30% for list copying, and 35% for GC.

(f) **body-intcheck** Body-intcheck performs interference checking of two solid models. This is an application level function important to the solid modeling. The function consists of hundreds of functions and methods including vector/matrix operations, scanning lists, sorting, message sending, etc. It requests frequent memory allocation for conses, vectors, and objects of various sizes. Two solid model data are read out from a shared data structure.

concurrency	1			2			4			8			16		
	T_{elapse}	T_{run}	T_{GC}	T_{elapse}	T_{run}	T_{GC}	T_{elapse}	T_{run}	T_{GC}	T_{elapse}	T_{run}	T_{GC}	T_{elapse}	T_{run}	T_{GC}
compfib	1.0	1.0	0.0	1.0	2.0	0.0	1.0	4.0	0.0	1.0	8.0	0.0	1.0	15.9	0.0
intfib	1.0	1.0	0.0	1.2	2.3	0.0	1.4	5.4	0.0	1.6	12.3	0.0	2.0	30.7	0.0
inner-prod	1.0	1.0	0.0	1.0	2.0	0.0	1.1	4.0	0.0	1.1	8.1	0.0	1.1	16.8	0.0
list-replace	1.0	1.0	0.0	1.1	2.2	0.0	1.2	4.7	0.0	1.3	9.9	0.0	1.6	23.5	0.0
copy-seq	1.0	1.0	0.4	2.3	2.3	0.8	7.3	12.2	1.6	18.3	43.8	3.2	45.5	146.3	6.3
body-intcheck	1.0	1.0	0.2	2.1	2.1	0.5	14.5	36.1	1.1	37.1	132.3	2.1	51.6	183.6	4.4

Table 2: Normalized parallel performance: Elapsed time (T_{elapse}), total run time (T_{run}), and garbage collection time (T_{GC}) measured at each concurrency and normalized by $T_{elapse}(1)$

Overall characteristics of these benchmarks are summarized in **Table 1**.

6.3   Memory arrangement

The total amount of memory needed for executing benchmarks is approximately 4MB. Since the machine is equipped with 8GB real memory, no disturbance by virtual storage management is expected. The heap is arranged to leave 40% free space after a GC.

6.4   Performance measurement

Benchmark programs are run on the CS6400 and the time elapsed (T_{elapse}), the sum of the execution time of all threads (T_{run}), and time for GC (T_{gc}) are measured at various concurrency (C). Timings are acquired in an exclusive use of the machine. T_{elapse} is acquired by the **gettimeofday** function which gives 0.1 s resolution, and T_{run} and T_{gc} are acquired by the **times** function at 0.01s resolution. Measurements were taken 10 times and the average was calculated. One to sixteen concurrency levels are measured by changing the number of threads in the **parlist** macro. In this method, when $C = n$, the total amount of the computation is n times greater than that of $C = 1$.

To simplify the comparison between benchmarks and machines, all timings were normalized by dividing by $T_{elapse}(1)$. The results are listed in **Table-2**. Since concurrency level is always lower than the number of physical processors, all threads can execute computation without being scheduled for allocating to available processors.

Next, to represent the effect of parallel computation in numbers, we computed the parallel gain at concurrency C, $P_{gain}(C)$, as follows:

$P_{gain}(C) = C \times T_{elapse}(1)/T_{elapse}(C)$

In other words, P_{gain} is the ratio of parallel computation to the corresponding sequential execution, and means how much speed-up can be obtained from a parallel

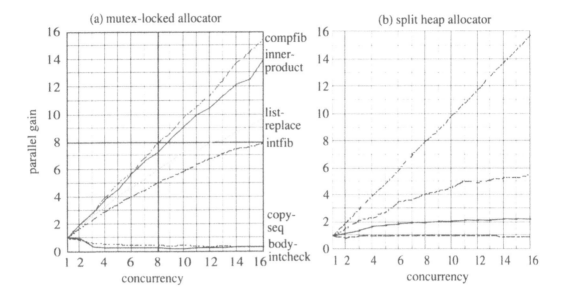

Figure 9: Parallel execution performance of six benchmarks

execution. P_{gain} for six benchmarks are plotted in **Fig. 9 (a)**.

6.5   Consideration

Factors affecting parallel performance are: (1) shared memory access, (2) overhead introduced by mutex, (3) serial part remaining in the memory management. Among our benchmark programs, *copy-seq* and *body-interference* are affected by (2) and (3), and others are only affected by (1).

6.5.1   (1) Bottleneck for shared memory access

On an SMP architecture machine like CS6400, both instruction access and data access compete for the shared memory. Programs with relatively a small working-set can decrease access to the shared memory by taking advantage of a cache memory, and higher performance can be expected. In **Fig. 9**, *compfib* exhibits ideal parallel gain growing almost linearly to the concurrency. *Inner-product, list-replace,* and *intfib* follow this top data.

Among these, *inner-product* is the second best, because the inner-most loop fits in the cache and the memory system can efficiently read out consecutively stored data. The increase of T_{run} more than the concurrency number in **Table-2** suggests shared memory access is often put in a wait state in a parallel execution. Thanks to the CS6400's big cache line size and four-way interleave memory bus, consecutive memory access is greatly sped up. On the other hand, *list-replace* shows a slight performance drop because of random data access. *Intfib* is worse because its instruction stream is not straight. Greater effect of linearized instruction stream than linearized data stream is observed.

6.5.2 (2) Mutual exclusion and (3) Serial part

In **Fig. 9(a)**, the performance of *Copy-seq* and *body-intcheck* are decreasing as the concurrency goes up. These benchmarks are different from others in that they request a great number of memory allocation and GC runs frequently.

The performance drop is understood as the effect of mutex-locks in `alloc`. Threads are racing for the access to the global buddy-base. As the concurrency increases, there is less chance to enter `alloc` without being blocked.

Fig. 9(b) depicts parallel performance gain when the split heap memory management is used. Comparing two graphs, we can conclude the split heap memory management can reduce mutex-lock drastically and exhibits better performance. However, it is also apparent that these two benchmarks are still very slow compared with other non-memory requesting benchmarks.

We can attribute these result to the high percentage of serial parts in GC. Looking at the timings when concurrency is one, we can estimate the serial part of an execution is more than 40% in *copy-seq* and 20% in *body-intcheck*. In our measurement, the amount of computation increases according to the concurrency. **Fig. 10** shows the increase of computation and proportions of GC according to the concurrency. When the concurrency is more than three, almost 60% of time for GC, which runs serially suspending other threads. If there exists 50% serial part, even a huge multiprocessor of an infinite number of processors can barely attain two times faster execution than the uniprocessor execution. If the serial part is 75%, no parallel gain is obtained from parallel execution. In this sense, **Fig. 9** shows reasonable results.

We observe another overhead in these benchmarks. Solaris-2's thread library implements mutex-lock with spin-lock using an atomic *load-store* instruction. This means CPU time increases even when the CPU is in a wait state, which is well observed in the extreme increase of T_{run} in **Table-2**. Finding that it is a waste of processor time after a certain number of spins to get lock, mutex-lock turns into a semaphore wait, which is handled by the OS kernel. At a marginal situation, this semaphore wait may be immediately satisfied and task switch happens. This also adds extra overhead both in T_{elapse} and T_{run}.

6.6 Applicability of parallel Lisp

From the above consideration, it is apparent that applicability of parallel computation is application dependent. Especially, it is very difficult to speed up memory hungry programs using the sequential memory manager. On a shared memory machine like CS6400, the application of parallel EusLisp should be limited to functions that do not request much memory, have a small inner loop, manipulate vectors rather than lists, etc. If we think about the task switch time, use of mutex-lock should be minimized, and operations of greater granularity are preferred. If these conditions

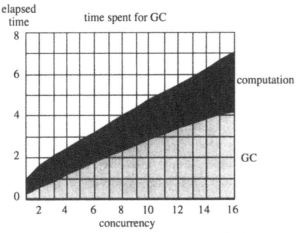

GC time increases more quickly than real computation time,
since there is substantial serial parts in GC.

Figure 10: GC time increase in the body-intcheck benchmark

are met, we can expect high performance gain as shown by *compfib*.

For greater range of applications, the memory management is a bottleneck, but
still we have good prospect for more practical applications using parallel GC as
described in [18].

As stated in the first section, the purpose of multithread EusLisp is not only in the
parallel performance gain but also in writing asynchronous programs. In this direction, an AI group at ETL applied multithread EusLisp to the organic programming
system, *GAEA*[20]. GAEA is a logic programming language with multiple concurrent
contexts.

7   Conclusion

The multithread computing model of the SMP architecture provides a natural extension toward parallel and asynchronous programming of Lisp while keeping the
software heritage from the sequential Lisp systems.

This paper described the design of the multithread EusLisp, putting the primary
focus on the memory management. Relatively small modifications to the classical
Fibonacci buddy memory management were sufficient to upgrade to a multithread
environment. Bench marking shows that the memory management has the greatest
effect on performance. By allocating free lists locally to threads, overheads of mutex
to access the global memory management database was avoided. The serial part in
GC, however, degraded the parallel performance greatly, and the partial marking
parallel GC is one of the most promising approaches. Other factors affecting performance are the working set and the access frequency to the global memory, which
are also true to all sequential processes on cache-based machines. From the view-

point of asynchronous programming, capabilities for multiple simultaneous system calls and concurrent signal handling will play important roles particularly in robotics applications.

Through writing multithread programs in EusLisp, we learned that the debugging environment is very important in parallel computing. Errors put threads in infinite loops unnoticeably, messages from threads are mingled on the screen, and it is unpredictable which thread will catch a keyboard interrupt. Without good debugging tools, multithreading can totally spoil Lisp's comfortable interactive programming.

EusLisp is open to public and available at the following URL:

`http://www.etl.go.jp/~matsui/eus/euslisp.html`.

EusLisp has been applied to many robotics problems and is currently used for implementing a multi-agent system on a talking mobile robot, Jijo-2 [21, 22], in our group.

Acknowledgement

We express sincere gratitude to Prof. Takase and Dr. Tsukune, Directors of Intelligent Systems Division, ETL, for giving us an opportunity to develop EusLisp. We were able to improve EusLisp with the implementation efforts by Dr. Tanakas' and others in Prof. Nakanishi's group at Keio University and with porting works by Dr. Hara of ETL and Mr. Konaka of Logic Design Corp., and with feed-backs from Dr. Hirukawa of ETL, Prof. Inaba and Dr. Kagami of Tokyo University.

Bibliography

1) T. Matsui and M. Inaba, EusLisp: an Object-based Implementation of Lisp, *Journal of Information Processing*, Vol. 13, No. 3, 1990, pp. 327–338.

2) T. Matsui and S. Sekiguchi, Design and Implementation of Parallel EusLisp Using Multithread, *Journal of Information Processing*, Vol. 36, No. 8, 1995, pp. 1885–1896, (in Japanese).

3) T. Matsui and I. Hara, EusLisp Reference Manual, version 8.00, Technical Report, Electrotechnical Laboratory, ETL TR95-2, 1995.

4) T. Matsui, "http://www.etl.go.jp/ matsui/eus/euslisp.html" 1997.

5) G. L. Steel, Jr., *Common Lisp the Language*, Digital-Press, 1984.

6) G. L. Steel, Jr., *Common Lisp the Language Second Ed.*, Digital-Press, 1990.

7) H. Onda, T. Hasegawa and T. Matsui, Collision Avoidance for a 6-DOF Manipulator Based on Empty Space Analysis of the 3-D Real World, *Proc. of IROS'90*, Tsuchiura, 1990.

8) T. Omata, Finger Position Computation for 3-dimensional Equilibrium Grasps, *Proc. of IEEE Int. Conf. on Robotics and Automation*, pp. 216–222, Atlanta, 1993.

9) H. Hirukawa, T. Matsui and K. Takase, Automatic Determination of Possible Velocity and Applicable Force of Frictionless Objects in Contact from Geometric Models under Translation and Rotation, *IEEE trans. on Robotics and Automation*, Vol. 10, No. 3, 1994.

10) T. Hasegawa, et al., An Integrated Tele-Robot System with a Geometric Environment Model and Manipulation Skills, *Proc. of Int. Conf. on Intelligent Robots and Systems (IROS-90)*, pp. 335-341, Tsuchiura, 1990.

11) S. Sakane, T. Sato, et al., A Distributed Sensing System with 3D Model-Based Agents, *Proc. of Int. Conf. on Intelligent Robots and Systems (IROS-93)*, pp. 1157–1163, 1993.

12) R. H. Halstead, Jr., Implementation of Multilisp: Lisp on a Multiprocessor, *Conference Record of the 1984 ACM Symposium on a Lisp and Functional Programming*, pp. 9–17, 1984.

13) G. L. Steele, Jr., *Common Lisp the Language*, Digital Press, 1984.

14) J. L. Peterson and T. A. Norman, Buddy systems, *Communication of the ACM*, Vol. 20, No. 6, 1977.

15) Multithreaded Programming Guide, In the manual set of Solaris 2.4, Sun Soft, 1994.

16) R. Jones and R. Lins, *Garbage Collection, Algorithms for Automatic Dynamic Memory Management*, John Wiley & Sons, 1996.

17) *Lisp Dictionary version 6.1, Thinking Machines, 1991.

18) Y. Tanaka, S. Matsui, A. Maeda and M. Nakanishi, Partial Marking GC: Generational Parallel Garbage Collection and its Performance Analysis, T. Yuasa, and H. G. Okuno eds., *Advanced Lisp Technology*, Gordon and Breach, 1998, pp. –.

19) The Multitasking facility, advanced user's guide, Lucid Common Lisp/Sun version 4.0, chapter 5, 1991.

20) H. Nakashima, I. Noda, K. Handa and J. Fry, GAEA Programming Manual, Technical Report, ETL-TR-96-11, Electrotechnical Laboratory, 1996.

21) T. Matsui, H. Asoh, et al., An Event-Driven Architecture for Controlling Behaviours of the Office Conversant Mobile Robot, Jijo-2, *Proceedings of IEEE International Conference on Robotics and Automation (ICRA-97)*, pp. 3367–3372, Albuquerque, 1997.

22) J. Fry, H. Asoh and T. Matsui, Natural Dialogue with the Jijo-2 Office Robot, *Proc. of IEEE/RSJ Int. Conf. on Intelligent Robots and Systems (IROS-98)*, pp. 1278–1283, 1998.

5

TUPLE: An Extended Common Lisp for SIMD Architecture

Yuasa Taiichi

Graduate School of Informatics
Kyoto University

Yasumoto Taichi

Faculty of Integrated Arts and Sciences
Aichi University of Education

Yoshitaka Nagano

NTN Corporation

Katsumi Hatanaka

Oki Electric Industry Co., Ltd.

ABSTRACT

An extended Common Lisp language and system, called TUPLE, for SIMD (Single Instruction stream, Multiple Data) architectures is presented. Unlike other Lisp languages on SIMD architectures, TUPLE supports the programming model that there are a huge number of subset Common Lisp systems running in parallel. For this purpose, each PE (processing element) of the target machine has its own heap in its local memory. In addition, there is a full-set Common Lisp system with which the user interacts to develop and execute parallel programs. This paper briefly introduces the TUPLE language and system, and then reports the implementation on the SIMD machine MasPar MP-1 with at least 1024 PEs, together with the performance evaluation.

1 Introduction

Several computation models have been proposed for the so-called massively parallel computation, in which thousands or more PEs (processing elements) run in parallel. The SIMD (Single Instruction, Multiple Data) model seems one of the most promising

81

models for applications with regular structures. In fact, some commercial SIMD machines are available and are being used for realistic applications.

So far, SIMD machines have been mainly used for numeric computation, and thus most languages in use are extensions of Fortran and C. On the other hand, parallel computation is highly required in the application areas of symbolic computation or list processing, where Lisp languages have traditionally been used.

In this paper, we present TUPLE, which is a Lisp language and system to develop application programs of symbolic computation on SIMD architectures. Our goal is to verify the feasibility of the SIMD model for symbolic computation. For this purpose, we need an efficient Lisp implementation on SIMD architectures, as the platform to develop and test massively-parallel symbolic algorithms. Thus, TUPLE was designed so that it can be implemented efficiently on SIMD architectures.

So far, several Lisp languages and systems have been developed for SIMD architectures, such as Connection Machine Lisp [7, 8, 13], Paralation Lisp [4, 5], *Lisp [15], and Plural EuLisp [2]. These languages provide new data structures that can be handled in parallel. For example, *xappings* in Connection Machine Lisp are vector-like data structures with parallel operations defined on them. These languages share the same computation model that the front-end processor dominates the entire control flow and the PEs are used for parallel execution of operations on the extended data structures. By taking a different approach, TUPLE allows flexible and efficient programming on SIMD architectures.

In SIMD machines, PEs do not have their own instruction streams but they simply execute instructions supplied by the front-end. Except for this point, each PE can be regarded as an ordinary uni-processor. This means each PE has the ability to run a Lisp system. Because of the small size (typically a few kilo bytes) of the local memory in actual SIMD machines, the Lisp system on each PE ought to be very compact, but it should be powerful enough to allow symbolic computation and list processing. The front-end, on the other hand, is a general-purpose machine such as a Unix workstation and thus has the ability to run a modern Lisp system.

The computation model of TUPLE reflects these features of SIMD architectures. That is, there are a huge number of Lisp systems called *PE subsystems* running in parallel. These PE subsystems execute programs in a subset Common Lisp [6]. In addition, there is a full-set Common Lisp system, called the *front-end system*, with which the user interacts to develop and execute parallel Lisp programs. This model of TUPLE has the following advantages.

- Parallel programs can be described in the same notation as ordinary sequential programs.

- Performance of a program can be estimated easily, since the model reflects the underlying SIMD architecture. This increases the possibility of tuning up program performance.

- The programmer can make use of the efficient programming environment supplied by the front-end system.

In this paper, we first introduce the TUPLE language and system in Section 2. Section 3 gives an example of parallel list processing in TUPLE. The entire language of TUPLE is made clear in Section 4. In Section 5, we present the implementation of TUPLE on the MasPar MP–1 and finally in Section 6, we report some results of performance measurements of TUPLE.

2 An Overview

This section introduces the language and system of TUPLE, through simple examples. We use a simple function **abs** which computes the absolute value of the given argument. In Common Lisp, this function can be defined as follows.

```
(defun abs (x)
   (if (>= x 0) x (- x)))
```

That is, if the argument is greater than or equal to zero, then the function simply returns the argument. Otherwise, the function returns the negative of the argument. By replacing **defun** with **defpefun**, the similar function will be defined in the PE subsystems.

```
(defpefun abs (x)
   (if (>= x 0) x (- x)))
```

When this *PE function* is invoked, all PEs receive independent values, one value per PE. Then those PEs that receives non-negative numbers will return the arguments. The other PEs will return the negatives of the arguments.

TUPLE runs on SIMD architectures, where no two PEs can execute different instructions at the same time. What actually happens is the following. When the PE function **abs** is invoked, those PEs that do not satisfy the condition becomes inactive while the other PEs (i.e., those PEs that satisfy the condition) evaluate the *then* clause. Then the activity of each PE is reversed and the previously inactive PEs evaluate the *else* clause, while the previously active PEs are inactive.

Below is an example interaction between the user and the TUPLE system. The top-level of TUPLE is similar to that of ordinary Common Lisp systems. The user can input any Common Lisp form at the top-level. Then the form is (sequentially) evaluated and the result is displayed.

```
% tuple
TUPLE (Massively Parallel KCL)

>(defun abs (x)
    (if (>= x 0) x (- x)))
ABS
>(abs -3)
3
```

Table 1: Reductions.

some-pe	some-penumber	some-pevalue
every-pe	not-any-pe	not-every-pe
reduce-max	reduce-min	reduce-char-max
reduce-char-min	reduce-logand	reduce-logior
reduce-logxor	reduce-+	reduce-*
reduce		

Here, the lines with lower case letters are inputs from the user and the lines with upper case letters are outputs from the system. The symbol '>' at the beginning of a line is the prompt from the system.

In order to start a parallel computation, the user has to supply a form in the extended language of TUPLE.

```
>(defpefun abs (x)
    (if (>= x 0) x (- x)))
ABS
>(ppe penumber)
#P(0 1 2 3 ...)
>(ppe (abs (- penumber 2)))
#P(2 1 0 1 ...)
```

In this example, the user uses the **ppe** form that passes a *PE form* to PE subsystems for evaluation and displays the results. Such **ppe** forms are mainly used at the top-level of TUPLE to supply a top-level form to the PE subsystems.

The **penumber** in the above example is a built-in constant in PE subsystems which holds the processor number for each PE. The "first" processor has 0 as the value of **penumber**, the "second" has 1, and so on. The second **ppe** form computes the absolute value of **penumber** − 2 by calling the PE function **abs**. Thus, the first processor, for instance, returns 2 as the value.

Note that TUPLE uses distinct name spaces for ordinary sequential functions and PE functions. In the example, **abs** names both the sequential function and the PE function. This is because a PE function is defined in the PE subsystems, whereas a sequential function is defined in the full-set Common Lisp system on the front-end with which the user interacts.

The **ppe** form in the example displays the values returned by the PEs, but it does *not* return the values. Actually, it returns "no value" in the terminology of Common Lisp. The so-called "parallel values" or "plural values" are not first-class objects in TUPLE. In order to obtain a single value from the values of PEs, the user has to use a *reduction* operation. Table 1 lists reduction operations of TUPLE. The function **reduce-max**, for example, returns the maximum value among the values that are returned by all active PEs. The function **reduce** is a general-purpose reduction operation, which accepts the function that is used for reduction. For example,

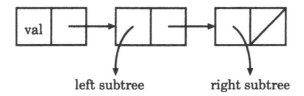

left subtree   right subtree

Figure 1: A node of a binary search tree.

```
(reduce #'max x)
```

is equivalent to

```
(reduce-max x)
```

3   Parallel List Processing

As a typical example of parallel list processing, we will show how binary search trees can be handled in TUPLE. In Lisp, each node of a binary search tree can be represented as a list of three elements (see Figure 1). The first element is the value of the node, and the second and the third elements are respectively the left and the right subtrees of the node. Node values in the left subtree are all less than the current node value, and node values in the right subtree are all greater than the current node value. Ordinary binary search function can then be defined so that it recursively descends the given binary search tree, to find the given item in $\log n$ time, with n being the number of nodes in the tree. In Common Lisp, the binary search function can be defined as follows.

```
(defun binary-search (tree item)
  (if (null tree)
      nil
      (if (= (car tree) item)
          t
          (binary-search
            (if (> (car tree) item)
                (cadr tree)
                (caddr tree))
            item)))))
```

In order to parallelize the binary search function, we assume that the entire binary search tree is represented by disjoint *PE trees*, one per PE (see Figure 2). Each PE tree of a PE is itself a binary search tree that is constructed with cons cells in the PE subsystem of the PE. If any pair of two PE trees are disjoint (i.e., have no common node value), then we can regard the whole collection of the PE trees as a large binary search tree. We will show later how such PE trees can be constructed in TUPLE.

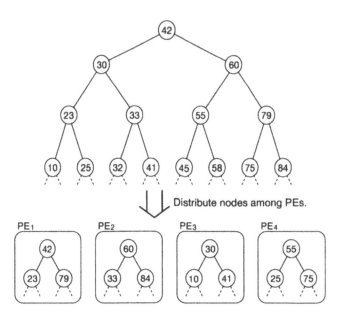

Figure 2: PE trees (for 4 PEs).

The parallel version of the binary search function can be defined as follows.

```
(defpefun binary-search (tree item)
  (if (null tree)
      nil
      (exif (= (car tree) item)
            t
            (binary-search
              (if (> (car tree) item)
                  (cadr tree)
                  (caddr tree))
              item)))))
```

The point here is that, when one of the PEs finds the item in its PE tree, the other
PEs need not go further. Rather, we would like to stop computation as soon as a
PE finds the item. Since this kind of processor synchronization is common to many
parallel algorithms, we introduce a new construct **exif** (exclusive if). The **exif** form

(exif *condition then-clause else-clause*)

is similar to the ordinary if form, but if some PEs satisfy the *condition*, then the
other PEs do not evaluate the *else-clause*. The parallel binary search function above
returns immediately if the current node value for some PE is equal to the item, in
which case that PE returns the true value t and the rest of the PEs return the false
value nil.

In order to perform efficient binary search, each PE tree must be balanced. In addition, the entire PE trees among PEs must be balanced. Therefore, when adding an item into one of the PE trees, the best choice will be the PE tree of the PE that first reaches a leaf during binary search. Based on this idea, we define the following PE function **bs-add**, which inserts an item into one of the PE trees.

```
(defpefun bs-add (place item)
  (cond ((some-pe (null (car place)))
         (exif (binary-search (car place) item)
               nil
               (when (= (some-penumber
                          (null (car place)))
                        penumber)
                 (rplaca place
                   (list item nil nil)))))
        ((some-pe (= (caar place) item))
         nil)
        (t (bs-add
             (if (> (caar place) item)
                 (cdar place)
                 (cddar place))
             item))))
```

This function behaves as follows:

1. If some PEs reach a leaf, the other PEs begin to simply search the item.

   (a) If one of the PEs finds the item, then all PEs return false.

   (b) Otherwise, one PE is selected among those PEs that first reached a leaf, and the item is added there.

2. If one of the PEs finds the item, then all PEs return false.

3. Otherwise, all PEs traverse their PE trees recursively.

To simplify the algorithm, we pass to the function the place holders of the current subtrees. Each place holder is a cons cell whose **car** part points to the current subtree. The predicates **some-pe** and **some-penumber** are reduction functions. The predicate **some-pe** returns the true value to all PEs if its argument is true for some PE, and **some-penumber** returns the processor number of such a PE to all PEs. If more than one PEs receive true, then **some-penumber** chooses one of the PEs and returns the processor number. The expression

```
(some-pe (null (car place)))
```

in the second line tests where there is a PE that reaches a leaf. In the **else** clause of the **exif** expression, **some-penumber** is used to select one PE among those PEs that have reached a leaf.

Initially, each PE has an empty tree. This initialization can be done by the following top-level form.

```
>(defpevar pe-tree (list nil))
```

This form defines a *PE variable* named **pe-tree**, whose initial value is the place holder for the empty tree for each PE. By invoking the PE function **bs-add**, the specified item will be inserted into one of the PE trees. For example,

```
>(ppe pe-tree)
#P((NIL) (NIL) (NIL) (NIL) ...)
>(ppe (bs-add pe-tree 503))
#P(T NIL NIL NIL ...)
>(ppe pe-tree)
#P(((503 NIL NIL)) (NIL) (NIL) (NIL) ...)
```

By repeatedly invoking the function, we can construct PE trees in the PE local memories.

4   The Language

In this section, we briefly present the language of TUPLE. Remember that TUPLE is an extension of Common Lisp. This means TUPLE supports all features of Common Lisp and any Common Lisp program runs on the TUPLE system, though such a program runs sequentially.

4.1   Data Objects

All data objects defined in Common Lisp are also defined in TUPLE. In addition, TUPLE supports the following data objects for parallel computation.

- PE conses

  PE conses are cons objects that are allocated in the PE subsystems. We have already seen how these objects are handled in TUPLE programs. Like ordinary conses, a PE cons can hold any TUPLE object in its **car** and **cdr** fields.

- PE vectors

  PE vectors are one-dimensional arrays allocated in the PE subsystems. Like ordinary vectors, a PE vector can hold any TUPLE object as its element.

- PE function objects

  Like ordinary functions, PE functions are also first-class objects. This allows TUPLE programs to dynamically determine a function to be invoked. Since TUPLE runs on SIMD architectures, only one PE function can be invoked at a time.

Both front-end variables and PE variables can hold any TUPLE objects. In particular, a front-end variable can hold a PE cons, a PE vector, or a PE function object, and a PE variable can hold any Common Lisp object.

As in many Common Lisp systems, fixnums, short-floats, and characters are immediate data in TUPLE. Operations on these objects are performed in parallel by the PE subsystems. The other Common Lisp data objects, such as symbols, are represented as a pointer to the data cell in the front-end heap. In SIMD architectures, no two PEs can access different locations of the front-end memory simultaneously. Thus, accessing the front-end heap from the PE subsystems is inevitably a sequential operation, one access at a time. The only parallel operation on front-end objects is the pointer comparison **eq**.

4.2   PE Forms

Forms that are input to the TUPLE top-level are regarded as *front-end forms*, or *FE forms* for short. Any ordinary Common Lisp forms are FE forms. FE forms are evaluated in the front-end system, until TUPLE encounters forms for parallel computation. If a FE form does not contain such a form, then TUPLE behaves in exactly the same way as a Common Lisp system does.

We have already seen the following form for parallel computation.

   (ppe *form*)

This *forms* is not an ordinary (i.e., front-end) form, but is a form that is intended to be executed by the PE subsystems in parallel. Such forms are called *PE forms*. Since a form is usually input at the top-level, PE forms are represented by objects in the heap of the front-end system.

The followings are valid PE forms.

- List forms

    - Special forms
    - Macro forms
    - Function call forms

- Variables

- Self-evaluating forms

This classification of PE forms is exactly the same as for front-end forms (or, Common Lisp forms).

TUPLE is designed so that each PE subsystem be as close to the front-end Common Lisp system as possible. Table 2 lists special forms in the PE subsystems, that have counterparts in Common Lisp. The syntax of each special form is similar to that of the corresponding Common Lisp special form, and the semantics is also similar, except that execution of these *PE special forms* are performed in parallel by PE subsystems.

Table 2: Special PE forms.

and	dolist	labels	macrolet	psetq
case	dotimes	let	or	quote
cond	flet	let*	prog1	setq
declare	function	locally	prog2	unless
do	if	loop	progn	when
do*				

There are some additional special forms. We have already seen **exif** (exclusive if) in the previous section. TUPLE has only a few such special forms. Presumably, **exif** will be the only one that is frequently used in actual TUPLE programs. In other words, most TUPLE programs can be described by using **exif** and those PE special forms listed above.

As usual, a macro form is expanded to another PE form, which is then evaluated. Since PE forms are usually represented by front-end objects, macro expansion is an operation of the front-end system.

A function call form for the PE subsystems is a list whose first element is either a function name or a lambda list. Arguments to a function are evaluated by the PE subsystems in parallel and then the function is invoked simultaneously by the PE subsystems.

As in Common Lisp, a PE variable is represented by a symbol. By evaluating a symbol, the value of the PE variable named by the symbol is returned to each PE subsystem simultaneously. The PE subsystems do not share PE variables. Each PE subsystem has its own variable named by the symbol, and the value of the variable is returned to the PE subsystems.

Any TUPLE object other than lists and symbols is regarded as a self-evaluating form when evaluated as a PE form. When evaluated, the object is broadcast to the PE subsystems. If the object is represented as a pointer to a data cell in the front-end heap, then only the pointer is broadcast and the data cell is not copied into the PE subsystems.

5   Implementation

The TUPLE system is implemented by extending KCL (Kyoto Common Lisp [9]), a full-set Common Lisp system developed by the group including the first author. The system is currently running on the MasPar MP–1, a SIMD parallel computer with at least 1024 PEs. As the original KCL is written partly in C and partly in Common Lisp, the TUPLE system on the MasPar is written partly in MPL [16], the extended C language on the MasPar, and partly in TUPLE itself. Thus the TUPLE system can be easily ported to other SIMD or SPMD (Single Program, Multiple Data stream) architectures.

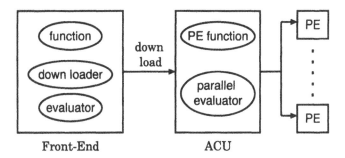

Figure 3: Implementation on MP–1.

The MasPar MP–1 consists of two parts: the front-end UNIX workstation and the back-end. The back-end consists of the array control unit (ACU), which broadcasts instructions to PEs, and the PE array, where PEs are aligned in a two-dimensional array. A program on the MasPar consists of front-end functions and ACU functions. Parallel computation begins by invoking an ACU function from a front-end function. The memory size in each component is relatively small. The size of the data memory in the ACU is 128 Kbytes and the size of the memory in each PE is 16Kbytes. Virtual memory is not supported on these memories.

5.1 Heaps

In MP–1, communication between the front-end and the back-end is very slow. In order to perform high performance, the TUPLE system is designed to avoid frequent communication between the front-end and the back-end. For this purpose, all PE functions are stored in the ACU and the parallel evaluator runs also in the ACU (see Figure 3). When the user defines a new PE function, the *downloader* in the front-end puts the function definition into the ACU memory. Some front-end forms such as **ppe** downloads PE forms into the ACU memory before passing control to the parallel evaluator. Thus, once triggered by the front-end, the entire parallel computation is performed solely in the ACU and no communication takes place between the front-end and the back-end.

The implementation of TUPLE on the MasPar MP–1 uses three kinds of heaps:

- the *font-end heap* where ordinary Common Lisp objects are allocated

- the *PE heaps* where PE cons cells are allocated

- the *ACU heap* where those objects common to all PE subsystems, such as PE function objects (including built-in functions, user-defined functions, and function closures) and PE vector headers, are allocated

Any object in one of these heaps can be referenced from any component of the MasPar system. For example, an object in the front-end heap may be referenced from the

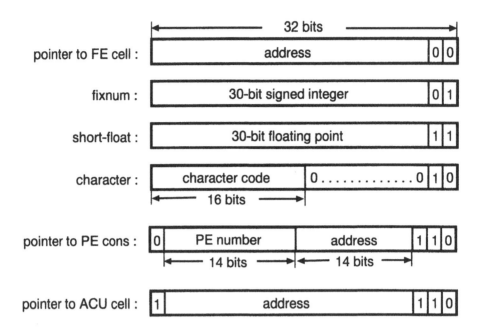

Figure 4: Object representation of TUPLE.

ACU (as part of a user-defined function) and PEs (by broadcasting). Also, a cons cell in a PE heap may be referenced from the front-end (by reductions), the ACU, and the other PEs (by PE communications).

5.2   Data Representation and Allocation

Figure 4 illustrates data representation of TUPLE. This representation is common to all components of the MasPar system. By having the same representation, we can avoid data conversion in communications among the components. The first four formats are those used by the original KCL. As indicated in the Figure, the two least significant bits are used to distinguish these four formats. Since the third significant bit of a character object is always 0, we extended the data representation of KCL so that pointers to the ACU and PE heaps are distinguished by the bit pattern 110 at the three least significant bits.

Figure 5 shows the data area of each PE that TUPLE handles directly. The run-time stack of MPL is not shown in the Figure. The first words of the memory area are used to allocate built-in constants nil, t, and penumber. Next to these words is the PE global area, where user-defined global PE variables, constants, and vectors are allocated. This global area expands dynamically as the user defines PE variables etc. Next is the PE stack area where local PE variables are allocated and temporary values (including arguments to PE functions) are stored. Then there is a heap area where PE cons cells are allocated. A parallel garbage collection [10] is implemented

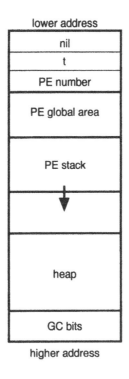

Figure 5: The PE data area.

in TUPLE, which will be reported in another paper.

The total size of the data area is 8 Kbytes for the MasPar system that has 16 Kbytes of local memory per PE. Half of the data area is used as the heap. Since each cons cell occupies 8 bytes (i.e., 2 words), 512 cells are available per PE.

5.3 Symbol Cells

Global PE variable bindings and global PE function bindings are represented by ACU cells called *ACU symbol cells*. Each ACU symbol cell corresponds to an ordinary front-end symbol, and no two ACU cells correspond to the same front-end symbol. When a global PE variable is defined (typically by **defpevar**) or when a global PE function is defined (typically by **defpefun**), a new ACU symbol cell is created that corresponds to the name of the PE variable or the PE function if and only if there exists no such ACU symbol cell. The downloader converts all references to global PE variables and global PE functions in a PE form, to pointers to the corresponding ACU symbol cells.

Each ACU symbol cell contains the address of the global PE variable in the PE global area, the PE function object (pointer to an ACU cell), and the pointer to the corresponding front-end symbol. The pointer to the front-end symbol cell is mainly used in error messages in case unbound variables and undefined functions are detected. On the other hand, each front-end symbol cell contains a pointer to the corresponding ACU symbol cell, if one exists. This pointer is used mainly by the downloader for conversions from front-end symbols to back-end symbols.

Front-end symbol cells are extended so that they can contain information on parallel computation such as the ACU routine that handles a PE special form, and the pointer to the corresponding ACU symbol cell. Thus modification of the front-end system was surprisingly small.

6   Performance Measurements

We have measured the run time of the function **bs-add** in Section 3, by supplying several random numbers as the arguments. We used the MasPar MP–1 with 1024 PEs and with the VAXstation 3520 as the front-end. The result is shown in Figure 6. The Figure shows that the parallel version is only four to five times faster than the equivalent sequential version on the front-end. Roughly speaking, each call of **bs-add** requires $\log_2 n$ time for the sequential version, and $\log_2 \frac{n}{2^k}$ time for the parallel version, with n being the number of items and 2^k being the number of PEs. (According to our experiences with the MasPar MP–1, the performance of the front-end is almost the same as a single PE.) In this experiment, we used 1024 PEs, and thus $k = 10$. If $n = 2^{12} = 4096$, for example, the sequential version runs in time 12 whereas the parallel version runs in time 2. Thus the maximum speed up will be 6. This means that the performance of the TUPLE system is very close to the theoretical upper bound. Another reason for this small gain is that each expansion of a tree is performed for only a single PE. Obviously, tree expansion is one of the most time-consuming operations in the program because cons cells must be allocated in the PE heap. On SIMD architectures, all PEs except one have to wait while the selected PE expands its PE tree. We can possibly increase the performance by modifying the program so that tree expansions are deferred until many (or all) PEs become ready to expand their PE trees.

Figure 7 shows the result of another test for the same program. This time, we change the number of PEs that participate in the parallel computation. Note that the program is independent of the number of PEs. When we used only one PE, the performance of the "parallel" program was a little bit better than the sequential version. This means TUPLE is well implemented for each PE. As seen in the Figure, the runtime decreases steadily as the number of PEs increases, but the runtime seems to converge. The convergence point indicates the time for the essentially sequential part of the program.

To see the performance of the TUPLE system for more practical applications on SIMD architectures, we wrote a TUPLE program to simulate fluid flow by solving Navier-Stokes Equations. As is well known (see [1] for example), the computation is performed by dividing the entire field into small regions and then by repeating a loop body that updates values of the regions. Table 3 shows the result of this performance test.

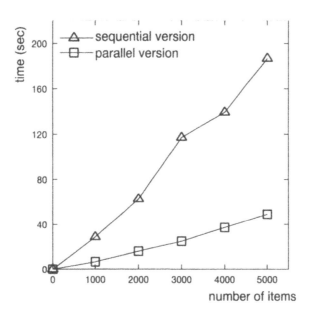

Figure 6: Adding items with 1024 PEs.

Currently, TUPLE does not have a compiler, and thus runs programs interpretively. Compared with the interpreted execution of the sequential version, it is clear that the parallel version runs quite fast. Even if compared with the compiled version on the SPARC, the parallel version is more than five times faster. It is obvious that TUPLE programs are slower than equivalent MPL programs. Nevertheless, the runtime of this TUPLE program is not very far from the runtime of the MPL version.

7 Concluding Remarks

In this paper, we introduced the TUPLE language for SIMD architectures and presented the current implementation of TUPLE on a SIMD machine MasPar MP-1. We have shown that the TUPLE system has a high performance for typical SIMD applications.

TUPLE is currently being used for research purposes to exploit parallel algorithms in some application areas of symbolic computation, such as computer algebra and term rewriting. TUPLE is also used for education. The highly interactive parallel environment of TUPLE helps the students write their first parallel programs. Since we have only one MasPar MP-1 available for education, we have developed a TUPLE simulator that runs on Unix workstations. The students prepare their programs by using the simulator and test the performance on the real TUPLE system. This enables efficient use of the computation resource.

In our experience with TUPLE, the heap size (8 Kbytes) of each PE subsystem is too small for real applications, or even for experimentation. This small size is the

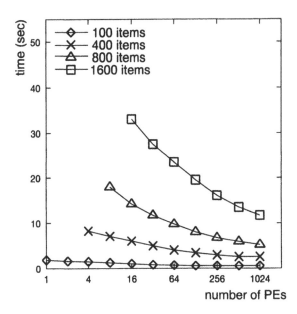

Figure 7: Adding items with various number of PEs.

major obstacle to develop parallel programs in TUPLE. On the MasPar MP–1 with 1024 PEs, the total size of 8 Mbytes seems satisfactory in many cases. However, it is hard to distribute the entire data among the PE heaps. The binary tree search program in this paper is one of the few programs that succeeded in balanced data distribution. A SIMD machine with much more local memory is highly expected to solve this inessential problem.

Acknowledgements

Takashi Okazawa implemented a prototype version of TUPLE [1]. Toshiro Kijima joined the design of the parallel algorithm and gave many useful suggestions based on his experiences of designing and implementing his extended C language for SIMD parallel computation. The project of TUPLE is supported partly by Sumitomo Metal Industries., Ltd. and partly by Digital Equipment Corporation.

Bibliography

1)   Grosch, C.: Adapting a Navier-Stokes Code to the ICL-DAP, *SIAM J. SCI. STAT. COMPUT.*, Vol.8, No.1 (1987).

2)   Okazawa, T.: Design and Implementation of a Common Lisp System Extended for Massively Parallel SIMD Computer. Master's thesis (in Japanese), Toyohashi Univ. of Tech. (1992).

Table 3: Time for 200 iterations

C version
| VAXstation 3520 | 108.8 sec |
| SPARCstation 1+ | 32.9 sec |

| MPL version | 3.0 sec |

KCL version (interpreted)
| VAXstation 3520 | 1700.4 sec (49 GCs) |
| SPARCstation 1+ | 390.3 sec (49 GCs) |

KCL version (compiled)
| SPARCstation 1+ | 44.4 sec (no GC) |

| TUPLE version | 8.0 sec (no GC) |

3) Padget, J.: Collections and Garbage Collection. *Proceedings of the International Workshop IWMM 92*, St. Maro, Springer Lecture Notes in Computer Science No. 637 (1992).

4) Sabot G.: Introduction to Paralation Lisp. Technical Report PL87-1, Thinking Machines Corporation (1987).

5) Sabot G.: *The Paralation Model: Architecture Independent Parallel Programming*. MIT Press (1988).

6) Steele, G.: *Common Lisp the Language*. Digital Press (1984).

7) Steele, G., Hillis, D.: Connection Machine Lisp: Fine-Grained Parallel Symbolic Processing. *Proceedings of 1986 ACM Conference on Lisp and Functional Programming* (1986).

8) Wholey, S., Steele, G.: Connection Machine Lisp: a dialect of Common Lisp for data parallel programming. *Proceedings of Second International Conference on Supercomputing* (1987).

9) Yuasa, T.: Design and Implementation of Kyoto Common Lisp. *Journal of Information Processing*, Vol.13, No.3 (1990).

10) Yuasa, T.: Memory Management and Garbage Collection of an Extended Common Lisp System for Massively Parallel SIMD Architecture, it Proceedings of the International Workshop IWMM 92, *Lecture Notes in Computer Science 637*, pp.490-506, Springer-Verlag(1992).

11) Yuasa, T.: TUPLE - An Extension of KCL for Massively Parallel SIMD Architecture - Draft for the Second Edition. available from the author (1992).

12) Connection Machine Lisp Reference Manual. Thinking Machines Corporation (1987).

13) Introduction to Data Level Parallelism. Technical Report PR86-14, Thinking Machines Corporation (1986).

14) *Lisp Reference Manual. Thinking Machines Corporation (1988).

15) MasPar Parallel Application Language (MPL) User Guide. MasPar Computer Corporation (1991).

6

An Efficient Evaluation Strategy for Concurrency Constructs in Parallel Scheme Systems

Takayasu Ito

Department of Computer and Mathematical Sciences
Graduate School of Information Sciences
Tohoku University, Sendai, Japan

ABSTRACT

In Scheme-based parallel Lisp systems there are proposed a number of structured concurrency constructs like **pcall**, **par**, **par-and** and **plet**. A standard evaluation strategy for these structured constructs has been the eager task creation (ETC) that creates child processes in executing their argument expressions whenever these structured constructs are encountered. But the ETC strategy for structured concurrency constructs is known to be inefficient because of overhead caused by excessive process creation. In this paper we propose an efficient evaluation strategy for structured concurrency constructs, called the steal-help evaluation (SHE) strategy, which suppresses excessive process creation. SHE enables to suppress excessive process creation, since it creates processes only when an idle processor is available in evaluating a parallel expression. Also, the ideas of the SHE-based **future**, **stealable** and **pdelay** are proposed. **pdelay** is a parallelized version of **delay**, which allows parallel realization of stream computation.

1 Introduction

Parallel Lisp languages and systems have been designed and implemented on shared-memory parallel architectures. There are at least two different kinds of Scheme-based parallel Lisp languages: Multilisp and PaiLisp. Multilisp[3] may be considered to be a minimal extension of Scheme into concurrency, introducing only a single concurrency construct **future**, while PaiLisp[8] is an extension of Scheme with a rich set of structured concurrency constructs like **pcall**, **par**, **par-and**, **par-or** and **plet** in addition to **future** and the basic concurrency constructs of its kernel language PaiLisp-Kernel.

The **future** construct is a powerful and convenient construct to create a new process for parallel evaluation of its argument expression, and *lazy task creation* (LTC) is proposed as an efficient evaluation strategy for the **future** construct[13]. However, **future** creates asynchronous and unstructured parallel Scheme processes. In parallel Scheme programming using **future** the central concern has been *where* to insert the **future** construct to increase parallelism, suppressing the cost of excessive process creation. This problem of finding *where* to insert **future** is known to be a hard problem[4]. Using the structured concurrency constructs of PaiLisp it is easy to decide *where* to insert them to obtain a parallel program. *Eager task creation* (ETC) has been considered as a standard evaluation strategy for structured concurrency constructs, but the ETC strategy incurs a serious problem of excessive process creation in evaluating (recursive) parallel Scheme programs that create large numbers of fine-grained processes[12].

The *Steal-Help Evaluation* (SHE) strategy in this paper is proposed as an efficient evaluation strategy of concurrency constructs in parallel Scheme systems. SHE enables to suppress excessive process creation, since it creates processes only when an idle processor is available in evaluating a parallel expression. SHE is introduced by extending the idea of lazy task creation used for an efficient implementation of **future**. However, note that the SHE-based implementation of **future** differs from the LTC-based **future**, as is explained in Section 4.

In this paper we discuss the idea of SHE in detail and explain its implementation strategy. Structured concurrency constructs like **pcall**, **par**, **par-and** and **plet** will be efficiently evaluated using the SHE strategy so as to reduce excessive process creation. Under the SHE strategy a parallel Scheme program written with structured concurrency constructs can be executed as efficiently as the corresponding optimal future-based parallel program. Also, the ideas of the SHE-based **future**, **stealable** and **pdelay** are proposed, and their implementation strategies are explained.

2   PaiLisp and Its Concurrency Constructs

PaiLisp[8] is an extension of Scheme[1] into concurrency with a rich set of structured concurrency constructs **pcall**, **par**, **par-and**, **plet** etc. In addition it contains the **future** construct and the basic concurrency constructs **spawn**, **suspend**, **call/pcc** and **exlambda** of PaiLisp-Kernel[8], where **call/pcc** is an extension of the sequential **call/cc** of Scheme into concurrency to support PaiLisp's $\mathcal{P}$-continuation. PaiLisp-Kernel is a kernel language in which the meanings of PaiLisp constructs can be described, and it is Scheme + {**spawn**, **suspend**, **call/pcc**, **exlambda**}. Note that in the previous papers on PaiLisp[8, 10, 11] we had only one **call/cc** which is the extended **call/cc** that supports $\mathcal{P}$-continuations. But in this paper, **call/pcc** is used to denote the extended **call/cc** that supports $\mathcal{P}$-continuations, and **call/cc** is the one that supports sequential continuations in Scheme.

The major concurrency constructs in PaiLisp have the following meanings.

(**pcall** f e_1 $\cdots$ e_n): After evaluating e_1, $\cdots$, e_n in parallel, the expression f is evaluated, and then its resulting value is applied to the values of e_1, $\cdots$, e_n.

(**par** $e_1 \cdots e_n$): The processes of evaluating $e_1, \cdots, e_n$ in parallel are created, and the **par** construct terminates when the executions of all the child processes of evaluating $e_1, \cdots, e_n$ terminate.

(**par-and** $e_1 \cdots e_n$): $e_1, \cdots, e_n$ are evaluated in parallel, and if one of them yields *false* then the **par-and** expression returns false, killing all the remaining processes created in evaluating the argument expressions $e_1, \cdots, e_n$. If none of $e_1, \cdots, e_n$ yields false then the value of e_n is returned as the value of the **par-and** expression.

(**plet** $((x_1\ e_1) \cdots (x_n\ e_n))\ E_1 \cdots E_m$): After evaluating $e_1, \cdots, e_n$ in parallel, the resulting values of $e_1, \cdots, e_n$ are sequentially bound to $x_1, \cdots, x_n$, respectively[1]. Using the updated environment including the bindings of $x_1, \cdots, x_n$, the expressions $E_1, \cdots, E_m$ are evaluated in parallel. After their completion the value of E_m is returned as the value of this **plet** expression.

(**call/pcc** e): **call/pcc** creates $\mathcal{P}$-continuation, which is a procedure of one argument that packages up the process-id and the current continuation. The one-argument procedure e will be applied to the $\mathcal{P}$-continuation. When $\mathcal{P}$-continuation is invoked by the same process that captured it, the resulting behavior is the same as in the invocation of a sequential continuation in Scheme. When the $\mathcal{P}$-continuation is invoked by a different process, the process to execute the rest of computation is the process that captured it, discarding its current continuation, and the process that invoked the $\mathcal{P}$-continuation continues its own execution.

(**future** e): When this expression is evaluated the future-value for e is returned, and a new child process to compute e is created concurrently. The parent process continues its execution using the future-value for e. If an operation on the future-value for e requires its true value, it is suspended until the true value of e is obtained. This action of obtaining the true value for the future-value is called **force**. **future** is the construct introduced into Multilisp by Halstead[3]. Note that the future-value for e is a virtual symbolic value for e, while the true value for e is the actual computed value of e.

Consider a simple example to parallelize the following sequential Fibonacci function, using the concurrency constructs **pcall** and **future**.

```
(define (fib n) (if (< n 2) n (+ (fib (- n 1)) (fib (- n 2)))))
```

Using **pcall** the following parallel program can be obtained.

```
(define (pfib n) (if (< n 2) n (pcall + (pfib (- n 1)) (pfib (- n 2)))))
```

Using the **future** construct we can think of the following three parallelizations of (fib n) according to the places where **future** is inserted.

---

[1] The cost of binding a value to a variable is very small; about $2[\mu sec]$ in the PaiLisp/MT system[16]. Hence, *sequential binding* is used, avoiding the overhead incurred in *parallel binding*.

Table 1: Experimental results for parallelizations of (fib n)

programs	ETC	LTC	SHE
(pfib 20)	0.767	–	0.167
(ffib1 20)	0.519	0.162	–
(ffib2 20)	2.011	1.867	–
(ffib3 20)	0.922	0.210	–
(fib 20)	0.655 (in sequential)		

[sec]

```
(define (ffib1 n) (if (< n 2) n (+ (future (ffib1 (- n 1)))
                                   (ffib1 (- n 2)))))

(define (ffib2 n) (if (< n 2) n (+ (ffib2 (- n 1))
                                   (future (ffib2 (- n 2))))))

(define (ffib3 n) (if (< n 2) n (+ (future (ffib3 (- n 1)))
                                   (future (ffib3 (- n 2)))))))
```

In a sequential Scheme, functional arguments are typically evaluated from left to right. Taking into account this left-to-right evaluation rule in a sequential function application, we can make the following observations on the three **future**-based parallel versions of **fib**. **ffib1** is the most efficient, and **ffib2** does not benefit from the insertion of **future**, which incurs an additional overhead of process creation caused by **future**. **ffib3** is fairly good but it is no better than **ffib1**, since the second **future** that wraps up (ffib3 (- n 2)) incurs an additional overhead.

For the **future** construct an efficient evaluation strategy LTC is known, but as seen from the above example the effectiveness of **future** depends on *where* it is inserted to increase parallelism. It is known that this problem of finding an optimal place to insert **future** is not easy to solve.

It is easy to decide where to use **pcall**, since **pcall** should be used to parallelize function application, although we have to avoid its use when argument expressions are very lightweight. The problem with **pcall** involves its efficient evaluation. As far as we know, the standard evaluation strategy for **pcall** has been the *eager task creation* (ETC) strategy, but ETC incurs considerable overhead caused by excessive process creation. One of the main purposes of this paper is to present an efficient evaluation strategy, called the *steal-help evaluation* (SHE) strategy, for **pcall** and other structured concurrency constructs.

Table 1 shows experimental results obtained by evaluating the parallelized versions of (fib 20) to compare ETC, LTC and SHE. This experiment was done, using the PaiLisp/MT interpreter[16] on a DEC7000 with six Alpha processors.

As is seen from this example the ETC-based parallel evaluations of parallelized Fibonacci functions for n=20 are no better than the sequential evaluation of (fib 20) except the case of (ffib1 20). This is because of excessive process creation caused by the ETC evaluation. The SHE evaluation of (pfib 20) and the LTC evaluation of (ffib1 20) are definitely better than the sequential evaluation. But even with the LTC strategy (ffib2 20) is no better than the sequential (fib 20). This is because (ffib2 20) is evaluated essentially in a sequential manner according to the left-to-right evaluation of argument expressions, and moreover it adds some extra overhead caused by inserting **future** into a useless place.

The above result tells that the **pcall**-based program under the SHE strategy is as efficient as the optimal **future**-based program under the LTC strategy. Moreover, this result also shows that a careless use of **future** is not better and, in fact, is even worse than the sequential case. As we mentioned already, it is often hard to decide the optimal place(s) to insert **future** to get an efficient program. With these observations we propose the steal-help evaluation (SHE) strategy for structured concurrency constructs.

Remark: The current version of PaiLisp/MT[16] is a multi-threaded implementation of PaiLisp on a DEC7000 with six Alpha processors under OSF/1 OS. According to the preliminary implementation of the SHE strategy on the PaiLisp/MT interpreter, the SHE strategy of (pfib 20) and the LTC strategy of (ffib1 20) created only 51 and 66 processes, respectively, while the ETC strategy of (pfib 20) and (ffib1 20) created 21,890 and 10,945 processes, respectively. Thus we can see an actual effect of suppressing excessive process creation using the SHE strategy. This effect is also observed in the PaiLisp/MT compiler[16].

3   Steal-Help Evaluation Strategy for Structured Concurrency Constructs

The steal-help evaluation (SHE) strategy is an efficient parallel evaluation strategy that can suppress excessive process creation. It was originally called the steal-based evaluation[15], but in this paper we call it as the steal-help evaluation, since an idle processor helps evaluation of the home processor, stealing unevaluated expressions.

3.1   Basic Idea of Steal-Help Evaluation Strategy

We consider the ETC and SHE evaluations of (**pcall** f e_1 $\cdots$ e_n) assuming use of a shared-memory multi-processor with a small number of processing elements.

(1) ETC for pcall

ETC is a straightforward way to implement **pcall**. In the case of ETC the child processes of evaluating e_1, $\cdots$, e_n are created when (**pcall** f e_1 $\cdots$ e_n) is encountered. After obtaining the values of the argument expressions the function f is evaluated, and its resultant value is applied to the values of the argument expressions e_1, $\cdots$, e_n. A process creation means creation of a process to evaluate an argument expression. An argument expression may be a parallel Scheme expression defined recursively as in (pfib n). Then recursive function call will create new processes when **pcall** is encountered. Thus the ETC strategy for a recursive parallel Scheme program will create excessively many processes. For example, in case of the ETC evaluation of (pfib 20), more than 20,000 processes were created in PaiLisp/MT. However, since the number of processors is six in PaiLisp/MT, the actual argument-expression evaluations in most of the created processes must be suspended until a processor for evaluating them becomes available. The cost of this excessive process creation has been the major source of degradation in the ETC evaluation of (pfib 20).

(2) SHE for pcall

Intuitively speaking, the SHE strategy for (**pcall** f e_1 $\cdots$ e_n) starts evaluating (f e_1 $\cdots$ e_n) in a sequential manner, and when an idle processor is available an argument expression will be stolen for evaluation by the idle processor. In this case a process creation occurs only when an idle processor is available, so we may expect suppression of excessive process creation. The SHE strategy for (**pcall** f e_1 $\cdots$ e_n) should work in the following way. Assume that one processor, called the *home processor*, will become responsible in evaluating (**pcall** f e_1 $\cdots$ e_n). When the **pcall** expression is encountered the home processor will start evaluating it as if the sequential evaluation of (f e_1 $\cdots$ e_n) will take place on the home processor. That is, the evaluation on the home processor will proceed from e_1 towards e_n as follows:

```
        evaluate(e₁);
    then evaluate(e₂);
        ...
    then evaluate(f), after obtaining all the values of e₁, ···, eₙ;
    then apply the resultant value of f to the values of e₁, ···, eₙ.
```

During the course of evaluation of argument expressions, if an idle processor – called *helper* – is available, then the helper can steal an argument expression that is not evaluated yet. The stolen expression will be evaluated on the helper, but in order to realize this strategy we must have a mechanism that a helper steals and evaluates argument expressions. We assume that the evaluation on the home processor proceeds from e_1 towards e_n. Then the possibility that an argument expression is not evaluated is higher in the order from e_n towards e_1. The steal action by a helper will be effective if expressions are stolen in this order *from e_n towards e_1*. Even if more than one helper is available, a steal-help evaluation by a helper may proceed essentially in the same manner, although we explain its details in Section 3.2. Note that in this mode of evaluation a process creation occurs only when a steal action is taken, so that excessive process creation will not occur.

After evaluating all the argument expressions the home processor evaluates the function f, whose resultant value will be applied to the values of the argument expressions e_1, $\cdots$, e_n.

Based on the above idea of the SHE strategy we give an implementation strategy of SHE for (**pcall** f e_1 $\cdots$ e_n). Before explaining it we would like to remark here several points for such an implementation.

1. We assume that the order of evaluation of functional arguments has no effect on evaluation of a function application (f e_1 $\cdots$ e_n). This means that we are concerned here about the steal-help evaluation of functional program with no side-effect.

2. When an argument expression is evaluated by a helper it must be evaluated under the proper environment with enough information. For the purpose the shared object is introduced as explained below.

3. In order to realize the sequential and steal-help evaluation modes for argument expressions we introduce the mechanism of the *stealable stack* (SST). A home processor will evaluate expressions from the top of SST, and a helper will steal an expression from the bottom of the SST.

4. When the number of unevaluated argument expressions becomes 0 then the function f will be evaluated and its resultant value will be applied to the values of argument expressions on the home processor.

5. An implementation for the SHE strategy of **pcall** must be applicable to the evaluation of a nested **pcall** expression like (**pcall** f e_1 (**pcall** g e_2 e_3) (**pcall** h e_4 e_5)). Also, the implementation must support multiple sequential and steal-help evaluations, when several helpers are available.

A nested **pcall** expression may be regarded as forming a tree structure of expressions. The home processor will evaluate argument expressions from left to right in the sequential mode, while a helper will steal argument expressions from the SST of the home processor from bottom towards top. Thus a sequential evaluation on the home processor proceeds in *depth-first style* to search a tree structure, while a steal action on a helper will proceed in *breadth-first style* to create a new process. Hence, process creation is quite limited since only an idle processor can steal an expression to create a new process.

3.2 On Implementation of the SHE Strategy for (pcall f $e_1 \cdots e_w$n)

In this subsection we describe the SHE strategy of evaluating (**pcall** f $e_1 \cdots e_n$) under an environment *env* on a shared-memory multi-processor system. As was explained in Section 3.1 the home processor proceeds to evaluate the expression in its sequential evaluation mode as if the sequential evaluation of (f $e_1 \cdots e_n$) will take place. If an idle processor is available it steals an argument expression to help evaluation on the home processor; thus, the idle processor will be called a **helper**. We have to specify which argument expression will be stolen by a helper, and the helper must be provided enough information to evaluate the stolen expression, including the environment under which the stolen expression should be evaluated. For this purpose of providing enough information we introduce the following shared object.

- a pointer to the environment which gives a list of bindings of variables and their corresponding values.

- an identifier denoting the concurrency construct in the expression.
  In case of (**pcall** f $e_1 \cdots e_n$) the identifier PCALL is used to denote that **pcall** is the concurrency construct under consideration.

- the identifier of the parent process to the expression.

- the number of unevaluated argument expressions.

These information is necessary for a helper to steal and evaluate an expression and to return to its parent process after evaluating the expression on the helper.

We assume that a pair of each argument expression and its current shared object is pushed into the stealable stack SST in the following way.

$$\texttt{<top>} \quad (e_1 \, . \, SO) \; (e_2 \, . \, SO) \; \cdots \; (e_n \, . \, SO) \quad \texttt{<bottom>}$$

where SO is the shared object at the point where (**pcall** f $e_1 \cdots e_n$) is encountered. The home processor HP pops SST to get an expression from the top of the SST to evaluate, while a helper TP steals an expression and its shared object from the bottom of the SST of the home processor. The pointer to the list of the resultant values evaluated by the home processor and the helper will be saved into the argument register *argl*. The home processor and the helper should work in the following way.

Home Processor

A pair of each argument expression and its current shared object will be pushed into the stealable stack SST, and the argument register *argl* is a register to hold the list of argument expressions. The home processor pops the SST to get an expression from the top of SST and evaluates it, saving the resultant value into *argl* and decrementing the number of unevaluated argument expressions. It continues this *pop and evaluate* process on the SST until all the argument expressions are evaluated. This evaluation process on the home processor is called the **sequential evaluation mode**. During this sequential evaluation mode there might occur a situation that the home processor would become idle in spite that there remain some expressions in the SST of a helper that had stolen an expression like a **pcall** expression. In this case the home processor that has become idle can behave like a helper to steal and evaluate an expression in the SST of the helper. When the number of unevaluated expressions becomes 0, saving the values of all the arguments expressions into *argl*, the function f is evaluated, and its resultant value is applied to the values in *argl*. Then, the resultant value of this function application is returned as the value of the **pcall** expression.

Helper

An idle processor becomes a helper which can steal an expression and its shared object from the stealable stack SST of the home processor, and it evaluates the stolen expression under the environment recorded in the shared object. Since the identifier of the concurrency construct under consideration is PCALL, the SHE strategy for **pcall** on a helper will be invoked, performing the *steal and evaluate* actions as follows.

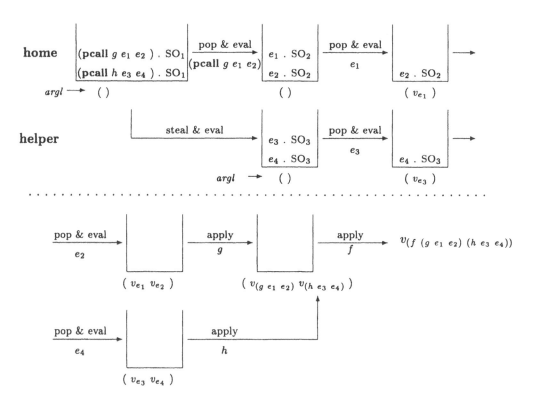

Figure 1: Evaluation of (**pcall** f (**pcall** g e_1 e_2) (**pcall** h e_3 e_4))

A helper TP steals a pair of an expression and its shared object from the bottom of the SST of the home processor, removing the pair from the SST. The stolen expression will be evaluated on TP with the corresponding environment saved in the shared object, and the number of unevaluated expressions will be decremented. The resultant value of the expression must be saved into the corresponding place in *argl*.

If another helper TP1 becomes available it can steal and evaluate the bottom element of the SST of the home processor. If there is no stealable expression in the SST of the home processor, TP1 may steal an expression from the SST of the helper TP, and TP will behave as a home processor to TP1. This process to steal and evaluate an expression by a helper will be continued until the number of unevaluated argument expressions becomes 0, saving the values of argument expressions into the corresponding places in the argument register *argl*.

Figure 1 is an example showing how the home processor and a helper behave when evaluating (**pcall** f (**pcall** g e_1 e_2) (**pcall** h e_3 e_4)), where e_1, e_2, e_3 and e_4 are assumed to be Scheme expressions with no side-effect. Also, v_e means the value of an expression e.

Note that the effectiveness of the SHE strategy will be guaranteed/increased, taking into account costs of handling shared objects and stealable stacks. In the

PaiLisp/MT interpreter[16] the cost of stealing a shared object and creating the corresponding process object is 70 [μsec], so that it would be better that an expression whose cost is smaller than 70 [μsec] would be evaluated in the sequential evaluation mode, disallowing its stealing by an idle processor. This kind of considerations should be incorporated into an efficient implementation of the SHE strategy.

3.3 On SHE Strategies for Other Concurrency Constructs

We explained above the SHE strategy for the **pcall** expression. The SHE strategy for other structured concurrency constructs can be given in a similar manner with modifications based on their meanings. In this section we explain how **par**, **par-and** and **plet** can be implemented in the SHE strategy. We use a *shared object*, the *stealable stack* SST and the argument register *argl*. We assume that for each structured concurrency construct the corresponding identifier is recorded in the shared object; PAR for **par**, PARAND for **par-and**, PLETBIND and PLETBODY for **plet**.

(1) SHE for (par $e_1 \cdots e_n$)

The SHE strategy of (**par** $e_1 \cdots e_n$) is slightly simpler than that of the **pcall** expression, since we do not need saving the values of the argument expressions $e_1, \cdots, e_n$ and the application of a function. Besides these actions of not saving values and not applying a function, the behaviors of the home processor and a helper should be the same as under the SHE strategy for the **pcall** expression.

(2) SHE for (par-and $e_1 \cdots e_n$)

We assume that the argument expressions $e_1, \cdots, e_n$ and their shared objects are saved in the stealable stack SST of the home processor. The home processor and a helper should behave as follows.

Home Processor : The home processor pops the SST to get an expression from the top of the SST and evaluates it, saving the resultant value into *argl* and decrementing the number of unevaluated argument expressions. If the resultant value is *false* the **par-and** expression returns *false* as its value, killing the rest of the computation[15]. If the value is not *false* the home processor pops the SST again to get an expression from the top of the SST and evaluates it, saving the resultant value into *argl* and decrementing the number of unevaluated argument expressions, and if this value is *false* the **par-and** expression returns *false*, killing the rest of the computation. The home processor continues this process of popping the SST to get an expression from the SST and to evaluate it, decrementing the number of unevaluated argument expressions until the number of unevaluated argument expressions becomes 0. When no expression stored in the SST returns *false*, the **par-and** expression returns the value of e_n saved in *argl*. Note that the actions of saving the values of argument expressions may be omitted except for the value of e_n.

Helper : A helper steals the bottom element of the SST, and it evaluates the stolen expression under the environment recorded in the shared object, saving its value into *argl* and decrementing the number of unevaluated argument expressions in the shared object. If the resultant value is *false* the **par-and** expression returns *false* as its value, killing the rest of the computation. If the value is not *false* a helper again steals the bottom element from the SST and evaluates it, saving its value into *argl*, removing it from the SST and decrementing the number of unevaluated argument expressions in the shared object. This process of evaluating expressions by a helper continues until the number of unevaluated argument expressions becomes 0. When none of the argument expressions returns *false* the **par-and** expression returns the value of e_n saved in *argl*.

(3) SHE for (plet $((x_1\ e_1)\ \cdots\ (x_n\ e_n))\ E_1\ \cdots\ E_m)$

The **plet** expression has two evaluation phases: *binding phase* and *body evaluation phase*. During the *binding phase* the shared object records the phase name PLETBIND, a pointer to *env* and the number of unevaluated argument expressions, while during the *body evaluation phase* the shared object records the phase name PLETBODY, a pointer to *new-env* and the number of body expressions.

Binding Phase

Home Processor : Assuming that the argument expressions $e_1, \cdots, e_n$ are stored in the SST together with their shared object, the home processor pops the SST to get the top element of the SST and evaluates it under the current environment *env*, saving the resultant value into *argl* and decrementing the number of unevaluated argument expressions. This process of evaluating argument expressions on the home processor continues until the number of unevaluated argument expressions becomes 0. After evaluating all the argument expressions the current environment *env* will be extended by binding the values of the argument expressions e_i to the corresponding variables x_i to form a new environment *new-env*.

Helper : A helper can steal the bottom element of the SST, and it evaluates the stolen expression under the current environment *env* recorded in the shared object, saving the resultant value into the argument register *argl* and decrementing the number of unevaluated argument expressions. This process of stealing and evaluating an expression from the SST continues until the number of unevaluated argument expressions becomes 0.

Body Evaluation Phase

The body evaluation phase is initiated after completing the binding phase of forming a new environment *new-env*, and the information recorded in the shared object must be updated before evaluating $E_1 \cdots E_m$.

Home Processor : Assuming that the body expressions $E_1, \cdots, E_m$ are stored in the SST together with the updated shared object, the home processor pops the SST to get its top element and evaluates it under *new-env*, saving the resultant value into *argl* and decrementing the number of unevaluated body expressions. This process continues until the number of unevaluated body expressions becomes 0. After evaluating all the body expressions the value of E_m saved in *argl* is returned as the value of the **plet** expression.

Helper : An idle processor (that is, a helper) can steal the bottom element of the SST that saves the body expressions together with the updated shared object, and it evaluates the stolen body expression under *new-env* recorded in the shared object, saving its resultant value into the argument register *argl* and decrementing the number of unevaluated argument expressions. This process of stealing and evaluating the body expressions on a helper will be continued until the number of unevaluated argument expressions becomes 0.

4   SHE-based Implementation of future

future is an interesting concurrency construct, successfully used as a major concurrency construct in Multilisp[3]. In this section we give the SHE-based implementation strategy of **future**, and we compare the SHE-based **future** and the LTC-based **future**.

4.1   SHE-based Implementation of future

The SHE-based implementation of **future** will be realized as follows, taking into account that (**future** e) means returning the future-value for e and creating a new process for evaluating e.

Home processor for (future e)

When the home processor HP evaluates (**future** e), the following actions are performed:

1. Firstly, the future-value for e is created.

2. The future object consisting of the following entities is formed:

    - the expression field, which is sometimes used as the value field.
    - the environment field.
    - the state field, which consists of a state information of the future object.
    - the process list, which consists of a list of processes requesting a true value for a future-value.
    - the pointer to SST.

3. The future object is stored into the SST, and the future-value fv is returned as a temporary virtual value of the expression e.

4. The home processor continues its evaluation, using the future-value fv.

5. When the true value for the future-value fv is required,

    - if e is not stolen by an idle processor, e is evaluated in a sequential mode, and after its termination the future-value fv is replaced by the resultant value of e.
    - if e is stolen by a helper (an idle processor), the evaluation of the home processor will be suspended until the helper that had stolen e finishes its evaluation.

A future object is in one of three states: *future*, *executing*, and *determined*. The force operation of obtaining the true value for the future-value fv is performed in the following way, depending upon the state contained in the future object.

- When the state is *future*, the home processor evaluates e using the environment *env* contained in the future object, and the state changes from *future* to *executing*. At this point the expression field of the future object changes to *no expression*. After evaluating e, the resultant value is stored into the *value field* of the future object, and the state changes from *executing* to *determined*.

- When the state is *executing*, the home processor is suspended until the true value of the future-value fv is obtained, because the expression e corresponding to the future-value fv is being executed by certain other processor. When the true value for fv is obtained, the execution of the processes in the process list of the future object is resumed with the true value for fv, and the corresponding process-id is removed from the process list.

- When the state is *determined*, the remaining computation on the home processor is performed, using the true value for the future-value fv.

Helper for (future e)

An idle processor that works as a helper obtains the future object from the bottom of the SST of the home processor HP. At this point the state of the future object must change from *future* to *executing*. A new process that evaluates the expression e is created, using the information contained in the future object. In case of evaluating $(f \ (\textbf{future} \ e))$, the following two processes $P1$ and $P2$ are evaluated in parallel.

$P1$: the process of evaluating $(f \ fv)$, which is the rest of computation after encountering (**future** e) on the home processor

$P2$: the process of evaluating e on a helper.

Immediately after obtaining the value of e (say, v_e), fv is replaced by the value v_e, and the state must change from *executing* to *determined*. Then the home processor continues the remaining computation $(f' \ v_e)$, where f' is the value of f at the point when fv was replaced by v_e.

4.2 Comparisons between the LTC-based future and the SHE-based future

LTC (Lazy Task Creation)[13] was introduced as an efficient evaluation strategy of **future**. Here we compare the LTC-based **future** and the SHE-based **future**. When $(f \ (\textbf{future} \ e))$ is evaluated with LTC, the following actions are taken:

- The home processor starts evaluating the expression e sequentially; that is, the expression e is evaluated in the sequential evaluation mode on the processor.

- When an idle processor is available, it creates the future-value fv for the expression e, and moreover the remaining computation $(f\ fv)$ is stolen by the idle processor, which obtains $(f\ fv)$ from the stack of the home processor.

- If no idle processor is available, the argument expression e is firstly evaluated, and after evaluating f, the resultant value of f is applied to the value of the expression e.

When LTC and SHE are compared in evaluating (**future** e), the behaviors of the home processor and an idle processor differ as follows.

1. The home processor in LTC evaluates the argument expression e in the sequential evaluation mode, while the home processor in SHE evaluates the remaining computation $(f\ \Box)$ using the future-value fv for the context $\Box$.

2. When an idle processor is available, in the LTC strategy a new process of evaluating $(f\ fv)$ is created by a stealing action on the idle processor, while in the SHE strategy a new process of evaluating e is created by a stealing action on the idle processor.

3. When no idle processor is available and only the home processor is available, LTC and SHE work as follows:

   - According to the LTC strategy, the expression e is firstly evaluated, and then f is evaluated, and the resultant value of f is applied to the value of the expression e. Thus $(f\ (\textbf{future}\ e))$ is evaluated like a call-by-value sequential evaluation of $(f\ e)$.

   - According to the SHE strategy, $(f\ fv)$ is evaluated, and when the actual value of fv is needed the expression e is evaluated, suspending the evaluation of $(f\ fv)$. Thus in this case (**future** e) behaves like (**delay** e).

Thus, the LTC-based **future** and the SHE-based **future** differ in what they create, and moreover they behave differently when no idle processor is available. (**future** e) has the following original meaning: when this expression is encountered

1. return the future-value for e,

2. create a new process for evaluating e.

Thus from the standpoint of process creation the SHE-based **future** may be considered to be more natural than the LTC-based **future**.

4.3   The stealable construct

stealable is a unique construct introduced for the SHE strategy. (**stealable** e) means that an expression e annotated by **stealable** may be stolen by an idle processor under the SHE strategy. In this sense (**stealable** e) may be considered to be the SHE-based **future** *without* returning the future-value. **stealable** would become effective and efficient, when no future-value is required.

Using **stealable** a function application (f e_1 e_2) can be parallelized as follows:

(f (**stealable** e_1) e_2)
(f e_1(**stealable** e_2))
(f (**stealable** e_1) (**stealable** e_2))

These expressions specify that the argument expressions annotated by **stealable** may be stolen by an idle processor. For instance, in case of (f (**stealable** e_1) e_2), (f $\Box$ e_2) will be evaluated concurrently with the expression e_1, when e_1 is stolen by an idle processor. Note that an implicit placeholder for the context $\Box$ will be used in evaluating (f $\Box$ e_2), and the value of e_1 must be saved into such a placeholder after its actual evaluation on an idle processor.

How to use stealable in parallelization

When we write (**stealable** e), process creation of e occurs when an idle processor is available. The annotation **stealable** would be better to be used only when the cost of evaluating e is larger than the cost of the stealing action. When the functional form (f e) with only one argument is given, (f (**stealable** e)) will not be effective, compared to (f e), because (**stealable** e) adds some extra cost of handling an implicit placeholder. Also, it may not be effective to annotate all possible argument expressions in (f e_1 $\cdots$ e_n) by **stealable** in the the following form,

(f (**stealable** e_1) $\cdots$ (**stealable** e_n))

even if the cost of each argument is larger than the cost of a stealing action, since at least one of the argument expressions may be evaluated on the home processor.

A simple-minded parallelization using **stealable** can be done in the following way. Let {(**stealable** e)} be defined as follows:

$$\{(\textbf{stealable}\ e)\}\ =\ \textbf{if}\ \text{cost}[e]\ \geq\ C_{\text{steal}}\ \textbf{then}\ (\textbf{stealable}\ e)\ \textbf{else}\ e$$

, where C_{steal} is the cost of the stealing action in a SHE-based system. Then (f e_1 $\cdots$ e_n) will be parallelized in the following way, assuming use of the left-to-right evaluation rule in evaluating function application.

$$(f\ e_1\ \cdots\ e_n)\ \Longrightarrow\ (f\ \{(\textbf{stealable}\ e_1)\}\ \cdots\ \{(\textbf{stealable}\ e_{n-1})\}\ e_n)$$

On implementation of stealable

stealable can be implemented by modifying the SHE-based implementation of **future**.

Home processor for (stealable *e*)

When the home processor encounters (**stealable** *e*), the following actions are performed:

1. The stealable object consisting of the following entities are formed:

   - the expression field, which is sometimes used as the value field.

   - the environment field.

   - the state field, which contains one of the states: *stealable, executing* and *obtained*.

   - the list of processes of waiting for the value of the argument expression *e*.

   - the pointer to SST, in which a pointer to the argument list is saved.

2. The stealable object is saved into the SST.

3. The home processor continues its evaluation, and the resultant value will be saved into the argument list.

4. If *e* is not stolen by an idle processor, *e* is evaluated in a sequential mode.

5. If *e* is stolen by a helper (an idle processor) or there is no expression in SST, the evaluation on the home processor is suspended until the helper that had stolen *e* finishes its evaluation.

Helper for (stealable *e*)

An idle processor that works as a helper obtains the stealable object from the bottom of the SST of the home processor. At this point the state of the stealable object must change from *stealable* to *executing*. A new process that evaluates the expression *e* is created, using the information contained in the stealable object. When the value of *e* is obtained the state changes from *executing* to *obtained*, and the resultant value is saved into the argument list.

5   Parallelization of delay and Stream Computation

The **delay** construct in Scheme is an explicit construct to realize *lazy evaluation*, together with the **force** construct. The benefit of lazy evaluation realized by **delay** and **force** is of efficiency that comes from performing only the needed computation. Also, the **delay** construct is important to implement *stream computation* in Scheme.

The **delay** and **force** constructs have the following syntax and meanings[14].

(**delay** *exp*), which returns *promise* for *exp*.

(**force** *promise*), which returns the result of forcing *promise*.

In Scheme programming a stream can be defined using the **delay** construct, usually in the form of (**delay** (<constructor> e_1 (f e_2))), where <constructor> must be a list constructor like **cons** and **list**, and f is a function of creating a new *stream* element.

A simple-minded approach of parallelizing **delay** is to replace it by **future**. However, this approach does not work well; for example, if we replace **delay** in (**delay** (**cons** e_1 (f e_2))) by **future**, the resultant expression creates non-terminating computation in evaluating (**cons** e_1 (f e_2)), where f is assumed to be a recursively-defined function.

Also, note that lazy evaluation in functional programming and lazy task creation in parallel programming are different; the former is a method of evaluating a function in *call-by-need*, and the latter is a method of creating a new process as explained in the previous section.

We consider here a parallel evaluation strategy of **delay** and stream computation. Assume that the home processor HP evaluates (**delay** (**cons** e_1 (f e_2))), in which f is a recursive function of creating a next stream element. Then we can make the following observation in a step-wise creation and evaluation of a stream element. The promise *promise-1* is returned when encountering **delay**. If an idle processor TP is available, TP steals and evaluates a promise expression corresponding to *promise-1*, and a new promise *promise-2* is created encountering **delay** in evaluating f. This *unfolding* evaluation of obtaining promise values must be done with *restriction* for preventing non-terminating evaluation. The resultant values of promises after evaluating the corresponding promise expressions are saved into the *stream stack* (STR) as explained below. A **force** action on *promise* gets its corresponding value from STR. With this observation we introduce **pdelay** as follows.

(**pdelay** *depth exp*)

where *depth* is the number of promises to be created in forced evaluation of this expression. (**pdelay** n *exp*) has the following meaning.

(1) (**pdelay** 1 *exp*)

The home processor returns *promise-1*, and an idle processor evaluates the promise expression *exp*. Then the pair of *promise-1* and the value of *exp* is saved into the stream stack STR.

(2) (**pdelay** 2 *exp*)

The *promise-1* is returned, and an idle processor forces to evaluate the promise expression. Then the pair of *promise-1* and the value of the promise expression is saved into the STR. In evaluating the promise expression *promise-2* is created when **pdelay** is encountered, and the promise expression for *promise-2* is evaluated by an idle processor. Then the resultant value and *promise-2* is pushed into the STR.

(n) (**pdelay** n *exp*)

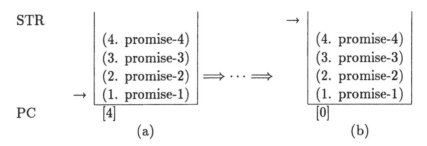

Figure 2: Behavior of the stream stack STR

The above process is repeated, and this repetitive process is suspended when a pair of *promise-n* and the value of the corresponding promise expression is saved into the STR.

In another words, (**pdelay** *n exp*) returns the promise (*promise-1*), and *exp* is unfolded $(n-1)$ times returning a promise each time when **pdelay** is encountered in the unfolding process. Thus, n promises {*promise-1, promise-2, $\cdots$, promise-n*} are created, and their corresponding promise expressions are evaluated by idle processors. n promises and their corresponding true values are saved into the STR. Consider the following example with *depth* $= 4$.

```
(define p-counters (let next ((n 1))
                      (pdelay 4 (cons n (next (+ n 1))))))))

(define stream-car (lambda (str) (car (force str))))
(define stream-cdr (lambda (str) (cdr (force str))))
```

The home processor returns *promise-1* when **pdelay** is encountered, and it continues to evaluate the rest of computation using *promise-1*. An idle processor (helper) can steal and evaluate the corresponding promise expression. In this case the idle processor evaluates the promise expression (**cons** **n** (**next** (+ **n** 1))) with the binding (n . 1). The promises *promise-2, promise-3* and *promise-4* and their values are successively created by forced evaluation of the corresponding promise expressions, and they will be pushed into the stream stack STR as in Fig. 2 (a).

This means that the first 4 elements of the **counters** stream is obtained by an idle processor, whose evaluation is suspended at this stage. When a promise is forced, the corresponding value is obtained from the STR stack, and then the STR pointer is moved up, decrementing the *promise counter* (PC) whose initial value is 4. When the *promise counter* (PC) becomes 0 as in Figure 2(b), an idle processor can start to evaluate the rest of stream after setting *promise counter* to be 4. But evaluation of the promise expressions on the idle processor must be suspended when PC reaches to 4. To keep the original idea of **delay** the promise values must be remembered to avoid their re-evaluation, and this remembrance will be performed using the STR stack that saves all the pairs of promises and the values of the corresponding promise expressions. However, when no idle processor is available a regular sequential delayed evaluation will be performed, regarding **pdelay** as **delay** and neglecting *depth*, but pairs of promises and their values must be saved into the STR.

We can generalize the above strategy to programs that contain several **pdelay** and streams[15].

6 Conclusion

We explained the Steal-Help Evaluation strategy for concurrency constructs of parallel Scheme languages, including SHE implementation strategies of **pcall**, **par**, **par-and**, **plet** and **future**. Also, we introduced **stealable** and **pdelay**, explaining their implementation strategies. A multi-threaded PaiLisp system with interpreter and compiler based on the SHE strategy is implemented on a system of DEC7000 with six Alpha processors[16], and its preliminary experimental results show that the SHE strategy is actually an effective and efficient parallel evaluation strategy superior to the ETC and LTC strategies. But the ideas of **stealable** and **pdelay** are not fully implemented yet, and their implementation and experimental justifications are left for future study. This paper is an updated version of the reference 15), focusing some detailed explanations on the SHE strategy. In the reference 15) a number of other issues are discussed and proposed, including a programming style of *structured parallel symbolic programming* (SPSP), the Restricted Eager Task Creation, and an idea of Constraint-based Automatic Parallelization (CAP). But their fuller developments are also left for study.

In this paper we explained only the basic ideas of the SHE strategy. For actual implementation of the SHE strategy, we have to consider some implementation issues to increase the performance keeping the idea of SHE. For example, the home processor can evaluate the expression e_1 immediately, pushing the argument expressions $e_2, \cdots, e_n$ into the SST together with their shared object. If an argument expression e_j is one of a constant, a variable and a quote expression, its evaluation cost is much smaller than the cost of the steal action. Thus the home processor should evaluate such a low cost expression directly, disallowing its stealing by an idle processor, as mentioned at the end of 3.2. The current PaiLisp/MT system[16] is realized, taking into account these implementational aspects.

Acknowledgements

The author would like to thank S. Kawamoto and M. Umehara for their discussions on the SHE strategy. They implemented the SHE strategy of this paper in implementing PaiLisp interpreter and compiler. Special thanks go to R. H. Halstead, Jr. who made various insightful and useful comments to clarify the ideas presented in this paper.

Bibliography

1) Abelson, H. and Sussman, G.: *Structure and Interpretation of Computer Programs*, MIT Press (1985).

2) Gabriel, R. and McCarthy, J.: Queue-based Multiprocessing Lisp, *Conference Record of ACM Symposium on Lisp and Functional Programming*, pp.25-44 (1984).

3) Halstead, Jr., R.: Multilisp: A Language for Concurrent Symbolic Computation, *ACM Trans. on Programming Languages and Systems*, Vol.4, No.7, pp.501-538 (1985).

4) Halstead, Jr., R.: New Ideas in Parallel Lisp: Language Design, Implementation, and Programming Tools, *Lecture Notes in Computer Science*, Vol.441, pp.2-57, Springer (1990).

5) Halstead, Jr., R. and Ito, T.: *Parallel Symbolic Computing: Languages, Systems, and Applications*, Lecture Notes in Computer Science, Vol.748, Springer (1993).

6) IEEE Computer Society: *IEEE Standard for the Scheme Programming Language* (1991).

7) Ito, T. and Wada, S.: Models of Parallel Execution of Lisp Functions and their Evaluations, *SIG Report of Symbolic Processing*, SYM26-5, Information Processing Society of Japan (1983) [in Japanese].

8) Ito, T and Matsui, M.: A Parallel Lisp Language PaiLisp and its Kernel Specification, *Lecture Notes in Computer Science*, Vol.441, pp.58-100, Springer (1990).

9) Ito, T. and Halstead, Jr., R.: *Parallel Lisp: Languages and Systems*, Lecture Notes in Computer Science, Vol.441, Springer (1990).

10) Ito, T. and Seino, T.: On PaiLisp Continuation and its Implementation, *Proceedings of ACM Workshop on Continuations* (Eds. O. Danvy, C. Talcott), pp.73-90 (1992).

11) Ito, T. and Seino, T.: P-Continuation based Implementation of PaiLisp Interpreter, *Lecture Notes in Computer Science*, Vol.748, pp.108-154, Springer (1993).

12) Kawamoto, S. and Ito, T.: Multi-Threaded PaiLisp with Granularity Adaptive Parallel Execution, *Lecture Notes in Computer Science*, Vol.907, pp.97-117, Springer (1995).

13) Mohr, E., Kranz, D. A. and Halstead, Jr., R.: Lazy Task Creation: A Technique for Increasing the Granularity of Parallel Programs, *IEEE Trans. Parallel and Distributed Systems*, Vol.2, No.3, pp.264-280 (1991).

14) Springer, G. and Friedman, D.: *Scheme and the Art of Programming*, MIT Press (1989).

15) Ito, T.: Efficient Evaluation Strategies for Structured Concurrency Constructs in Parallel Scheme Systems, *Lecture Notes in Computer Science*, Vol.1068, pp.22-52, Springer (1995).

16) Ito, T., Kawamoto, S. and Umehara, M.: A Multi-Threaded Implementation of PaiLisp Interpreter and Compiler based on the Steal-Help Evaluation Strategy, *this volume*.

This work was partially supported by Grant-in-Aid for Scientific Research 09245102 under the Ministry of Education, Science and Culture, Japan.

7

Extended Continuations for Future-based Parallel Scheme Languages

Tsuneyasu Komiya

Taiichi Yuasa

Graduate School of Informatics
Kyoto University

ABSTRACT

A continuation represents the rest of computation from a given point. Scheme, a dialect of Lisp, provides a function to generate a continuation as a first-class object. Using Scheme continuations, we can express various control structures such as non-local exits and coroutines. The `future` construct, which provides the mechanisms of process creation and synchronization, is supported in many parallel Scheme languages. However, continuations of these languages are not powerful enough to describe parallel programs. This paper proposes an extension to Scheme continuations to make them adaptable to parallel environment based on the `future` construct.

1 Introduction

A continuation represents the rest of computation from a given point. Scheme [1, 2], a dialect of Lisp, provides a function to generate a continuation as a first-class object. Using Scheme continuations, we can express various control structures such as non-local exits and coroutines.

The `future` construct [3] provides the mechanisms of process creation and synchronization. There are many `future`-based parallel Scheme systems including Multilisp [4], MultiScheme [5] and PaiLisp [6, 7].

Each of these parallel Scheme systems has its own semantics of continuations since the semantics of Scheme continuations is not defined in parallel environment except PaiLisp continuations. However, continuations of these languages are not powerful enough to describe parallel programs besides PaiLisp continuations as will be remarked in Section 9.

In this paper, we propose an extension to Scheme continuations to make them adaptable to parallel environment based on the `future` construct. The rest of this paper is organized as follows. First, we overview Scheme continuations and the future construct, respectively in Sections 2 and 3. Then, in Section 4, we discuss the problems of continuations in the parallel environment. In Sections 5 through 7, we present the extended continuations and some applications of the extended continuations. Finally, we compare the continuations of popular parallel Schemes and explain why they are not powerful enough to describe these applications.

2   Continuations

A continuation represents the rest of computation from a given point. For example, consider the following expression.

        (+ 1 (* 2 3))

When (* 2 3) is being evaluated, there exists a continuation, which represents the computation after the evaluation of (* 2 3), namely adding the result of (* 2 3) to 1. Continuations are a concept to control program execution, and this concept exists in any programming language. In Scheme, continuations are first-class objects, created by the function call-with-current-continuation (call/cc for short). Using Scheme continuations, we can express various control structures such as non-local exits and coroutines.

A continuation can be captured by the following form:

        (call/cc ⟨function⟩)

In this paper, ⟨A⟩ denotes an expression which evaluates to an A, and ⟨⟨A⟩⟩ means that A itself appears in that position. When the above expression is evaluated, call/cc generates a continuation object, which contains all information that is necessary to resume the computation after the call of call/cc. Then call/cc calls the single-argument function ⟨function⟩ by passing the continuation as the argument. The continuation object itself is a kind of function with a single argument. By calling the continuation, the computation after the call to call/cc will be resumed, with its value being the argument to the continuation. The action to call a continuation object is said "throwing the continuation." If the continuation is not thrown during the execution of ⟨function⟩, then whatever ⟨function⟩ returns will be used as the value of the call to call/cc.

3   Futures

The future construct provides mechanisms for process creation and synchronization. The future construct has the following format:

        (future ⟨⟨expression⟩⟩)

When evaluated, this expression immediately returns an object called *promise*, and creates a process to evaluate ⟨⟨expression⟩⟩. The process that evaluates (future

⟨⟨*expression*⟩⟩) is called the *parent* process and the process to evaluate ⟨⟨*expression*⟩⟩ is called the *child* process. These processes can be executed in parallel. When the value of ⟨⟨*expression*⟩⟩ is obtained, that value replaces the promise and the execution of the child process terminates. We say that, by this action, the promise is *determined to* the value. When a process needs the value of ⟨⟨*expression*⟩⟩, the process is suspended until the promise is determined. Thus, synchronizations of the two processes is automatically done by the system. If the programmer wants to determine the promise explicitly, then he can use the function **touch** as follows.

(touch ⟨*promise*⟩)

If ⟨*promise*⟩ is not determined yet, the caller of (touch ⟨*promise*⟩) will be suspended until ⟨*promise*⟩ is determined and then when ⟨*promise*⟩ is determined, the value of ⟨*promise*⟩ is returned. If ⟨*promise*⟩ is already determined, the value of ⟨*promise*⟩ is immediately returned.

The semantics of (future ⟨⟨*expression*⟩⟩) is equivalent to the semantics of ⟨⟨*expression*⟩⟩, if ⟨⟨*expression*⟩⟩ has no side effects. Hence, by replacing any ⟨⟨*expression*⟩⟩ in a sequential program that has no side effects with (future ⟨⟨*expression*⟩⟩), we can obtain a parallel program whose semantics is equivalent to the sequential program. If the sequential program has side effects, the semantics of the parallel program may be different from the sequential program since the order of execution of the side effects may be changed.

4 Interaction of Continuations and Futures

In the parallel environment in which multiple processes exist, the process which created a continuation and the process which throws the continuation may be different. For this case, the behavior of the continuation is not defined because it is not obvious which process should execute the thrown continuation. Moreover, the meaning of "the rest of computation" is not defined in the parallel environment because when a child process creates a continuation, the parent process may be executing the rest of computation after the **future** expression that created the child process.

In the following, we review two behaviors of continuations suitable for the parallel environment. One is the behavior that a parallel program using continuations, which has no side effects, and the sequential program, which is obtained by removing **future** construct from the parallel program yield the same result. We say continuations have the *sequential semantics*, when they behave in this way. The merit of this behavior is that the feature of **future** construct, which is described in the last paragraph in Section 3, is preserved, even if a parallel program uses continuations.

The second behavior is adapted to express parallel control structures. In this behavior, a continuation has only the rest of computation of the process that creates the continuation. In other words, a continuation represents the computation from the call of **call/cc** to the determining of the promise. If a process throws this continuation, the process executes the continuation without discarding its own current continuation. After the execution of the thrown continuation, the process continues its own computation, with the result of the execution of the continuation. That is, a call of a continuation behaves as if it were a function call, and the behavior after the determining of the promise is specified by the process which throws the continuation.

In the following, we show that Multilisp [4] and MultiScheme [5], which are popular future-based parallel Scheme systems, cannot express these continuations. In Multilisp, continuations are created and thrown in the same way as in sequential Scheme. Call/cc captures the continuation of the current process, and the execution of a continuation is performed by the process that throws the continuation. The future construct (future 《*expression*》) is implemented as follows.

```
(let ((p (make-promise)))
  (fork (begin
          (determine! p 《expression》)
          (quit)))
     p)
```

The function make-promise creates an undetermined promise object and returns it, and the function quit terminates the execution of the current process. The form (fork X) creates a child process to evaluate X, while the parent process continues its own execution without waiting for the termination of the child process. The form (determine! p 《*expression*》) determines the promise p to the value of 《*expression*》.

Let us consider the behavior of processes when a process A throws a continuation created by another process B. Assume that B is created by the following future expression:

```
(future 《expression for B》)
```

This future expression is equivalent to:

```
(let ((pB (make-promise)))
  (fork
    (begin
      (determine! pB 《expression for B》)
      (quit)))
     pB)
```

The continuation created by B in 《*expression for B*》 executes the rest of computation of 《*expression for B*》, determines the promise pB, and then terminates the current process. Assume that A is also created by future. Then the continuation created by B will be thrown at somewhere in 《*expression for A*》 of the following expression.

```
(future 《expression for A》)
  ≡
(let ((pA (make-promise)))
```

```
(fork
  (begin
    (determine! pA ⟨⟨expression for A⟩⟩)
    (quit)))
  pA)
```

If the continuation is thrown, *A* discards its own continuation and executes the thrown continuation. This means that *A* will execute the rest of computation of ⟨⟨*expression for B*⟩⟩, determine the promise pB, and terminate. Therefore, *A* cannot receive the result of the execution of the continuation nor can continue the rest of computation of ⟨⟨*expression for A*⟩⟩. Accordingly, pA will never be determined and the processes waiting for the determining pA will be blocked forever. This complicated behavior makes it difficult to describe parallel programs that uses continuations.

On the other hand, MultiScheme implements the **future** construct (**future** ⟨⟨*expression*⟩⟩) as follows.

```
(let ((p (make-promise)))
  (fork (begin
          (set-process-waiting-for! p)
          (let ((value ⟨⟨expression⟩⟩))
            (determine! (process-goal) value))
          (quit)))
  p)
```

The function **set-process-waiting-for!** establishes the promise that is to be determined by the current process, and the form (**process-goal**) returns that promise.

The method of MultiScheme to determine a promise is different from that of Multilisp. After executing the rest of computation of ⟨⟨*expression for B*⟩⟩, *A* in Multilisp determines the promise pB, whereas *A* in MultiScheme determines the promise pA of the current process *A*. After that, the execution of *A* terminates in the same way as in Multilisp. Thus pA will eventually be determined, but *A* cannot continue its own computation after the call to the continuation.

In both cases, the reason why a process cannot continue its own computation is that the execution of the process terminates after determining a promise. Thus these parallel Schemes cannot implement the sequential semantics of continuations.

5 Extended Continuations

In order to adapt continuations to the parallel environment, we propose an extension to Scheme continuations. We use Multilisp's **future** implementation, and extend continuations so that they can be invoked with an additional argument ⟨*function*⟩.

    (⟨*continuation*⟩ ⟨*datum*⟩ [⟨*function*⟩])

The optional argument ⟨*function*⟩ can be any function (including continuations) that receives a single argument. If ⟨*function*⟩ is not given, the above form behaves in the

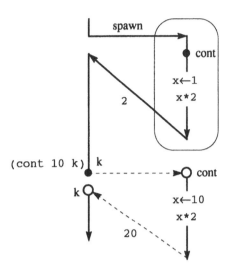

Figure 1: Behavior of the extended continuation

same way as in Multilisp. If ⟨*function*⟩ is given, however, the above form evaluates
(⟨*continuation*⟩ ⟨*datum*⟩), determines the promise, and then calls ⟨*function*⟩ with
the result of (⟨*continuation*⟩ ⟨*datum*⟩). That is, with the extended continuation,
the programmer can specify the behavior after the determining of a promise by
⟨*function*⟩. By this extension, we can realize two behaviors of continuations described
in Section 4 as will be explained in Sections 6 and 7.

For example, consider the following expressions.

```
(define cont #f)
(future
   (let ((x (call/cc (lambda (k) (set! cont k) 1))))
     (* x 2)))
```

The continuation cont represents the computation that doubles a given number and
returns the result. If this continuation is thrown as

```
(call/cc (lambda (k) (cont 10 k)))
```

then the thrower of the continuation can receive the result of the execution of the
continuation. Thus this call/cc expression will return 20. Figure 1 illustrates
the control flow of this example. In the figure, a black circle represents a point of
continuation capturing and a white circle represents a point to resume execution,
i.e., the point immediately after the call/cc expression. The continuation k, which
is created just before the call of cont, represents the computation that returns the
value of the argument to k as the value of the call to call/cc. By supplying k as
the argument to the call of cont, the call/cc expression can return the result of the
execution of cont.

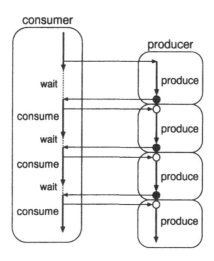

Figure 2: Producer and consumer

6   Application 1: Producer and Consumer

In this section, we give an example of applying the extended continuations to implement a producer and a consumer.

In this implementation, the producer produces one value at a consumer's request so that the producer can avoid producing unnecessary values. This producer can be implemented as a function which produces one value and returns a pair of the value and the current continuation which produces the next value. If the consumer calls this function, the consumer will obtain a value and a continuation of the producer. Then, by calling this continuation, the producer will be resumed and then return the next value and another continuation. Each time the consumer calls a continuation of the producer, the consumer can obtain a new value. Before the consumer consumes a value, if the consumer calls the continuation of the producer through future, the producer can generate the next value in parallel with the consumer.

Figure 2 illustrates the control flow of the producer and the consumer when the above operations are repeated. Although the consumer may have a long wait for the first value, the waiting time for the next values becomes shorter than the first time or even none.

This problem can be written as follows.

```
(define (consumer)
  (let loop ((m (future (producer #f))))
    (let ((n (future (call/cc (lambda (c) ((cdr m) #f c))))))
      (consume (car m))
      (loop n))))
```

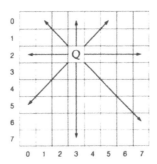

Figure 3: Movement of a queen

```
(define (producer x)
  (if x
      x
      (producer (call/cc
                  (lambda (k) (cons (produce) k))))))))
```

When calling a continuation of **producer**, **consumer** creates a continuation c and passes it as an optional argument to the continuation of **producer** so that **consumer** can obtain the promise which will be determined to a pair of the next value and a continuation.

In the following, we show a simple but concrete application of the above use of the extended continuations. There are multiple producers that find all solutions of the eight-queen problem in parallel, and a consumer, which prints the solutions.

A queen in chess can move along the column, the row, and the two diagonals through her present position as shown in Figure 3. The eight-queen problem is the problem to place eight queens on an 8×8 chessboard so that they do not threaten each other. There are many solutions in this problem. Figure 4 illustrates one of the solutions.

We parallelize this problem as follows (see Figure 5).

1. A parent process (a consumer) creates eight child processes (producers), and places a queen in column j of row 0 on the board of the j-th process ($j = 0, 1, \ldots, 7$). Each child process tries to place seven queens in the other rows.

2. If the child process finds a solution, it returns the solution to the parent process and then terminates.

In order to find all solutions, we use the extended continuations as follows.

1. When the child process finds a solution, the child process returns the current continuation to the parent process together with the solution. This continuation represents the computation that tries to find the next solution.

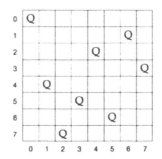

Figure 4: Sample solution for the eight-queen problem

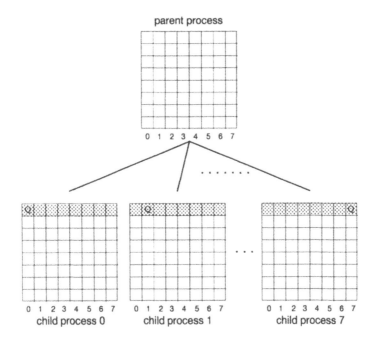

Figure 5: Parallelization of the eight-queen problem

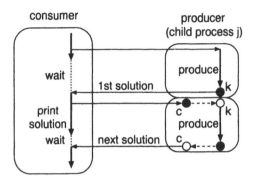

Figure 6: Finding next solutions in parallel

2. If the parent process receives the continuation and the solution from the child process, the parent process asks a child process to execute the continuation in parallel (by using **future**, as explained above) in order to obtain the next solution, and then prints the solution. This is repeated until all solutions are found.

The child process can pass one solution and its continuation to the parent process by using the extended continuations (see Figure 6).

We present the program for this problem in the appendix. We do not pay any attention to the efficiency of the program in order to simplify the program. Note that the function **8queen** in the program is just the same as the function for the sequential version.

7   Application 2: Sequential Semantics

In this section, we show how to realize the sequential semantics described in Section 4.

Let us consider the following expression [8]:

```
(let ((v (future (call/cc (lambda (k) k)))))
  (if v (v #f) v))
```

If the **future** in this expression is removed, this expression initially binds the variable v to a continuation. This continuation rebinds v to the value of its argument, and then evaluates the **if** expression again. Thus, the above expression without **future** rebinds v to **#f**, and then returns **#f**.

On the other hand, the above expression with **future** may behave in a different way. In Multilisp and MultiScheme, by throwing the continuation, the execution of the current process terminates after determining its promise.

Sequential semantics of continuations is proposed by Katz and Weise [9]. In their proposal, (**future** ⟪*expression*⟫) is implemented as follows.

```
(call/cc
  (lambda (cont)
    (let ((p (make-promise))
          (first-return? #t))
      (fork (cont p))
      (let ((result ⟪expression⟫))
        (if first-return?
            (begin (set! first-return? #f)
                   (determine! p result)
                   (quit))
            (cont result))))))))
```

The continuation **cont** represents the computation after the **future** expression. The variable **first-return?** has **#t** as the initial value. In this implementation, a process is created to evaluate the rest of computation after the **future** expression rather than to evaluate ⟪*expression*⟫. When the evaluation of ⟪*expression*⟫ is finished, the value of **first-return?** is changed to **#f**. Then the promise is determined in the same way as in Multilisp and the execution of the process terminates. However, if the continuation that is created during the evaluation of ⟪*expression*⟫ is thrown after determining the promise, **cont** will be thrown with the result of ⟪*expression*⟫ as an argument. This means that the continuation created in ⟪*expression*⟫ includes also the rest of computation of the parent process.

In their continuations, each time a process is created by **future**, a continuation must be created, though most of such continuation are never used. As the result, the process creation is a heavy operation.

With the extended continuations, we can realize the sequential semantics of continuations. In order to realize this, a process needs to create its current continuation (parent's continuation) right before a process creation, and the continuation created by a child process is thrown as follows.

(⟨*child's continuation*⟩ ⟨*datum*⟩ ⟨*parent's continuation*⟩)

For example, the first example of this section can be rewritten as follows.

```
(let ((v (call/cc
           (lambda (kk)
             (future
               (call/cc (lambda (k) (lambda (x) (k x kk)))))))))
  (if v (v #f) v))
```

In our proposal, process creation will be a light operation since parent's continuations are needed only when we need a sequential semantics.

8 Implementation of Extended Continuations

Our implementation of the extended continuations uses stacks to store ⟨*function*⟩'s (i.e., the second argument to continuation calls), one stack for each process. We call

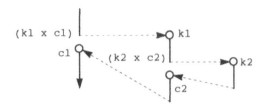

Figure 7: Control flow of the extended continuations

these stacks *continuation stacks*. When a continuation is thrown with a ⟨*function*⟩, the ⟨*function*⟩ is pushed onto the continuation stack of the current process, and then the process executes the continuation. A process checks its own continuation stack after determining a promise. If the continuation stack is empty, then the execution of the current process terminates. Otherwise, the process pops a ⟨*function*⟩ from the continuation stack, and executes it. A continuation stack is used for saving the control information of ⟨*function*⟩'s. This control information cannot be saved in the control stack because when a continuation is thrown, all the current contents of the control stack will be discarded and the contents of the control stack at the time of the continuation creation will be restored. For this reason, the control information of those functions must be saved into another stack, i.e., the continuation stack.

The extended continuations are implemented by saving the contents of the continuation stack and the control stack into the heap when a continuation is created and by restoring the continuation stack and the control stack from the heap when the continuation is thrown without the optional argument. If the optional argument ⟨*function*⟩ is given, only the control stack is restored and ⟨*function*⟩ is pushed onto the continuation stack.

Figure 7 illustrates the control flow of the extended continuations. When (k1 x c1) is evaluated, the process evaluating (k1 x c1) pushes c1 onto the continuation stack and executes k1. Later, when (k2 x c2) is evaluated, the process pushes c2 onto the continuation stack. After the execution of k2, the process pops c2 from the continuation stack and executes it. Similarly, after the execution of c2, the process pops c1 and executes it.

We have implemented the extended continuations in our **future**-based parallel Scheme, which is a parallel version of TUTScheme [10] and is running on Mach OS [11] and Solaris 2.

9   Comparisons with Other Parallel Scheme Systems

The producer and consumer problem described in Section 6 is one of the most important applications expressed by the extended continuations. In this section, we explain why the continuations of popular parallel Scheme systems and Katz-Weise continuations are not powerful enough to solve this problem.

9.1 Multilisp

In Multilisp, if a process A throws a continuation created by another process B, A will execute the rest of computation of B, determine the promise associated with "B," and terminate. Therefore, a continuation of the producer will determine the promise associated with the process that creates this continuation, rather than the current process, and the consumer cannot receive the next value.

9.2 MultiScheme

In MultiScheme, if a process A throws a continuation created by another process B, A will execute the rest of computation of B, determine the promise associated with "the current process," and terminate. Therefore, the consumer can receive the next value. However, if the producer creates a child process to parallelize the producer and a continuation is created in the child process, this created continuation has only the rest of computation of the child process although this continuation should include the rest of computation of the parent process.

Moreover, if the consumer calls a continuation of the producer in sequential execution, i.e., without `future`, the promise associated with the consumer process is determined, and then the execution of the consumer terminates. Thus the consumer cannot continue the computation after that call.

9.3 PaiLisp

In PaiLisp [6, 7], continuations can control execution of processes. If the continuation that is created by a process is thrown by another process, the current execution of the process that creates the continuation will be aborted and then the process that creates the continuation will execute the continuation. But if the process that creates the continuation has already been terminated, the call of the continuation is ignored. In either case, the process that throws the continuation continues its own execution.

The producer and consumer problem can be implemented by using PaiLisp continuations that extend Scheme continuations into concurrency in a direct and honest manner.

9.4 Katz-Weise Continuations

From the viewpoint of the feature of `future` which can parallelize a program by replacing ⟨⟨*expression*⟩⟩ in the program with (`future` ⟨⟨*expression*⟩⟩), their approach is desirable. However, since a continuation represents all the rest of computation that includes the rest of computation of parent processes, the producer continues the execution of the consumer after execution of the producer. Therefore, Katz-Weise continuations cannot realize the application described in Section 6.

Their proposal introduced a property of processes called *legitimacy* [9] so that parallel execution always follows control flow of the sequential execution of a program. Our system cannot implement legitimacy, because the implementation requires handling promises directly.

10   Conclusions

In this paper, we proposed an extension to Scheme continuations to make them adaptable to the parallel environment based on the `future` construct. The extended continuations are expected to improve the ability to describe parallel programs. They also enable implementation of the sequential semantics without overhead to process creation.

Bibliography

1) Yuasa, T.: *Introduction to Scheme* (in Japanese), Iwanami Shoten (1991).

2) IEEE Standard for the Scheme Programming Language, IEEE (1991).

3) Baker, H.: Actor Systems for Real-Time Computation, TR-197, Laboratory for Computer Science, MIT (1978).

4) Halstead, R.: Multilisp: A Language for Concurrent Symbolic Computation, *ACM Trans. Prog. Lang. Syst.*, Vol. 7, No. 4, pp. 501–538 (1985).

5) Miller, J.: MultiScheme: A Parallel Processing System Based on MIT Scheme, TR-402, Laboratory for Computer Science, MIT (1987).

6) Ito, T. and Matsui, M.: A Parallel Lisp Language PaiLisp and Its Kernel Specification, *Lecture Notes in Computer Science 441*, Springer-Verlag, pp. 58–100 (1990).

7) Ito, T.: Efficient Evaluation Strategies for Structured Concurrency Constructs in Parallel Scheme Systems, *Lecture Notes in Computer Science 1068*, Springer-Verlag, pp. 22–52 (1995).

8) Halstead, R.: New Ideas in Parallel Lisp: Language Design, Implementation, and Programming Tools, *Lecture Notes in Computer Science 441*, Springer-Verlag, pp. 2–57 (1990).

9) Katz, M. and Weise, D.: Continuing Into the Future: On the Interaction of Futures and First-Class Continuations, *Proc. 1990 ACM Conference on Lisp and Functional Programming*, pp. 176–184 (1990).

10) Yuasa, T., et al.: TUTScheme Reference Manual (in Japanese), Toyohashi University of Technology (1994).

11) Walmer, L. and Thompson, M.: A programmer's guide to the Mach system calls, CMU (1989).

Appendix: Parallel Program for Eight-Queen Problem, Using Extended Continuations

```
(define (all-queens)
  (let loop ((sols (map (lambda (j)
                          (future
                            (8queen 1 0 (cons j '())
                                        (cons j '())
                                        (cons (- j) '())))))
                        '(0 1 2 3 4 5 6 7))))
    (if (not (solution-exists? sols))
        'done
        (loop (map (lambda (sol)
                     (if sol
                         (let ((x (future
                                    (call/cc
                                      (lambda (c) ((cdr sol) #f c))))))
                           (print-solution (car sol))
                           x)
                         #f))
                   sols)))))

(define (8queen i j column left right)
  (cond ((= i 8) (call/cc (lambda (k) (cons column k))))
        ((= j 8) #f)
        ((or (member j column)
             (member (+ i j) left)
             (member (- i j) right))
         (8queen i (1+ j) column left right))
        ((8queen (1+ i) 0 (cons j column)
                          (cons (+ i j) left)
                          (cons (- i j) right)))
        ((8queen i (1+ j) column left right))))
```

8

Lightweight Processes for Real-Time Symbolic Processing

Ikuo Takeuchi

The University of Electro-Communications

Masaharu Yoshida

NTT-IT CORPORATION

Kenichi Yamazaki

NTT DoCoMo, Inc.

Yoshiji Amagai

NTT Network Innovation Laboratories

ABSTRACT

In order to construct a real-time symbolic processing system, it is indispensable to implement real-time garbage collection and an interrupt handling mechanism with small response delay. The latter needs to be based upon a preemptive lightweight process mechanism.

This paper describes a lightweight process implemented on the real-time symbolic processing system TAO/SILENT which is now being developed by us. The TAO/SILENT process is not only lightweight but it is also extensible so that it can accommodate arbitrary object-oriented semantics. It is implemented by microprogramming on the 33 MHz SILENT machine. The shortest elapsed time for process creation, activation, and deactivation is 16.91 microseconds. The best process switching time is 3.93 microseconds. A multiprogrammed recursive Fibonacci function that replaces the recursive calls by process spawning indicates that the TAO/SILENT lightweight process is about 50 times faster than SunOS4 LWP on the 60 MHz SuperSparc+ machine.

The performance figures and some implementation techniques for symbolic processing ensure that an urgent interrupt starts to be served by the corresponding process within at most 140 microseconds.

1   Introduction

It is a difficult challenge to fit symbolic processing to hard real-time systems[8]. However, increasing complex applications such as robotics in the real world environment, object-oriented real-time animation, and intelligent network control need a symbolic processing system that can cope with the real world in "nearly hard real-time".

In order to provide a symbolic processing system with real-time capabilities, it is indispensable to implement real-time garbage collection and interrupt handling with as small response delay as possible. It would, of course, be difficult to achieve hard real-time even if such a symbolic processing system exists, because of the inherent unpredictability of computation time of symbolic processing. However, it may be possible to make a sort of semi-hard real-time applications on such a system.

This paper describes lightweight processes implemented on a real-time symbolic processing system TAO/SILENT[12] which is now being developed by us. The design objective of our lightweight process was quite clear; it should be ensured that any urgent interrupt service could be started within 100 microseconds. We call the time between the moment when an interrupt happens and the moment when the interrupt service gets started, the interrupt response delay.[1] Because the value, 100 microseconds, is roughly an order of magnitude smaller than the response time presumed for various complex real-time multimedia applications[9] and robotics, say 1 to 5 milliseconds, there would be some margin for urgent interrupt disposal.

The SILENT[15] symbolic processing machine is a successor of the ELIS[5] symbolic processing machine that was developed by NTT and it came on the market in the mid 80s. The TAO language on SILENT is also a successor of the multiple paradigm programming language TAO[13] on ELIS, but it has been completely re-designed for further refinement.

The paper consists of the following sections: Section 2 outlines the SILENT machine, Section 3 describes the concepts and implementation of processes and interrupts in TAO, Sections 4 to 6 describe the microcoded kernel that manages process execution, Sections 7 and 8 describe the performance of the current implementation, which shows that our objective is almost achieved.

2   The SILENT machine

In order to differentiate our approach from other operating system research projects[1, 6], it is important to clarify that our research platform is not a conventional machine on the market, but a unique dedicated machine called SILENT that has been developed by us for real-time symbolic processing. We will briefly sketch the SILENT architecture in this section.

SILENT is a 40-bit tagged machine with an 8-bit tag inclusive and a 32-bit data field. The system bus is 80 bits wide and two Lisp pointers can be simultaneously

---

[1]It is difficult for the system to ensure the interrupt response completion time in symbolic processing.

read or written; that is, one Lisp cell can be accessed in one read/write operation.

SILENT is controlled by 80-bit-wide, 128K (or 256K) word microinstructions. The machine cycle is 30 nanoseconds, which is equal to the machine clock.

SILENT has no CPU mode such as kernel mode or user mode. The primitives written in microcode have the desired protection mechanism naturally because the usual interrupts are detected by the microinstruction explicitly and no raw address arithmetic is allowed in a user program written in TAO.

SILENT has a 128K (or 256K) word cyclic hardware stack other than the main memory. Consecutive pushes or pops can be performed at one word per machine cycle. A 2-bit dirty flag is equipped for each 128 stack words. Each stack word is accessed by a logical address that will be biased by a stack base register **spbas**. A stack boundary register **sbr** can automatically check the stack overflow in terms of the logical address. If the value of a stack pointer goes below the value of **sbr**, a **hap** condition is raised as an interrupt signal.

There are two levels of interrupts. The first ones, *micro-interrupts*, are interrupts at the microinstruction level, which are used for communication with other devices and for hardware error detection. The second ones are those that should be detected by the microinstruction explicitly. The latter are called **hap** interrupts since the branch instruction mnemonic to detect an interrupt is called **hap**. Events that raise **hap** conditions are stack overflow, timeout, communication through channels, and a simulated **hap** that is raised by the microinstruction explicitly.

It is assumed that a big main memory is equipped for the purpose of real-time symbolic processing to avoid virtual memory complications. The current machine is equipped with 640M bytes, or 64M cells. The 320K-byte cache memory is direct-mapped and write-through, with one clock wait for a hit access, and four clock wait for a non-hit access. Each cache entry consists of 80 bytes, or 8 cells. In wait cycles, any microinstruction other than main memory access can be executed in parallel with memory operation.

SILENT has a dozen 32-bit statistics counters to count machine cycles, cache hits/non-hits, branch successes/failures, and so on. A counter overflow will raise a micro-interrupt so that we can measure those statistics in arbitrary long precision. Of these, the machine cycle counter **timc** can be accessed as quickly as general registers so that we can measure the execution time of a microcode fraction by calculating the difference of two **timc** values at two program points. Since even one-step improvement can be observed precisely, **timc** boosted our microcode tuning a great deal.

3 TAO Processes

3.1 The concept of TAO process

The TAO/SILENT system is the pairing of a language and a dedicated machine, and there is only microcode in between. That is, there is no outstanding operating system. Those that are equivalent to system calls in other operating systems are implemented as language primitives of TAO. However, the basic part of the process management is done by a sort of kernel written in microcode. In that sense, we will call the kernel a *microkernel*. The microkernel is merely a runtime system, as well as the garbage collector, that guarantees the language performance.[2]

A set of SILENTs and conventional 32-bit machines can comprise a multiprocessor system with rather a limited amount of shared memory. However, we only focus on the multiprogramming on a SILENT uniprocessor in this paper.

To achieve real-time processing, it is necessary to be able to run a number of processes each of which has its own role, and to give the CPU resource to any one of these just in time when it is required. To satisfy timing conditions, it is mandatory to implement quick process control and quick interrupt service for a required process being awaken within as small a delay as possible. Consequently, lightweight processes need to be implemented.

Moreover, a process needs to be provided with sophisticated functionality so that it is a first class entity in a multiple paradigm symbolic processing language. For example, an autonomous concurrent object, or an agent, should be able to be programmed with any structure with which the user wants to model it.

To sum up, the TAO process should be lightweight and easy to extend in conjunction with other symbolic processing programming paradigms.

TAO processes are close to threads in UNIX operating systems, in the sense that the SILENT heap memory can be shared by any TAO process. However, a TAO process can have its own protected environment, and can be dealt as first class data, not only via pid. The word "process" was chosen to emphasize this independence and substantiality.

There are four protection levels, and 64 priority levels for processes; that is, from 0 to 63; the higher the number, the higher the priority. A simple priority inheritance mechanism is adopted to cope with priority inversion caused by semaphores. A process with lower protection level obviously cannot manipulate other processes with higher protection level.

The internal data structure of a process is fixed since the microkernel directly accesses it. A handle called an *adjoint object* is included in the process data structure, through which the user can give any object semantics to each process (See Fig. 1). If a process is sent a message in the object-oriented programming sense, the message is delegated to its adjoint object, if any. It is possible either to adjoin the same object to a set of processes or to adjoin individual object to each process, according to the user's policy.[3]

Concurrent objects implemented by the adjoint object semantics make it easier to improve the microkernel performance than other implementations such as inheriting,

---

[2]Needless to say, the garbage collector is merely a runtime system that guarantees there is virtually an infinite source of allocatable memory in the system.

[3]In TAO, a primitive data type that has a handle for the adjoint object is called a pseudo-object. Vectors, arrays, and bounded buffers for interprocess communication are pseudo-objects. A buffer with an appropriate adjoint object will behave like an I/O stream of Common Lisp in the context of message passing computation.

say, the system "Process" class, or storing a process in one of the instance variables of an object, since the access to the internal structure of a TAO process is always quite direct from the microkernel, even if the process is given an object semantics.

The function that creates a process is **make-process**. [4]

> (**make-process** [*priority*] [*protection-level*] [*adjoint-obj*])

A process just created has no environment (that is, context and memory) and no task. We will not explain here how to enrich the environment proper to a process. To give a task to a process, a function **task** is used:

> (**task** *process chore*)

Here, *chore* is a pair (cons) of a function and its argument list.[5] A chore once given to a process is called a *task*. The task is queued in the chore queue of the process. A process executes the tasks in the queue one after the other, and it becomes dormant when no task remains.

The microkernel employs preemptive priority-based scheduling with round robin CPU rotation for processes of the same priority.[6]

3.2 Process Implementation

As shown in Fig. 1, a piece of process data is represented by consecutive eight cells. These eight cells are allocated in binary buddy areas of the heap memory so that they fit the SILENT cache boundaries. That is, once a process data is accessed, any further field access will hit the cache. The CPU time field for a process needs 64 bits because 32 bits can only accommodate about two minutes for the 30 nanosecond time grain.

The *symtab* (from symbol table) in Fig. 1 is a sort of hash table that utilizes a simple hash instruction **mash** of SILENT. Searching a symtab for a symbol key will, independent of the number of entries, end up on the average within 0.35 microsecond if all caches are hit, and within 1.1 microseconds if no cache is hit.

For the simple priority inheritance mentioned above, pairs of the process and semaphore that caused the inheritance are recorded in a list data so that the inherited process can move to the next appropriate priority when it releases a semaphore. For simplicity, however, priority inheritance is not rippled down. For example, if a process P_2 inherits the priority of process P_1, and then P_1 inherits the priority of process P_0, P_2 does not inherit the priority of P_0.

The process status field has three 5-bit priority subfields in order to cope with the priority inheritance and casual priority change initiated by the user. These are an inherent priority which is a default priority when a process starts to execute a

---

[4]Arguments enclosed in long brackets are optional.

[5]In this paper, we do not refer to the multiple paradigms of TAO. Hence, it is not needed here to consider the case where a chore is a pair of a logic predicate and its argument patterns.

[6]The real-time garbage collector consists of eight concurrent processes. They are not scheduled by the priority; instead, they are specially scheduled according to the urgency of the garbage collection.

adjoint object*	status
CPU time* (a unit is 30 nanoseconds)	
symtab for context variables	primordial object table
symtab for dynamic variables	process symtab
event interrupts	priority inheritance*
chore queue*	stack management info
saved stack pointer	pid etc.
swapped block list	stack status

The asterisked fields and the word "symtab" are explained in the text. The process status is a 32-bit bit-table that represents the characteristics and current status of the process. Context variables are variables global within the process. They can be shared among processes and they survive even when the process becomes dormant; that is, they have an indefinite extent scope. Dynamic variables are those similar to the special variables of Common Lisp. Their bindings will disappear when the process becomes dormant.

The primordial object table may contain an object that corresponds to a primitive data type such as integer and list, which provides a message sent to the primitive data type with an object semantics, individually to the process. The process symtab behaves like a property list of the process.

The event interrupts are a queue that accepts interrupts raised by eventboxes (See Section 3.3). The stack management info has subfields for the proper amount of stack, tickets, and a stackometer (See Section 5). The other four slots are also used for the stack management.

Many of these slots are empty at the moment of process creation, and they are filled on demand with pointers to certain data structures. For example, the swapped block list gets a variable sized vector that will hold a set of system memory blocks, when the stack of the process is being swapped out to the main memory.

Figure 1: The process structure

task, a dynamic priority that can be changed dynamically within a permitted range according to its inherent priority, and a temporary priority which holds the inherited priority but normally equals to the dynamic priority. The process is scheduled on the temporary priority.

The chore queue is sorted by the priority of the processes that gave the tasks. It also contains interprocess interrupts that are similar to those invoked by the **process-interrupt** of Lisp Machine Lisp[14]. Interprocess interrupts are highly asynchronous and not well-structured, but they are prioritized in the chore queue and take over the current task, using its environment. That is, an interprocess interrupt is executed on top of the stack of the current task. It may resume the overtaken task or simply abort it.

Process data themselves are managed in a similar way to other primitive data.

There is a system global process table of 65534 entries that prevents the running processes from being garbage collected.

3.3 Concurrent Primitives

In this subsection, we introduce the concurrent primitives of TAO to clarify the concurrent programming style intended in TAO. The data types for concurrency are semaphore, locker, mailbox, buffer, and eventbox.

The semaphore is binary, and its primitive operations are P and V as usual, with additional non-blocking **P-no-hang** and other privileged primitives for the crisis recovery management.[7]

The locker is a lockable data type that can cope with the so-called readers and writers problem. Its primitive operations are R and UR for read lock and unlock, and W and UW for write lock and unlock, respectively.[8] Only when a process gets the lock of a locker, it can access the data encapsulated in the locker.

The mailbox is an unbounded buffer with non-blocking write and blocking/non-blocking read. Its primitive operations are **send-mail**, **receive-mail**, **receive-mail-no-hang** and so on. It also supports memory-less write **signal-mail**. The input port (sender's side) and output port (receiver's side) of a mailbox are strictly distinguished so that processes with different protection levels can communicate safely with one another.[9]

The buffer is a bounded buffer that synchronizes the transmission of, say, bytes, 16-bit character codes, or 32-bit integers between processes. It consists of an eight cell header and a buffer body (vector or string). Its input/output ports are distinguished in the same way as those of the mailbox.

The eventbox is best explained as a substitute that waits for a specific event on behalf of a process. A process can continue its computation once it lets an eventbox wait for an event. Eventboxes can be enqueued into any kind of queue that accommodates processes. If an eventbox in a queue is to be waken up as if it were a process, an interrupt to the client process that let the eventbox be enqueued is raised, so that the client process can be made aware that the specified event has happened. Events handled by eventboxes are semaphore P operation, receiving data in a mailbox, timeout in terms of milliseconds, and user event raised by the function **raise-event**. Eventboxes make synchronous operation such as P of a semaphore asynchronous. Interrupts caused by an eventbox can be accepted only within the program construct, or special form, **event-alert** and **timeout-alert** that let the eventbox hook interrupts, so that the syntactic structure and the interruptible range coincide; that is, eventboxes realize well-structured interrupt handling.

For example, the following program waits for data in a mailbox within 50 milliseconds, while doing some background job;

---

[7]TAO symbols are case-sensitive.

[8]These are similar to **StartRead**, **EndRead**, **StartWrite**, and **EndWrite**, respectively, in the operation system literature.

[9]Both sides have the same 32-bit address but are distinguished by a bit in the tag.

```
(let ((evbx-mbx (make-eventbox :mailbox mbx)))
     (timeout-alert 50 (op* (_) (exit let #f))
          (eventbox-alert evbx-mbx (op* (_ mail) (exit let mail))
               (do-some-background-job) )))
```

where op* is almost equivalent to **lambda** of other Lisps and a "_" means an ignored argument. Other details are omitted here, however.

Other than those mentioned above, there are some important primitives with respect to interrupts. The following privileged program construct disables any **hap** interrupt detection and achieves system-wide inseparable operations.

(**without-process-switch** *FORM ...*)

There is an absolute time limit for this mighty interrupt inhibition for the sake of system safety; 50 microseconds in the current implementation. Interrupt disabling that is local within a process can be programmed as follows.

(**without-interrupt** *FORM ...*)

4 Microkernel

The runtime system, microkernel is responsible for the following.

(1) It keeps runnable processes in a multiple-level priority queue, and it decides the next process which will get the CPU. If a process wakes up another process by a synchronization primitive and the wakened process has a higher priority than the waking one, the waking process passes the control to the microkernel for preemption. Preemption is checked in the concurrency primitive rather than in the microkernel because it slightly reduces the number of dynamic steps for the check.

(2) It accepts **hap** interrupts at an entry in the microkernel which will be called from **hap** branch instructions in the microcode. To ensure the system safety, especially with respect to the garbage collector, **hap** branches are only (but as frequently as possible) placed after where inseparable primitive operations are settled so that no dangling pointers or dangerously incomplete data structures remain at the moment of process switching.

There are four types of **hap** conditions.

- *stack overflow*: When a process's stack gets bigger than a predefined limit, the microkernel tries to enlarge the stack. If this will result in collision with another process's stack, appropriate action should be taken as will be described in the next section.

- *timeout*: Timeout alarm requests issued by processes via eventboxes are queued after being sorted by the absolute time. The nearest timeout is set to a decremental counter that causes timeout **hap** when it reaches zero. A timeout event wakes up the corresponding eventbox and hence interrupts the process that has been alert to the timeout.

- *communication channel*: Communication channels with other processors (unused for the present).

- *simulated* **hap**: A **hap** condition that is signaled by a microinstruction. It is used when a certain interrupt is required to be signaled inside an inseparable program segment, or when a micro-interrupt wants to pass the low-level interrupt to the **hap** interrupt, since micro-interrupts may interleave at any point inside primitive operations.

(3) It keeps track of the system time every 500 microseconds. At these timings, round-robin scheduling is done if necessary. Its overhead is typically 5 to 10 microseconds.

(4) It guarantees that the whole stack of a process is on the hardware stack when the process is to be resumed. It involves swap-in and/or swap-out between the hardware stack and the main memory; it is a similar activity to the memory management across the memory hierarchy in conventional operating systems. However, there may be transfer within the hardware stack because of the peculiarity of the SILENT hardware stack. Swap and transfer are both time consuming. Hence, they are segmented into small fractions in order not to produce long inseparable sections.

(5) It allocates a process's stack to the hardware stack, and it deallocates the stack of a process that has gone into the dormant state. A sort of best-effort stack allocation algorithm makes stack collision less possible.

5 Stack management

The most complicated job of the microkernel is the stack management, since the hardware stack is one of the most precious resources of SILENT. Its puzzle-minded microprogram amounts to about 1,700 steps.

The current 128K word hardware stack is divided into 256 512-word stack blocks. The bottoms of process execution stacks are aligned to these block boundaries. The reason why the block size was chosen to be 512 words is as follows:

- We have statistics in the TAO/ELIS system that the stack memory amount of most processes is less than 200 words when they are inactive, and less than 500 words even when they are running.[10]

- Swapping between the hardware stack and main memory takes at most inseparable 70 microseconds for a 512-word block. Hence, 512 is the largest tolerable block size in order to achieve our objective, a 100-microsecond response delay.[11]

- Smaller stack block will load the stack management because the size of tables to be maintained will increase.

---

[10]Moreover, stack usage is more parsimonious in TAO/SILENT than in TAO/ELIS.

[11]It is, in fact, impossible to achieve the 100 microsecond response delay as can be easily guessed. But 140 microsecond response delay is at least guaranteed. As will be noted in Section 8, a sophisticated swapping algorithm will reduce the delay to about 110 microseconds.

Application programs that wish to be real-time are assumed not only to give high priority to urgent processes, but also to plan to reduce the stack size of those processes because urgent processes are expected to be resident in the hardware stack as steadily as possible. TAO assumes the amount of stack memory to be used properly by a process, according to its priority as follows:

priority	stack memory amount
48 – 63	1 block
32 – 47	2 blocks
16 – 31	4 blocks
0 – 15	more than 16 blocks

Note that the larger the number, the higher is the priority.

This seems to be too restrictive, but it is sufficient from our experience with TAO/ELIS. In fact, it is by no means a strict restriction. It is only for the purpose of guaranteeing performance. No error is caused if a process uses more stack blocks than expected. Only the number of violations is recorded in the *ticket* field in the process data (See Fig. 1). Ticket records would be useful for tuning application programs.

Unlike general memory management, the stack management should take into account the address consecutiveness of the SILENT hardware stack. If the hardware stack were equipped with an MMU (memory management unit), the microkernel load would be lessened, but it was too costly to install an MMU in our design phase to guarantee stack push/pop in one machine cycle.[12]

Any process that is not dormant has an execution stack. A process that gets the CPU should have the whole execution stack allocated on the hardware stack in order to guarantee the performance of TAO primitives such as dynamic variable access and function call/return.

The execution stack of a process may have one of the following three states.

whole: The whole stack of the process resides on the hardware stack.

absent: No stack block is on the hardware stack.

wane: Some of stack blocks are swapped out into the main memory or part of the stack is being transferred to other location in the hardware stack.

Stack transfer is twice as quick as swapping; 31 microseconds per block at most. Hence, stack transfer is considered first when stack collision occurs, if there is room elsewhere. However, stacks less than four blocks are only taken into account because big transfer will complicate the transfer algorithm and make it difficult to achieve our performance objective. When a three-block stack is to be transferred, the microkernel first transfers two of them inseparably (62 microseconds at most),

---

[12] Even today, since machine cycle is shortened than those days, it would still be too costly.

marks the remaining one as "to be transferred some time", and then checks **hap** and preemption.

There are two cases for stack collision. The first is caused by stack overflow, and the second is caused by swap-in of the stack blocks of a wakened process. The combination of these certainly complicates the stack management.

Stack overflow is detected by hardware comparing **sbr** and the main stack pointer **sp**. The stack overflow **hap** condition set by the hardware is detected by the **hap** branch instruction in the microcode only at the timing when there are no dangling structures, so that there may be cases where the stack is further deepened until the stack overflow is actually detected. Hence, **sbr** is set with a 64-word margin; that is, the top stack block is effectively $512 - 64 = 448$ words before stack overflow is detected. Every TAO primitive is regulated not to push the stack too rapidly and running over the margin without checking **hap**.

When a stack overflow is detected, the stack block just above the top is examined if vacant. If it is vacant, the overflowing stack is simply enlarged and some bookkeeping tables are updated. The *stackometer* (See Fig. 1) subfield of the stack management info field of the process that records the maximum stack block usage is incremented if necessary. The ticket subfield is also incremented if necessary.

There are three actions when a process's stack collides with another process's stack due to a stack overflow: it transfers itself to another stack location if it is small, the other stack is transferred if it is small, or the other stack is swapped out in the main memory. The worst case of these takes 62 microseconds.

If swap-in is needed to wake up a process, every time the swap-in of a stack block is completed, the microkernel checks **hap** and preemption. When swap-in causes simultaneous swap-out or stack transfer, they are pipelined so that they are done simultaneously utilizing memory wait cycles. The worst case needs 70 microseconds per block.

As described above, stack collision is resolved within inseparable 70 microseconds at most. As can easily be seen, small stack processes, especially, those with only one stack block probably reside in the hardware stack unless there are so many such processes. We can be sure that urgent processes are stack resident if application programs are adequately designed.

One of the two bits of the dirty flag associated with every 128 words of the hardware stack is used to omit each of their swap-outs, since unchanged 128 words need not be stored more than once. The other bit is used to detect the end of the marking phase of the garbage collection.

When a process needs to access another process's stack using some privileged primitives, the access is virtualized by a set of micro-subroutines.

Bookkeeping of the stack block usage is implemented by a set of bit-tables. SILENT has a microinstruction **fbit** that searches for the first non-zero bit position from left (or right) in a 32-bit register. It is quite easy to find consecutive vacant stack blocks using **fbit** instruction along with 64-bit double shift instructions.

The LRU algorithm adopted in the microkernel is slightly more sophisticated than usual. Four 256-bit LRU bit-tables are used to represent four recent generations cyclically. One of these represents the current generation, whose bits are all set to one initially. When a process gets the CPU, then the bits for the corresponding stack blocks are reset to zero.

When the number of zeros exceeds 1/4 of the total bits, generation change, namely a cyclic shift of the role of the LRU bit-tables, takes place at the next process switching. Thus, there is a record of stack usage for the current and the former three generations. The LRU bit-tables are referred to only if there is no room in the hardware stack when an execution stack is (re-)allocated. If there are non-zero bits in the bitwise AND of the bit-tables of the most recent three generations, the corresponding stack block has not been used for at least three generations. If there is no non-zero bit, the most recent two generations are examined. At worst, the current generation has 1/4 non-zero bits.[13]

The LRU tables are updated even when there is much room in the hardware stack. This updating brings in at least a 0.63 microsecond overhead to process switching, one of the main performance defect at present.

6   Process Switching

Process switching takes place when there is a synchronization by **send-mail** or a preemption. Process switching in TAO/SILENT only needs to store ten registers to save a process context, because **hap** interrupts are detected only when a unit of (sub-)primitive operation is completed so that most working registers need not be saved, and because SILENT is a stack machine that needs fewer working registers. Other overheads for process switching are storing information about the stack status and time measurement into the relevant slots of the suspended process (See Fig. 1).[14]

Here, we describe the exact number of dynamic microsteps that is needed to switch processes when process A becomes blocked by **receive-mail** on a mailbox, and the highest priority process B at that moment gets the CPU. We assume that process B's stack is *whole* (See Section 5). In the following, n and w in the notation $[n/w]$ denote, respectively, the number of machine cycles when all memory accesses hit the cache, and the number of wait cycles included in n that are never utilized by the microcode. In the actual microcode, the following stages are interleaved to exploit unused wait cycles.[15]

(1) Save ten registers and the return address on the execution stack of process A. [12/0]

---

[13]There is a case where the generation change is postponed until 3/4 of all the stack blocks are used. This may happen if a malicious process runs a simple stack overflowing program, since final stack overflow error will be reported if 1/2 of all the stack blocks are used by a single process.

[14]At this time, stack underflow, namely, stack shrink by releasing once used stack blocks, is detected, and the stack management tables are updated.

[15]For simplicity, we do not mention the preemption by the garbage collector. However, the figure does not change since there is a special branch instruction that examines the garbage collection status.

(2) Update A's slots (stack information and the CPU time). [20/3]

(3) Remove process A from the runnable queue. [12—19/2—5]

(4) Release stack blocks now released by A. [17—/1—] (17 if there is no release)

(5) Choose process B that gets the CPU next. [12—17/1—2] (The microkernel uses `fbit` to find the highest priority of the runnable processes on the 64-bit bit-table. Then it refers to the corresponding process queue in the multiple-level priority queue. The best 12 is a case where only one process is in a queue with a priority higher than 31. The worst 17 is a case where there is more than one process in a queue with a priority lower than 32. When the garbage collector runs concurrently, two more steps are needed, however.

(6) Set three registers `sp`, `spbas` and `sbr` for process B. [10/0]

(7) Update the LRU tables. [21—/4—] (21 for the case where there was no change in stack block usage.)

(8) Accumulate the kernel CPU time consumption and set the starting time for B's resumption.

(9) Recover ten registers for B and give the CPU to B.

We can obtain a minimal process switching time of 3.93 microseconds by summing up these steps. Note that time measurement and LRU table updating consume more than 30 percent (1.26 microsecond) of the time. Note that `fbit` instruction is essential to speed up the next process choice.

7 Evaluation

It is necessary to evaluate at least two performance figures if one wants to advocate lightweight processes.

- (1) The time for process creation, activation, and deactivation

- (2) The time for process switching

As was described in the former section, the process switching time is 3.93 microseconds for the best case. The total elapsed time for process creation, activation, and deactivation was measured using the following iterative program:[16]

```
(task (make-process) trivial-chore)
(task (make-process) trivial-chore)
......
```

---

[16]The reclamation of an unreferenced process that is dormant is the garbage collector's job.

where `trivial-chore` is the chore of a trivial function with no argument which returns only `#t`. A number of such processes run one after another. Their average life-time is 16.91 microseconds. This can be called the shortest life-time of a TAO process. The microkernel overhead is 7.94 microseconds of the 16.91 microseconds. This means that the time for `make-process`, `task` and `trivial-chore` is less than 9 microseconds.

Other than these, however, the time for process synchronization and communication, and the time for manipulating the process environment need to be evaluated. Here, we only show the relevant time for the former. We used the following program:[17]

```
(defun mfib (n)
   (if (<= n 1) 1
       (let (((s r) ..(make-mailbox)))
          (task (make-process)
                (make-chore #'fs (list s (1- n))) )
          (task (make-process)
                (make-chore #'fs (list s (- n 2))) )
          (+ (receive-mail r) (receive-mail r)) )))

(defun fs (mb n) (send-mail mb (mfib n)))
```

This is a multiprogrammed variation of the well-known recursive Fibonacci function:

```
(defun fib (n)
   (if (<= n 1) 1
       (+ (fib (1- n)) (fib (- n 2))) ))
```

that is, the recursive calls are replaced by child process creation, and value returning is replaced by interprocess communication by mailboxes.

The form (`mfib` n) creates $2v - 2$ processes if the value of (`fib` n) is v. We measured up to (`mfib 22`), which is shown in Table 1. The time is in milliseconds and OH is the microkernel overhead. As a reference, the time for (`fib 22`) is 56.92 microseconds.

The reason why the microkernel overhead increases rapidly from (`mfib 13`) is that stack swapping begins to take place from there. However, this overhead saturates at 61 percent.

The CPU time for processes that create two child processes fluctuates from 26 to 32 microseconds according to given task and cache status. The average percentage of wasted wait cycles where nothing is done ranges from 26.7 to 28.9 percent, and the average cache hit rate ranges from 93.7 to 89.0 percent (decreasing as n increases).

In the above program, `send-mail` does not cause preemption because all processes have the same priority. Modifying the program so that child processes have lower priority than the parent, we can force preemption every time `send-mail` is executed, and as a result swapping and process switching happen more frequently.

---

[17]The declaration part of the `let` construct has a TAO peculiar form in this program. This reads as follows: let `s` and `r` be, respectively, the output port and the input port of a mailbox which are returned as two values by (`make-mailbox`).

n	total time	net time	OH(%)	number of processes
9	2.95	1.64	44.5	108
10	4.83	2.68	44.5	176
11	7.93	4.36	45.0	286
12	12.89	7.06	45.2	464
13	23.70	11.74	50.5	752
14	45.12	19.26	57.3	1218
15	80.18	32.66	59.3	1972
16	135.92	54.24	60.1	3192
17	227.87	89.56	60.7	5166
18	377.20	147.33	60.9	8360
19	617.07	240.95	61.0	13528
20	1011.03	393.33	61.1	21890
21	1646.18	639.08	61.2	35420
22	2671.89	1036.73	61.2	57312

The time is in milliseconds.

Table 1: The performance for (mfib n)

However, this increases the elapsed time only by 10 to 6 percent (as n increases), and increases the microkernel overhead by 5 to 2 points. Contrary to intuition, the net CPU time for processes also increases by 0.6 — 0.8 percent. The reason is that preemption checking and small related overwork is done in the synchronization primitive, send-mail in this case.

TAO/ELIS can only run up to (mfib 9) because it accommodates only 128 concurrent processes at maximum. (mfib 9) on TAO/SILENT is 530 times faster than that on TAO/ELIS. This extreme difference is caused by the fact that stack swapping occurs frequently on TAO/ELIS even for this small $n = 9$, while no swapping occurs on TAO/SILENT. Rather, the lightweightness of the TAO/SILENT processes is highlighted by the fact that (mfib 9) on TAO/SILENT is only two times slower than compiled (fib 9) on TAO/ELIS, whereas SILENT only has a clock six times faster than ELIS.

In order to allow comparison with other current systems, we converted mfib as directly as possible to Allegro Common Lisp (ACL), Sun OS4 LWP, KLIC, and CML. The measurement shown in Table 7 was done by (mfib 22).

Allegro Common Lisp[4] has the concept of stack group. We converted mfib to a program that uses the stack group. The measurement excluded the garbage collection time. However, the converted program did not use synchronization primitives such as send-mail so that the time obtained here may be shorter than that of an accurately converted one.

system	time	machine
TAO	2.67	SILENT 33MHz
ACL	12.86	HP9000/755 125MHz
LWP	138.6-	SS-20 SuperSparc+ 60MHz
KLIC	0.65	SS-20 SuperSparc+ 60MHz
CML	2.10	SS-20 SuperSparc+ 60MHz

The time is in seconds.

Table 2: Comparison of performance with other systems

In the conversion to SUN OS4 LWP[10], we implemented the TAO mailbox, converted `mfib` to a C program and compiled it by `gcc` with a -O4 option. If we did not use the converted mailbox, instead using natural value returning from child to parent like the stack group programming in ACL, the time would be about half that in the table.

It is not straightforward to convert `mfib` to KLIC[2]. We used **merger** to make a program that can be said to be similar to the TAO `mfib`.

CML[7] employs generational garbage collection so that every primitive has a certain overhead. We excluded this overhead in the measurement. If it is included, the time would be 4.66 seconds, twice as long. It may be correct to call the latter the elapsed time.

We have not mentioned the Solaris kernel thread[3] here, since it was too slow to refer to.

The reason why KLIC is much faster than TAO is that the KLIC process is very light in its semantics; that is, it is history-less so that no execution stack is needed. The speed of CML is close to that of TAO, but the CML process does not have priority or protection level, and cannot cope with real-time processing. Both kinds of processes are not what operating system people call a process. They are sorts of "processes" in a programming language framework. The TAO process can, however, behave flexibly both in a language framework and in an operating system framework.

In the `mfib` benchmark of TAO, the size of the execution stack swapped into the main memory is 31 words including the 10 registers mentioned previously. The size can be arbitrary increased if the program is modified to call `mfib` recursively in `fs` after `fs`'s stack is deepened by executing another simple recursive function, say, obtaining the sum of 1 to m as follows:

```
(defun fs (mb n) (fs2 mb n m))

(defun fs2 (mb n m)
   (if (<= m 1)
       (block (send-mail mb (mfib n)) 1)
       (+ m (fs mb n (1- m))) ))
```

If we set the size to 1350 words (three stack blocks), the microkernel overhead reduces to 34 percent from the original 61 percent. This is because the swapping time for the stack is less than the access time to the stack in this simple recursive summation. This suggests that about a 60 percent overhead is almost the worst case conceivable in real computation.

8   Interrupt Response Delay

As mentioned previously, we assume that an urgent process uses only one stack block, at least when it is waiting for an event. Such a process can resume within 70 microseconds at worst even if its stack has been swapped out into the main memory.

Theoretically, it is sufficient to set the maximum interval between successive hap checks to be a little less than 70 microseconds in order not to increase the interrupt response delay. However, we set the time at 30 microseconds to enhance the performance of actual computation. It is another important research topic to ensure that every inseparable operation other than swap-in/out runs within 30 microseconds.

Almost all primitive operations such as car and cons need very small inseparable computation, say, 0.1 to 10 microseconds. However, there are operations that need long inseparable computation; for examples, insert/delete operations in a long character string, and the bignum arithmetics. But these are not assumed to be necessary in most real-time applications. Hence, TAO has system parameters that prevent excessively long string or large bignums from appearing in real-time computation.

We have decomposed, in a safe manner, other long operations that are traditionally considered inseparable. For example, when the user claims a big vector from the heap memory, its elements may contain old garbage because the garbage collector does not clear vector elements for the sake of efficiency. During the initialization of the vector elements to the specified initial value, the system checks hap frequently. It would cause the garbage collector to get the CPU and mark the old garbage in the vector. But the vector has a flag that indicates the vector is in the course of initialization. Hence, old garbage will be guarded from being marked and it does not harm the real-time garbage collector.

A more complicated example is rehashing a *symtab* (hash table) when its entries increase over the threshold. If the entire rehashing is programmed inseparably, it is easy to violate the 30-microsecond rule. We made an incremental symtab rehashing program to break down the inseparability. In the rehashing phase, there coexist a new enlarged hash table and the old hash table in a symtab. Searching is done in both tables and new entries will be entered into the new one. Every time the symtab is accessed, a small number of entries are moved from the old to the new until there are no more entries to move.

There would be also long inseparable operations in real-time garbage collection, but it turns out that no inseparable operation exceeds 10 microseconds. In other words, the garbage collector is brisker than the microkernel.

The worst interrupt response delay will happen in the case shown in Fig. 2.

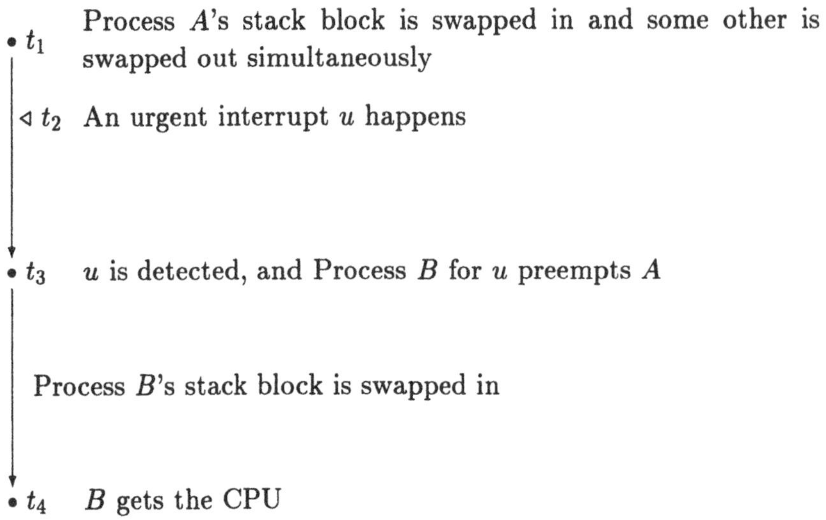

- t_1 Process A's stack block is swapped in and some other is swapped out simultaneously

◁ t_2 An urgent interrupt u happens

- t_3 u is detected, and Process B for u preempts A

Process B's stack block is swapped in

- t_4 B gets the CPU

Interrupt response delay $t_4 - t_2$ may be 140 microseconds at worst. However, it may be reduced to 110 microseconds if swap-in/out for A is rolled back shortly after t_2.

Figure 2: The worst interrupt response delay

Assume an urgent interrupt happens when process A is being swapped in. The swap-in takes inseparable 70 microseconds at most. The interrupt is detected just after it is finished and the swap-in of process B that has been alert to the interrupt is then started, which will take another 70 microseconds. Hence, 140 microseconds is the worst delay, which is larger than our objective, 100 microseconds.

A sophisticated swapping algorithm that checks **hap** more frequently and that rolls back A's swap-in on its way should reduce this 140 microseconds to 110 microseconds. We have not implemented this, however, because it would complicate the microkernel too much, but more because we are now developing a second generation SILENT chip with twice as fast a clock, which will achieve our objective without any microprogramming effort.

9   Conclusion

We described the concept and performance of the TAO/SILENT lightweight processes which are the fundamentals for the real-time garbage collection and for the interrupt disposal with minimum response delay. Since SILENT is a stack-based symbolic processing machine, we had to implement through microprogramming a number of features that are implemented by hardware in other conventional machines. The benefit is the tight coordination of the machine and language, as well as the tight coordination of the microkernel and the garbage collector.[18]

We think that the process spawning Fibonacci function is a good benchmark to measure the lightweightness of processes. The performance of TAO/SILENT is an order of magnitude higher than the lightweight processes of UNIX operating systems. This performance is achieved because the microkernel is written in a carefully handcoded microprogram, the total main memory throughput is important in this benchmark, and the semantics of the TAO process is inherently small, or more precisely, flexible to be able to be either simple or full-fledged according to their purpose and usage.

TAO/SILENT guarantees 70 microseconds to wake up a process that uses a stack below about 500 words at that time. If an interrupt is detected within about 70 microseconds, an urgent process with a small stack is guaranteed to resume within 140 microseconds. We chose 30 microseconds as the maximum interval to detect interrupts. This forced us to decompose a number of symbolic processing primitives into fractions of small inseparable operations. We described some of these in the paper.

TAO/SILENT is still being implemented. We think that the TAO/SILENT lightweight process described in the paper will ensure high-performance real-time symbolic processing.

Acknowledgment

We would like to thank Dr. Kazuhiko Kato (Tsukuba University) and Dr. Yoshikatsu Tada (The University of Electro-Communications) for their valuable suggestions. We also wish to thank Dr. Keiji Hirata (NTT) wand Mr. Kouji Sato (NTT) for their assistance in evaluating performance of KLIC and the Solaris kernel threads.

Bibliography

1) M. Accetta, R. Baron, W. Bolosky, R. Rashid D. Golub, A. Tevanian, and M. W. Young. Mach: A New Kernel Foundation for UNIX Development. *Proceedings of USENIX Summer 1986*, 1986, pp. 93–112.

2) T. Chikayama, T. Fujise, and D. Sekita. A Portable and Efficient Implementation of KL1. *Proceedings of PLILP'94*, Lecture Notes in Computer Science 844, Springer-Verlag, 1994, pp. 25–39.

3) J. R. Eykholt, S. R. Kleiman, S. Barton, R. Faulkner, A. Shivalingiah, M. Smith, D. Stein, J. Voll, M. Weeks, and D D. Williams. Beyond Multiprocessing... Multithreading the SunOS Kernel. *Proceedings of USENIX Summer 1992*, 1992, pp. 11–18.

4) Franz Inc. *Allegro Common Lisp User Guide, Version 4.2*. Franz Inc., 1994.

5) Y. Hibino, K. Watanabe, and I. Takeuchi. A 32-bit LISP Processor for the AI Workstation ELIS with a Multiple Programming Paradigm Language TAO. *Journal of Information Processing*, Vol. 13, No. 2, 1990, 156–164.

---

[18]This will be described in another paper, but was presented in an informal paper[11]).

6)   S. Inohara, K. Kato, and T. Masuda. 'Unstable Threads' Kernel Interface for Minimizing the Overhead of Thread Switching. *Proceedings of 7th International Parallel Processing Symposium*, 1993, pp. 149–155.

7)   J. H. Reppy. CML: A higher-order concurrent language. *Proceedings of ACM Conference on Programming Language Design and Implementation*, ACM, 1991, pp. 294–305.

8)   J.A. Stankovic. Real-Time Computing Systems — The Next Generation. *Proceedings. of Hard Real-Time Systems*, IEEE, 1988, pp. 14–37.

9)   R. Steinmetz and K. Nahrstedt. *Multimedia: Computing, Communications & Applications*. Prentice Hall, 1995.

10) Sun Microsystems, Inc. *SunOS Programming Utilities & Libraries*. Sun Microsystems, Inc., 1990.

11) I. Takeuchi, Y. Amagai, K. Yamazaki, and M. Yoshida. Lisp can be "Hard" Real-Time *Proceedings of Lisp User Group Meeting Japan*, 2000.

12) I. Takeuchi, Y. Amagai, and K. Yamazaki. Design of New TAO In *IPSJ SIG Notes*, 90-SYM-56, IPSJ, 1990.

13) I. Takeuchi, H. G. Okuno, and N. Ohsato. A List Processing Language TAO with Multiple Programming Paradigms. *Journal of New Generation Computing*, Vol. 4, No. 4, Ohmsha, 1986, pp. 401–444.

14) D. Weinreb, D. Moon, and R. M. Stallman. *Lisp Machine Manual*. LMI, 1983.

15) M. Yoshida, Y. Amagai, K. Yamazaki, M. Nakamura, I. Takeuchi, and K. Murakami. A List Processor SILENT. In *IPSJ SIG Notes*, 95-ARC-114, IPSJ, 1995, pp. 17–24.

9

Indefinite One-time Continuations

Tsuneyasu Komiya

Taiichi Yuasa

Graduate School of Informatics

Kyoto University

ABSTRACT

A continuation represents the rest of computation from a given point of program execution. Scheme provides a function to generate a continuation as a first-class object. Using Scheme continuations, we can express various control structures such as non-local exits, coroutines and multi-tasks. In stack-based Scheme implementations, continuations are implemented by saving the contents of the control stack into the heap when a continuation is created and by restoring the control stack from the heap when the continuation is called. Although several implementation techniques have been proposed, the operation of creating and calling continuations still takes time. In this paper, based on the fact that each continuation is called only once in most applications, we propose *indefinite one-time continuations* (or IOCs for short) which can be called only once but which can be called at any time. Using IOCs, performance of application programs of Scheme continuations will be significantly improved.

1 Introduction

A continuation represents the rest of computation from a given point of program execution. Scheme [9, 3] provides a mechanism to capture a continuation and to resume the computation later at any point of program execution. Using Scheme continuations, one can express various control structures such as non-local exit, coroutines [7], and multi-tasks [20].

A continuation is captured by calling the function `call/cc` (short for "call with current continuation"). The argument to `call/cc` must be a function f with a single argument. `Call/cc` generates a *continuation object* C, which contains all information that is necessary to resume the computation after the call of `call/cc`. Then `call/cc` calls the function f by passing C as the argument. The continuation object C is a kind of function with a single argument. By calling C, the computation after the call to `call/cc` will be resumed, with the argument to C being the value of the call. The action to call a continuation object is said "throwing the continuation" and the argument to the call is said "the thrown value". If C is not thrown during

the execution of f, then whatever f returns will be used as the value of the call to
`call/cc`.

A Scheme continuation can be thrown as many times as desired. This means
that the continuation information, i.e., the information that is necessary to resume
computation, must be saved so that the computation can be resumed any number
of times. In stack-based implementations of Scheme, such information is stored in
the control stack. Thus continuations are implemented by saving the contents of the
control stack into the heap when a continuation is captured and by restoring the
control stack from the heap when the continuation is thrown. Therefore, the cost
of creating and calling continuations is very high. Although several implementation
techniques have been proposed to reduce the cost, these operations are still expensive
and the programmer tends to avoid the use of continuations, in spite of the high
functionality.

Several programming languages provide mechanisms for non-local exit, which is
most important application of Scheme continuations. For instance, C [12] provides
the `setjmp` and `longjmp` mechanism and many Lisp dialects including Common
Lisp [19] provide the `catch` and `throw` mechanism. Non-local exit can be implemented
essentially by saving the stack pointer when the catcher is created and restoring the
stack pointer when the catcher is thrown. This is because these languages assume
that a throw occurs while the catcher information remains on the stack and that
each catcher is thrown at most once. Thus operations for non-local exit are much
efficient than continuation capturing and throwing.

In order to support such "light-weight" non-local exit in Scheme, PaiLisp [18, 10]
and T [17] provide *escape procedures*. In PaiLisp, escape procedures are created by
another function `call/ep` (short for "call with escape procedure") and are used in
the same way as continuation objects with the following restrictions[1].

1. An escape procedure may be thrown at most once.

2. An escape procedure may be thrown only during the execution of the argument
   f to `call/ep` that created the escape procedure.

If a continuation object satisfies these restrictions, then by replacing `call/cc` with
`call/ep`, the performance of the program will be significantly improved. Although
escape procedures of T are created by special form `catch`, their usage and restrictions
are the same as in PaiLisp.

In this paper, we propose *indefinite one-time continuations* (IOCs for short),
which are somewhat between continuations and escape procedures. An IOC is created
by yet another function `call/ioc`. IOCs differ from escape procedures in that they
do not need the second restriction on escape procedures. In other words, like a
continuation, an IOC may be thrown at any point during the program execution,
but it may be thrown at most once. Here, we regard a normal return from the

---

[1]`Call/ep` in PaiLisp is designed so that it can support concurrency. However, since we do not
deal with concurrency, we consider only the sequential feature of `call/ep`.

function f (the argument to `call/ioc`) as a throw to the IOC that was captured by the `call/ioc` call. That is, we regard

```
(call/ioc f)
```

as if

```
(call/ioc (lambda (k) (k (f k))))
```

The introduction of IOCs is motivated by the following observations based on our experiences with Scheme continuation.

1. Most continuations are thrown at most once. Although there exist programs that throw a continuation more than once, many of such programs can be easily modified so that each continuation be thrown at most once. We will give an example of such programs in Section 2.

2. There are significant applications of continuations that cannot be realized by escape procedures. Coroutines and multi-tasks are examples of such applications. In these applications, a continuation to resume the execution of a coroutine (or a task) f may be thrown when the call frame of f does not reside on the control stack.

IOCs can be implemented much more efficiently than ordinary continuations, and almost as efficiently as escape procedures. If a continuation is thrown at most once during execution of a program, then by replacing `call/cc` with `call/ioc`, the performance of the program will be significantly increased.

The rest of this paper is organized as follows. In Section 2, we discuss applications that cannot be realized by escape procedures and show why IOCs are useful for these applications, together with details of IOCs. In Section 3, we give the formal semantics of IOCs. Then in Section 4, we present an implementation of IOCs, which is actually incorporated into our Scheme system TUTScheme [21]. The purpose of that section is to show why IOCs are much more efficient than continuations and almost as efficient as escape procedures. In Section 5, we show how to implement tail-recursion optimization in a Scheme system with `call/ioc`. In Section 6, we compare the performances of IOCs, continuations and escape procedures.

2   Indefinite One-time Continuations

In most application programs of Scheme continuations, each continuation is thrown at most once. For example, consider coroutines that are one kind of valuable applications of Scheme continuations. In Scheme, coroutines can be realized by capturing a continuation when execution of a coroutine is suspended, and then by throwing the continuation in order to resume the suspended execution.

```
(define (f k)
```

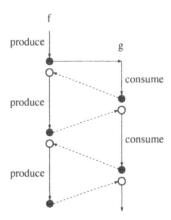

Figure 1: Control flow of the coroutine example.

```
(do ((k k (call/cc k)))
    ((terminate?))
  (produce)))

(define (g k)
  (do ((k k (call/cc k)))
      ((#f)
    (consume)))
```

This example defines two coroutines **f** and **g**. The coroutine **f** is supposed to produce
values, which are consumed one after another by the other coroutine **g**. Each time **f**
produces a value, execution of **f** is suspended and control is transferred to **g**. After
g consumed one value, execution of **g** is suspended and control is transferred back to
f. This process is repeated until a certain condition is satisfied.

Figure 1 illustrates the control flow when this program is initiated as (**f g**).
In the figure, solid lines represent control flow and dotted lines indicate control
transfer caused by continuation throws. Each black circle represents a point at
continuation capturing and each white circle represents a point to resume execution,
i.e., a point right after **call/cc** is called. As will be clear from this figure, each
coroutine generates a continuation object each time its execution is suspended, and
the continuation is thrown at most once to resume the suspended execution. Like
this example, each continuation is thrown at most once in many applications of
continuations. For instance, multi-tasks can be realized in Scheme in the same way
as this example, and can be easily found that each continuation is thrown at most
once.

Also in continuation applications, continuations are sometimes thrown when the
continuation information does not reside on the control stack. In the above example,
g's continuation information on the stack may be destroyed after control is transferred

back to f, since the stack area that has been used for g may be used by f. Thus when the continuation of g is thrown to resume the execution of g, the continuation information does not exist on the stack. Therefore, escape procedures cannot be used in this example. On the other hand, indefinite one-time continuations (IOCs) can be used successfully because the only restriction is that it can be thrown at most once.

From the above discussion, it should be clear that the application area of IOCs is much wider than that of escape procedures. Rather, it is hard to find a realistic application in which IOCs can *not* be used essentially. Even if an application throws a continuation more than once, often it can be modified so that each continuation is thrown at most once. As an example, consider the following function.

```
(define (try-them candidates)
  (let ((k #f))
    (call/cc (lambda (k1) (set! k k1)))
    (if (null? candidates)
        #f
        (let ((next-candidate (car candidates)))
          (set! candidates (cdr candidates))
          (try next-candidate k)))))
```

The function try-them receives some candidates and tries them one after another by calling try, until one of the candidates succeeds or all candidates fail. First, try-them establishes a backtracking point by capturing a continuation and stores it to k. As soon as the sub-function try determines that the candidate fails, the continuation is thrown and the next candidate is tried. Thus the continuation is thrown as many times as the number of failed candidates. This function, however, can also be defined as follows.

```
(define (try-them candidates)
  (if (null? candidates)
      #f
      (or (call/cc (lambda (k) (try (car candidates) k)))
          (try-them (cdr candidates)))))
```

With this definition, as many continuations as the number of tried candidates will be created, and each continuation is thrown at most once. Clearly, the latter definition is much more straightforward and easy to understand than the previous definition. Although the primary purpose of IOCs is to increase the program performance, use of IOCs is also recommended from the viewpoint of program readability.

Although IOCs can be used in most continuation applications, we do not intend to exclude continuations. If a Scheme system supports both of them, then an existing Scheme program can run on the system without modification. Then the programmer can incrementally replace call/cc with call/ioc wherever possible, to increase the performance.

Supporting both IOCs and continuations causes it difficult to determine whether an IOC is actually thrown at most once. Let us consider the following simple code:

```
(call/cc (lambda (k) (k (foo))))
```

At a glance, it seems obvious that the continuation k is thrown only once. However, there is the possibility that a continuation, say C, be captured during the execution of foo. If so, foo may return more than once and the continuation k may actually be thrown multiple times, each time foo returns. Note that each time foo returns, the continuation information for k resides on the control stack because it is restored each time C is thrown. Thus the system can resume the execution without problem.

For this reason, we specify IOCs as follows. Like escape procedures, an IOC can be thrown at most once. The system remembers the state whether each IOC has already been thrown, and if it is thrown more than once, the system signals an error. There is one exception. If a continuation is captured, then the current state of an IOC is saved in the continuation, and the saved state is used each time the continuation is thrown. In other words, if an IOC is not yet thrown when a continuation is captured, then the IOC can be thrown at most once each time the continuation is thrown. With this specification, the call/cc form in the above example, can safely be replaced by a call/ioc form. Incidentally, these discussions apply also for escape procedures when the system supports both escape procedures and continuations.

3 Formal Semantics of IOCs

In this section, we provide the formal denotational semantics of IOCs, using the notations in the IEEE Scheme standard [9]. The following notations, abstract syntax, and semantic domains are used in this section.

Notation

$\langle \ldots \rangle$	sequence
$s \downarrow k$	kth element of the sequence s
$\#s$	length of the sequence s
$s \ \S \ t$	concatenation of sequences s and t
$s \dagger k$	the subsequence of s without the first k elements
$t \to a, b$	McCarthy conditional "if t then a else b"
$\rho[x/i]$	substitution of i with x in ρ
x in D	injection of x into the domain D
$x \mid$ D	projection of x to the domain D

Abstract syntax

$K \in$ Con	constants, including quotations
$I \ \in$ Ide	identifiers (variables)
$E \in$ Exp	expressions
$\Gamma \in$ Com $=$ Exp	commands

$$\begin{aligned}
\text{Exp} \longrightarrow{} & \text{K} \mid \text{I} \mid (\text{E}_0\ \text{E*}) \\
& \mid (\texttt{lambda}\ (\text{I*})\ \Gamma\text{*}\ \text{E}_0) \\
& \mid (\texttt{if}\ \text{E}_0\ \text{E}_1\ \text{E}_2) \\
& \mid (\texttt{set!}\ \text{I}\ \text{E})
\end{aligned}$$

Semantic domain

$\alpha \in \text{L}$	locations
$\text{T} = \{\mathit{false},\ \mathit{true}\}$	booleans
$\phi \in \text{F} = \text{L} \times (\text{E*} \to \text{G} \to \text{C})$	procedure values
$\epsilon \in \text{E}$	expressed values
$\sigma \in \text{S} = \text{L} \to (\text{E} \times \text{T})$	stores
$\rho \in \text{U} = \text{Ide} \to \text{L}$	environments
$\theta \in \text{C} = \text{S} \to \text{A}$	command continuations
$\kappa \in \text{K} = \text{E*} \to \text{C}$	expression continuations
A	answers
X	errors
G	contexts

Since IOC can be called at most once, we need to express in the semantic domain whether an IOC has already been called or not. This makes it difficult to describe the semantics of IOCs in terms of expression continuations. Therefore, we use the notion of *context* [5] that was introduced to describe partial continuations [4, 11, 15, 14, 5].

A context is a list of *partial contexts*:

$\pi \in \text{P} = (\text{E*} \to \text{G} \to \text{C}) \times \text{L}$	partial contexts
$\gamma \in \text{G} = \text{P} \times \text{G} + \{\gamma_0\}$	contexts

where γ_0 is the initial context [5].

A partial context corresponds to a stack frame in a language implementation. The location of a partial context is used as a flag. Its value is *true* if the partial context is not yet called, and is *false* otherwise. Locations and the corresponding values are related by a store σ. As will be explained later, we use two kinds of stores, one for ordinary locations and the other for flag locations. Therefore, a store in our semantics consists of two stores of the ordinary Scheme semantics:

$$\sigma \in \text{S} = (\text{L} \to (\text{E} \times \text{T})) \times (\text{L} \to (\text{E} \times \text{T})) \quad \text{stores}$$

Accordingly, we need two *update* functions:

$$\begin{aligned}
& update1 : \text{L} \to \text{E} \to \text{S} \to \text{S} \\
& update1 = \lambda\alpha\epsilon\sigma\ .\ (\sigma \downarrow 1)[\langle\epsilon,\ \mathit{true}\rangle/\alpha]\ \S\ (\sigma \downarrow 2)
\end{aligned}$$

$$update2 : L \to E \to S \to S$$
$$update2 = \lambda\alpha\epsilon\sigma \,.\, (\sigma \downarrow 1) \,\S\, (\sigma \downarrow 2)[\langle\epsilon, true\rangle/\alpha]$$

The function *update1* is used to update the value of an ordinary location and the function *update2* to update the truth value of a flag location.

The following functions are used to handle contexts.

$$addframe : G \to P \to G$$
$$addframe = \lambda\gamma\pi \,.\, \langle\pi, \gamma\rangle$$

$$send : E \to G \to C$$
$$send =$$
$$\lambda\epsilon\gamma \,.\, \gamma = \gamma_0 \to$$
$$\quad \theta_0,$$
$$\quad \lambda\sigma \,.\, (\sigma \downarrow 2)((\gamma \downarrow 1) \downarrow 2) = true \to$$
$$\quad\quad ((\gamma \downarrow 1) \downarrow 1) \,\langle\epsilon\rangle\, (\gamma \downarrow 2)(update2\,((\gamma \downarrow 1) \downarrow 2)\,false\,\sigma),$$
$$\quad\quad wrong\ \text{``invalid invocation''}$$

The function *addframe* adds the partial context π in front of the context γ. The function *send* calls the first partial context of the context γ, if the partial context is not yet called, and in addition, updates the store σ of the partial context by *update2*. If γ is the initial context γ_0, then *send* calls the top-level command continuation θ_0.

By using contexts, the semantics of **call/ioc** is expressed as follows.

$$cwioc : E^* \to G \to C$$
$$cwioc =$$
$$\quad onearg\,(\lambda\epsilon\gamma \,.\, \epsilon \in F \to$$
$$\quad\quad\quad (\lambda\sigma \,.\, new\,\sigma \in L \to$$
$$\quad\quad\quad\quad applicate\,\epsilon$$
$$\quad\quad\quad\quad\quad \langle\langle new\,\sigma \mid L, \lambda\epsilon^*\gamma' \,.\, send\,\epsilon^*\gamma\rangle\ in\ E\rangle$$
$$\quad\quad\quad\quad\quad \gamma$$
$$\quad\quad\quad\quad\quad (update1\,(new\,\sigma \mid L)\,unspecified\,\sigma),$$
$$\quad\quad\quad\quad wrong\ \text{``out of memory''}\,\sigma),$$
$$\quad\quad\quad wrong\ \text{``bad procedure argument''})$$

The semantics of **call/cc** that can coexist with **call/ioc**, mentioned in Section 2, is expressed as follows.

$$cwcc : E^* \to G \to C$$
$$cwcc =$$
$$\quad onearg\,(\lambda\epsilon\gamma \,.\, \epsilon \in F \to$$
$$\quad\quad\quad (\lambda\sigma \,.\, new\,\sigma \in L \to$$
$$\quad\quad\quad\quad applicate\,\epsilon$$
$$\quad\quad\quad\quad\quad \langle\langle new\,\sigma \mid L,$$
$$\quad\quad\quad\quad\quad\quad \lambda\epsilon^*\gamma' \,.\, \lambda\sigma' \,.$$

$$send \; \epsilon^* \gamma \left((\sigma' \downarrow 1) \; \S \; (\lambda \alpha \, . \, (((\sigma \downarrow 2)\alpha = \bot \to \sigma', \sigma) \downarrow 2)\alpha)) \right)$$
in E$\rangle$

γ
$(update1 \, (new \, \sigma \,|\, \mathrm{L}) \; unspecified \, \sigma),$
$wrong$ "out of memory" $\sigma),$
$wrong$ "bad procedure argument")

When `call/cc` creates a continuation, it saves the store σ into the continuation. When the continuation is called, a new store will be constructed from the saved store σ and the current store σ', and will be used as the new current store:

$$(\sigma' \downarrow 1) \; \S \; (\lambda \alpha \, . \, (((\sigma \downarrow 2)\alpha = \bot \to \sigma', \sigma) \downarrow 2)\alpha)$$

Here, $\bot$ represents the "bottom" and $(\sigma \downarrow 2)\alpha = \bot$ means that the flag location α was not yet allocated when the continuation was created. Thus the new store uses $(\sigma' \downarrow 1)$ for the ordinary locations, $(\sigma \downarrow 2)$ for the flag locations of the partial contexts that existed at the continuation creation, and $(\sigma' \downarrow 2)$ for the other flag locations. This special handling of flag locations guarantees that, if a partial context π can be called at the time of a continuation creation, then each time the continuation is called, it becomes possible to call π even if π has already been called.

Some part of the semantics of primitive Scheme expressions expressed in terms of contexts is given below. The other part is the same as in [9].

$\mathcal{E}[\![(\mathrm{E}_0 \; \mathrm{E}^*) \,]\!] =$
$\quad \lambda \rho \gamma \, . \, \lambda \sigma \, .$
$\qquad new \, \sigma \in \mathrm{L} \to$
$\qquad\quad \mathcal{E}^*(permute(\langle \mathrm{E}_0 \rangle \, \S \, \mathrm{E}^*))$
$\qquad\qquad \rho$
$\qquad\qquad (addframe \, \gamma$
$\qquad\qquad\quad \langle \lambda \epsilon^* \gamma \, . \, ((\lambda \epsilon^* \, . \, applicate \, (\epsilon^* \downarrow 1) \, (\epsilon^* \dagger 1) \, \gamma)(unpermute \, \epsilon^*)), \, new \, \sigma \rangle)$
$\qquad\qquad update2 \, (new \, \sigma \,|\, \mathrm{L}) \; true \, \sigma,$
$\qquad\qquad wrong$ "out of memory" σ

$\mathcal{E}[\![(\mathtt{if} \; \mathrm{E}_0 \; \mathrm{E}_1 \; \mathrm{E}_2) \,]\!] =$
$\quad \lambda \rho \gamma \, . \, \lambda \sigma \, .$
$\qquad new \, \sigma \in \mathrm{L} \to$
$\qquad\quad \mathcal{E}[\![\mathrm{E}_0]\!] \, \rho \, (addframe \, \gamma$
$\qquad\qquad\qquad \langle single \, (\lambda \epsilon \gamma \, . \, truish \, \epsilon \to \mathcal{E}[\![\mathrm{E}_1]\!]\rho\gamma, \mathcal{E}[\![\mathrm{E}_2]\!]\rho\gamma), \, new \, \sigma \rangle)$
$\qquad\qquad (update2 \, (new \, \sigma \,|\, \mathrm{L}) \; true \, \sigma),$
$\qquad\quad wrong$ "out of memory" σ

$\mathcal{E}[\![(\mathtt{set!} \; \mathrm{I} \; \mathrm{E}) \,]\!] =$
$\quad \lambda \rho \gamma \, . \, \lambda \sigma \, .$
$\qquad new \, \sigma \in \mathrm{L} \to$
$\qquad\quad \mathcal{E}[\![\mathrm{E}]\!] \, \rho \, (addframe \, \gamma$

$$\langle single(\lambda\epsilon\gamma \,.\, assign \,(lookup \,\rho \,\mathrm{I}) \,\epsilon \,(send \,unspecified \,\gamma)), \,new \,\sigma\rangle$$
$$(update2 \,(new \,\sigma \,|\, \mathrm{L}) \,true \,\sigma),$$
$$wrong \text{ ``out of memory''} \sigma$$

$$\mathcal{E}^*[\![\,]\!] = \lambda\rho\gamma \,.\, send \,\langle\,\rangle \,\gamma$$

$$\mathcal{E}^*[\![\mathrm{E_0}\ \mathrm{E^*}]\!] =$$
$$\lambda\rho\gamma \,.\, \lambda\sigma \,.$$
$$\qquad new \,\sigma \in \mathrm{L} \rightarrow$$
$$\qquad (\lambda\sigma' \,.\, new \,\sigma' \in \mathrm{L} \rightarrow$$
$$\qquad\quad \mathcal{E}[\![\mathrm{E_0}]\!] \,\rho \,(addframe \,\gamma$$
$$\qquad\qquad\qquad \langle single(\lambda\epsilon_0\gamma \,.\, \mathcal{E}^*[\![\mathrm{E^*}]\!] \,\rho \,(addframe \,\gamma$$
$$\qquad\qquad\qquad\qquad\qquad \langle\lambda\epsilon^*\gamma \,.\, send \,(\langle\epsilon_0\rangle \,\S \,\epsilon^*)\gamma, \,new \,\sigma'\rangle)),$$
$$\qquad\qquad new \,\sigma\rangle)$$
$$\qquad\quad (update2 \,(new \,\sigma' \,|\, \mathrm{L}) \,true \,\sigma'),$$
$$\qquad\quad wrong \text{ ``out of memory''} \sigma')$$
$$\qquad (update2 \,(new \,\sigma \,|\, \mathrm{L}) \,true \,\sigma),$$
$$\qquad wrong \text{ ``out of memory''} \sigma)$$

As for auxiliary functions, the only difference is the following.

$$hold : \mathrm{L} \rightarrow \mathrm{G} \rightarrow \mathrm{C}$$
$$hold = \lambda\alpha\gamma\sigma \,.\, send \,((\sigma \downarrow 1)\alpha \downarrow 1)\gamma\sigma$$

4 Implementation

In this section, we describe an implementation of IOCs and explain why IOCs are more efficient than continuations. We start with a typical implementation of escape procedures [18] so that it becomes clear that IOCs, when used for non-local exit, are almost as efficient as escape procedures.

Escape procedures are essentially implemented by saving the stack pointer when an escape procedure is captured and restoring the stack pointer when the escape procedure is thrown. In many Scheme implementations, contents on the stack may be moved to another place on the stack because of their sophisticated algorithms to implement continuations [2]. This means the simple implementation above cannot be used actually. Instead, a marker is used to remember the stack position. When an escape procedure is created, a new marker is prepared and pushed onto the stack. The created escape procedure remembers the marker, rather than the stack pointer. When the escape procedure is thrown, the system searches the stack for the marker. If it is found, the stack pointer is set to the marker position and the execution will be resumed. If not, the system signals an error because the information to resume execution does not remain on the stack any more.

Implementation of IOCs also uses markers. When an IOC is created, a new marker is pushed onto the stack. When the IOC is thrown, the system searches the

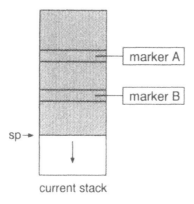

Figure 2: Before throwing an IOC.

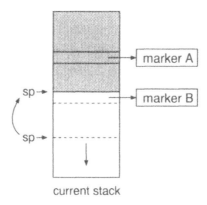

Figure 3: After throwing the IOC of the marker B.

stack for the marker and if found, moves the stack pointer to the marker position. For IOCs, the necessary information to throw other IOCs must be saved somewhere if the information may be lost by moving the stack pointer. Rather than using the heap, we use another stack to save the information. With this method, the information necessary to throw an IOC is always ready on a stack.

Suppose two IOCs have been captured so far (see Figure 2). In the figure, the markers A and B are those that was pushed on the stack when the first and second IOCs, respectively, were captured. Let us call the first IOC as A and the second as B. When B is thrown, there is no marker between the stack top and the position of B. This means that there is no continuation information that must be saved. Therefore, the system simply moves the stack pointer to the position of B (see Figure 3) and resumes the computation captured by B.

On the other hand, when A is thrown, there is another marker (marker B) on the

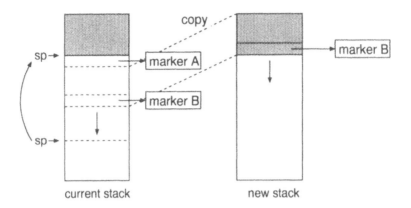

Figure 4: After throwing the IOC of the marker A.

stack between the stack pointer and the position of A. Since B may be thrown later, the system has to save its continuation information. That information is stored in the stack area between marker B and marker A. Therefore, the contents in that area will be copied from the current stack to a new stack. Then the system moves the stack pointer to the position of A and resumes the computation captured by IOC A. Later, when IOC B is thrown, the resumed computation is not allowed to return normally to the computation captured by IOC A, because IOC A has already been thrown. Therefore, the system stores the address of an error routine at the bottom of the new stack, so that an attempt to return normally can be trapped.

Figure 5 illustrates how this implementation of IOCs works for the example of coroutines in Section 2, when IOCs are used instead of continuations.

```
(define (f k)
  (do ((k k (call/ioc k)))
      ((terminate?))
    (produce)))

(define (g k)
  (do ((k k (call/ioc k)))
      ((#f))
    (consume)))
```

Let us trace the execution when this program is initiated by (f g).

1. f creates an IOC (of the marker 1) and calls g.

2. g creates an IOC (of the marker 2) as shown in Figure 5 (a).

3. Then g throws the first IOC (Figure 5 (b)). Since the marker 2 is found below the marker 1, the contents of the stack area between the two markers are copied into a new stack.

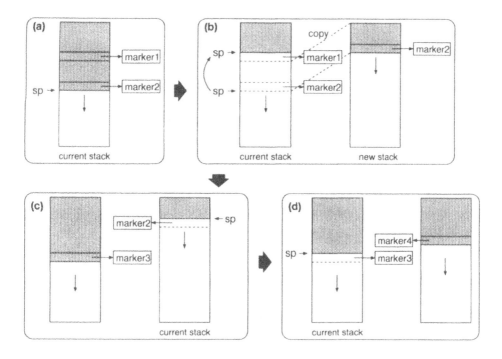

Figure 5: Execution of coroutines.

4. **f** creates another IOC (of the marker 3) and throws the IOC of the marker 2 (Figure 5 (c)). Since there is no marker below the marker 2, the system simply adjusts the stack pointer and uses the second stack as the current stack.

5. **g** creates another IOC (of the marker 4) and throws the IOC of the marker 3 (Figure 5 (d)). The system adjusts the stack pointer and uses the first stack as the current stack.

Only two stacks are used in this program, one stack for the execution of the coroutine **f** and the other for **g**. Since control transfer between the two coroutines is expressed as an IOC throw, the system only needs to switch the stacks and to adjust the stack pointer. Stack contents are not copied except for the first IOC throw.

Stacks are allocated each time a new stack is required. However, a stack that has been once allocated may become a garbage, i.e., it may contain no useful information to proceed program execution. A stack is a garbage if

1. it is not the current stack, and

2. it contains no marker at all or all its markers are garbage.

In order to recycle garbage stacks, the system keeps track of all garbage stacks in a free list. When an IOC is thrown and a new stack is required, the system uses one of the stacks in the free list. An actual stack allocation takes place only if the free list is empty.

In order to collect garbage stacks efficiently, we use a reference count for each stack. This reference count represents the number of markers on the stack, and is updated when an IOC is created or thrown. A stack that is not the current stack becomes a garbage if its reference count is zero. Therefore, when the system switches the current stack to another stack by throwing an IOC, if the reference count of the old current stack is zero, the system immediately collect this stack as a garbage.

Each stack also has a slot which is used to remember the position of the stack top. The stack top is nesessary for the system to search the stack for a marker or to scan the stack during garbage collection. Note that for the current stack, this slot is not used for these operation, because the stack pointer always remembers the position of the stack top.

5   Tail-Recursion Optimization

In Scheme, tail-recursive calls are handled as iterations. This tail-recursion optimization is implemented by overwriting the current call frame on the stack with a new call frame when a function is called at a tail-recursive position. This causes a problem when we implement call/ioc as described in Section 4, because if the overwritten frame contains a marker, the marker will be lost and therefore the IOC of the marker cannot be thrown.

In ordinary stack-based implementations of Scheme, each call frame has a slot to store the return address. When a function is called tail-recursively, the call frame of the caller is overwritten by the call frame of the callee. However, the slot for the return address remains untouched, because the return address is the same for the caller and the callee. In order to solve the above problem, we use the same technique.

To each call frame, we add a *marker slot* to store a marker. Like the slot of the return address, the marker slot of a call frame remains untouched when the frame is overwritten with another call frame for a tail-recursive call. For ordinary call frames, the marker slot contains no marker, i.e., its value is the null pointer. When call/ioc is invoked, it creates a new marker, saves the marker into the marker slot of its own call frame, overwrites the frame with the call frame for its function arguments, and then invokes the function. There is one exception for this. If the marker slot already contains a marker, then call/ioc does not create a new marker, but uses the marker in the slot as the marker of the created IOC. This means that, when tail-recursive calls to call/ioc are performed successively, the created IOCs share the same marker, which is generated by the first call of call/ioc. It is obvious that this implementation guarantees tail-recursive implementation, even for tail-recursive calls to call/ioc.

Let us explain this implementation is a valid implementation of call/ioc. Consider the following sequence of tail-recursive function calls:

$$\texttt{call/ioc} \rightarrow f_1 \rightarrow f_2 \rightarrow \cdots \rightarrow f_n \rightarrow \texttt{call/ioc}$$

where each f_i is a function other than `call/ioc`. With our implementation, the two calls of `call/ioc` share the same marker. Once the IOC of the first `call/ioc` is thrown, the IOC of the second `call/ioc` cannot be thrown, since the marker does not exist on the stack any more. However, this causes no problem because it is an error to throw the second IOC. If it is thrown, control eventually returns from f_1 to the first call of `call/ioc`, which has already been thrown. On the other hand, if the second IOC is thrown before the first IOC is thrown, control returns immediately from the first `call/ioc`. Semantically, the second `call/ioc` simply returns to f_n which then simply returns to f_{n-1}, and so on, and finally, the first `call/ioc` simply returns. Thus our implementation correctly handles this case as well. The same arguments hold for a sequence of successive tail-recursive calls of `call/ioc`:

$$\text{call/ioc} \to \cdots \to \text{call/ioc} \to \cdots \to \text{call/ioc} \to \cdots$$

Once one of the IOCs is thrown, it is an error to throw any IOC later. Also, by throwing one of the IOCs, control returns immediately from the first `call/ioc`, but this is a correct behavior. Incidentally, these discussions and techniques apply also for escape procedures.

6   Performance Evaluation

We have implemented IOCs in our Scheme implementation, called TUTScheme [21]. In this section, we evaluate the performance of IOCs by using benchmark programs. We use the following benchmarks for continuations.

ctak the `tak` function, modified so that the function returns by throwing a continuation [2].

coroutine the program with two coroutines mentioned in Section 2.

same fringe a program to traverse leaves of two trees and test if the leaf values appear in the same order [15]. This program consists of two coroutines, one for each tree. When the first coroutine finds the next leaf value, control is transferred to the second coroutine which then searches the second tree for the next leaf value. If the two leaf values are the same, then control is transferred back to the first coroutine.

mfib a function to calculate the n-th value of the Fibonacci sequence, by using `future` [6]. In our benchmark test, we ran this program on a multi-task emulator [16] in which `future` is implemented by using continuations.

For each benchmark program, we used the `call/cc`, `call/ioc`, and `call/ep` versions. Table 1 lists the execution times on SPARCstation 10 model 30 and Table 2 lists the times for garbage collection. For the original `call/cc` version, we measured the times both on the original version of TUTScheme without the extension for IOCs and on the extended version. In the tables, "`call/cc`" means the times on the original version, while "`call/ioc`" means the times on the extended version.

Table 1: Execution times (sec).

program	call/cc	call/cc'	call/ioc	call/ep	speed up
ctak	4.26	4.31	3.26	3.15	1.31
coroutine	9.17	9.56	4.32	N/A	2.12
same fringe	483.90	494.82	64.45	N/A	7.51
mfib	13.10	13.9	7.54	N/A	1.74

Table 2: GC times (sec).

program	call/cc	call/ioc
ctak	1.67	1.08
coroutine	3.38	0.58
same fringe	276.07	34.90
mfib	7.80	2.30

The only change to the original benchmark programs for these tests is that call/cc is replaced by call/ioc or call/ep. Each speed up in Table 1 is the speed up ratio of the call/ioc version against the call/cc version. TUTScheme uses the incremental stack/heap method [2] to implement continuations. Note that for the call/ep version, only the time for ctak is given in the table. This is because escape procedures cannot be used for the other benchmark programs.

As is clear from the table, for all benchmark programs, the call/ioc version is faster than the call/cc version. One reason for this is that the time for garbage collection is much less for the call/ioc version than for the call/cc version. This is because the call/ioc version uses multiple stacks efficiently and thus avoids copying from the stack to the heap.

For the ctak program, the call/ioc version runs almost as fast as the call/ep version. The original ctak program always throws the continuation that has been generated most recently. Thus, when the call/ioc version throws an IOC, there is no marker between the stack pointer and the marker of the thrown IOC. This means only one stack is necessary to execute ctak and therefore the call/ioc version runs essentially in the same way as the call/ep version.

Comparing the times for the call/cc version and the call/cc' version, we can observe that the overhead of extending the system with IOCs is relatively small.

7   Concluding Remarks

In this paper, we proposed indefinite one-time continuations (IOCs), and explained why IOCs are much more efficient than conventional continuations. If an implementation supports IOCs, performance of application programs of Scheme continuations can be significantly increased simply by replacing `call/cc` with `call/ioc`, wherever possible.

Bruggeman, et al. proposed one-shot continuations and its implementation [1]. The one-shot continuations are very similar to our one-time continuations. Although the implementation of one-shot continuations also uses multiple stacks, those stacks are managed in a different way, since their implementation is based on the implementation of Scheme continuations by Hieb, et al. [8].

This paper is an extended English version of 13).

Bibliography

1) Bruggeman, C., Waddell, O. and Dybvig, R. K.: Representing Control in the Presence of One-Shot Continuations, *Proc. SIGPLAN 1996 Conference on Programming Language Design and Implementation*, pp. 99–107 (1996).

2) Clinger, W., Hartheimer, A. H. and Ost, E. M.: Implementation Strategies for Continuations, *Proc. 1988 ACM Conference on Lisp and Functional Programming*, pp. 124–131 (1988).

3) Clinger, W. and Rees, J., editors.: Revised[4] Report on the Algorithmic Language Scheme, *MIT AI Memo 848b*, MIT (1991).

4) Felleisen, M., Friedman, D. P., Duba, B. and Merrill, J.: Beyond Continuations, Technical Report No. 216, Indiana University (1987).

5) Felleisen, M., Wand, M., Friedman, D. P. and Duba, B. F.: Abstract Continuations: A Mathematical Semantics for Handling Full Functional Jumps, *Proc. 1988 ACM Conference on Lisp and Functional Programming*, pp. 52–62 (1988).

6) Halstead, R.: Multilisp: A Language for Concurrent Symbolic Computation, *ACM Trans. Prog. Lang. Syst.*, Vol. 7, No. 4, pp. 501–538 (1985).

7) Haynes, C. T., Friedman, D. P. and Wand, M.: Continuations and Coroutines, *Proc. 1984 ACM Conference on Lisp and Functional Programming*, pp. 293–298 (1984).

8) Hieb, R., Dybvig, R. K. and Bruggeman, C.: Representing Control in the Presence of First-Class Continuations, *Proc. SIGPLAN 1990 Conference on Programming Language Design and Implementation*, pp. 66–77 (1990).

9) IEEE Standard for the Scheme Programming Language, IEEE (1991).

10) Ito, T. and Matsui, M.: A Parallel Lisp Language PaiLisp and Its Kernel Specification, *Lecture Notes in Computer Science 441*, Springer-Verlag, pp. 58–100 (1990).

11) Johnson, G. F.: GL — A Denotational Testbed with Continuations and Partial Continuations, *Proc. SIGPLAN 1987 Symposium on Interpreters and Interpretive Techniques*, pp. 165–176 (1987).

12) Kernighan, B. W. and Ritchie, D. M.: *The C programming language second edition*, Prentice Hall (1988).

13) Komiya, T. and Yuasa, T.: Indefinite One-time Continuation (in Japanese), *Trans. Information Processing Society of Japan*, Vol. 37, No. 1, pp. 92–100 (1996).

14) Moreau, L. and Queinnec, C.: Partial Continuations as the Difference of Continuations— A Duumvirate of Control Operators, *Lecture Notes in Computer Science 844*, Springer-Verlag, pp. 182–197 (1994).

15) Queinnec, C. and Serpette, B.: A Dynamic Extent Control Operator for Partial Continuations, *Proc. Eighteenth Annual ACM SIGACT-SIGPLAN Symposium on Principles of Programming Languages*, pp. 174–184 (1991).

16) Queinnec,   C.:   Scheme   code   to   emulate   future   and   pcall, http://youpou.lip6.fr/queinnec/Programs/pcall.tar.gz (1992).

17) Rees, J. A., Adams, N. I. and Meehan, J. R.: The T Manual Fifth Edition—Pre-Beta Draft—, Yale University (1990).

18) Seino, T. and Ito, T.: On Implementations of Parallel Constructs of PaiLisp and Their Evaluations (in Japanese), *Trans. Information Processing Society of Japan*, Vol. 34, No. 12, pp. 2578–2591 (1993).

19) Steele, G. L. et al.: *Common Lisp: The Language*, Digital Press (1984).

20) Wand, M.; Continuation-based Multiprocessing, *Conference Record of the 1980 Lisp Conference*, ACM, pp. 19–28 (1980).

21) Yuasa, T., et al.: TUTScheme Reference Manual (in Japanese), Toyohashi University of Technology (1994).

10

A Parallel Lisp System which Dynamically Allocates CPUs to List Processing and GC

Satoko Takahashi

Media Technology Development Center
NTT Communications Corporation

Teruo Iwai

Department of Information and Computer Science
Keio University

Yoshio Tanaka

Electrotechnical Laboratory

Atusi Maeda

Institute of Information Sciences and Electronics
University of Tsukuba

Masakazu Nakanishi

Department of Information and Computer Science
Keio University

ABSTRACT

This paper reports an efficient implementation of Lisp in terms of processing speed in which parallel list processing is realized as well as parallel garbage collection. Parallel garbage collection enables realtime (i.e. non-stop) list processing. Despite the improvement of realtimeness, processing speed might be slower than stop-and-collect GC like generation scavenging GC. Parallel GC is currently adopted only by Lisp systems in which sequential list processing is performed. We have implemented a parallel Lisp where multiple list processing and GC processes are running in parallel to realize fast processing. The optimal number of list processing processes and

GC processes depends on the application and the machine, because the cell consumption rate varies from application to application and a different machine has a different number of CPUs. Therefore we provide a mechanism to determine the CPU allocation of list processing processes and GC processes dynamically monitoring the cell consumption rate and the remaining free cells. This mechanism enables a fast and realtime processing for the major Lisp applications. Our basic allocation strategy is to assign a maximum number of CPUs to list processing. As a result, list processing is not interrupted and the execution time decreases.

1   Introduction

Thanks to the recent development of general purpose multi-processor machines, various **parallel Lisp** implementations have been reported on them[9, 7, 3, 8]. Memory management is crucial in implementing Lisp systems, where vast memory is consumed and reused. Lots of efforts have been made on **garbage collection** (GC) aiming at shortening the interruption period. The interruption is inevitable in stop-and-collect GC, which is triggered when no more cells become available. Accordingly, numberof parallel GC methods, in which GC is performed along with list processing, have been developed so far[2, 19, 2, 13, 14, 15]. But none of parallel Lisp implementations mentioned above implement these parallel GC algorithms.

Although realtimeness is improved by employing parallel GC, the total execution takes longer time in some applications compared with the system with a fast stop-and-collect GC like the generation copy GC for instance. This takes place because overhead for parallel processing is larger than the GC cost. We propose a Lisp system equipped with parallel list processing as well as parallel GC. These two parallelisms are necessary since parallel list processing consumes free cells quicker.

Both multiple list processing processes (**mutators**) and multiple GC processes (**collectors**) run simultaneously in our system. When there exist much more mutators than collectors, list processing might stop due to shortage of cells[10, 11]. Thus the dynamic CPU allocation mechanism for mutators and collectors is also investigated and implemented[12].

2   Parallel Lisp system

Lisp is a versatile language by allowing functions with side effects. Implicit parallelism extracts fragments which can be executed simultaneously. It is difficult, however, to extract the expressions fully taking side effects in consideration. Explicit parallelism, on the other hand, is specified by the user himself/herself. The user is responsible for side effects. There are many parallel Lisp systems reported so far adopting explicit parallelism. In this paper, a unit indicated by the user as an explicit parallel execution is called a 'Lisp process.'

3 Parallel GC

Although development of such efficient algorithms as the generation scavenging GC has shortened the interruption period, stop-and-collect GC can not escape from it. **Realtime GC** [19], on the other hand, persues non-stop list processing. In the parallel GC paradigm, both list processing and GC are executed in parallel.

Famous realtime GC mechanisms include on-the-fly GC [2], incremental copy GC [2], snapshot GC [19], and partial marking GC [13, 14, 15] which is a refinement of snapshot GC.

Partial marking GC is a snapshot GC mixed with an empirical principle that most objects die soon after creation and the objects which have survived beyond several GC cycles tend to be alive for a longer time. In partial marking GC, objects to be marked are limited. As a result, GC time decreases and sweep efficiency improves.

It is reported that one collector with partial marking GC is equivalent to two collectors with snapshot GC [13].

4 Implementing a parallel Lisp system with parallel GC

Our goal is to implement a fast and realtime Lisp system equipped with parallel GC in which list processing is executed in parallel. Our Lisp system adopts explicit parallelism and the partial marking GC mechanism, and is implemented on SPARC Center 2000 with 16 CPUs running Solaris2.4. Its light weight process (LWP) system call is used.

We have to consider the following three points to make list processing parallel.

1. **Scheduling Lisp processes**

   It is very important to schedule Lisp processes in designing parallel systems. The scheduling strategy should avoid too much creation of Lisp processes.

   Mechanisms have to be given for the user to control the creation of Lisp processes by explicit parallelism.

2. **Access conflicts to shared memory**

   LWP's mutual access exclusion to the shared resources is necessary on a parallel computer.

   Each mutator shares such Lisp objects as symbols and lists allocated in the heap area. If multiple LWPs change the value of those objects simultaneously, unexpected phenomena might happen. It is unrealistic, however, to resolve the conflicts of all the objects. So we provide the user with a mechanism to exclude mutual access.

3. **Barrier synchronization for GC phase switch**

Partial marking GC, which our system adopts, consists of three phases: root insertion, marking, and reclaim. These three phases are performed sequentially and non-overlapping way. Therefore barrier synchronization has to be introduced among mutators and collectors.

Next we describe specific implementation of our system considering those points mentioned above.

5 Parallel list processing

For explicit parallelism, we provide statements for the user to specify parallel execution.

5.1 Statements for parallelism

Future mechanism is adopted from Multilisp[7] as a basic statement for parallelism. Function **future** takes an S-expression as an argument and creates a Lisp process to evaluate that S-expression. The Lisp process which has evaluated function **future** returns a **future object** as a temporary value and proceeds to the next S-expression. A mutator evaluates the Lisp process created by function **future** and stores a pointer to the evaluation result into the future object.

As a mechanism for the user to handle side effects, we provide function **touch** for the synchronization purpose. When the function **touch** takes a future object being evaluated as an argument, it returns after the evaluation is handle.

As a mechanism for the user to control the creation of Lisp processes, we provide function **futobj** which checks if the future object is being evaluated. It returns **T** if the argument is under evaluation and **NIL** otherwise.

5.2 Implementation of a mutator

Each mutator interprets and executes the codes of a virtual processor. Here, by codes we means those such as P-code of Pascal-P[16] or **bytecode** of Smalltalk[6] for instance. The compilers for these languages generate machine independent intermediate codes, which are almost similar for the stack-type virtual processors.

Our system adopts the bytecode for the virtual processor and our mutator is a stack machine. In this paper, the term 'compile' means to translate a Lisp program into its bytecode format.

5.2.1 Scheduling Lisp processes

Each mutator has its **local queue** and keeps executable Lisp processes in the queue. When function **future** creates a new Lisp process, the process is registered in the local queue. When a mutator finishes a process, the mutator picks another Lisp process up from the queue. When the queue is empty, the mutator gets a Lisp process from other mutator's local queue, and executes it (figure 1).

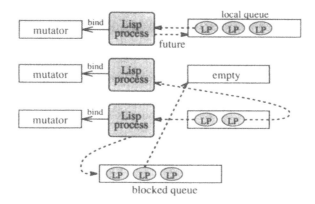

Figure 1: Scheduling of Lisp processes

As a characteristic of function **future**, a Lisp process is interrupted until the **future** object is evaluated (with the use of function **touch**) or until the semaphore is signalled. In that case the Lisp process is registered in a **blocked queue**, and the mutator picks a new Lisp process up from its local queue. The blocked queue must have a mutual exclusion mechanism because all the mutators can access it.

Suppose Lisp process A is interrupted waiting for another process B's termination. When B is terminated, process A is moved to a mutator's local queue from the blocked queue.

5.2.2   Managing information of a Lisp process

We have to manage the context for each Lisp process to execute them in parallel. The context holds intermediate results, argument values, a value stack for local variables, an execution stack for the register values, the stack pointer, the program counter, the process ID, etc. In our implementation, the context is handled as a **process structure**.

6   Memory management

Since multiple mutators and collectors are running in parallel, we have to resolve overhead of access conflicts to the shared area. This section especially describes how the heap area is managed where the access conflicts occur very often.

6.1   Managing heap area

There are five areas to which mutators might access in conflict: the **program area** where compiled bytecode programs are stored, the **constant area** where constants are held for bytecode execution, the **heap area** in which cells are stored, the **full**

word area where character strings are stored, and the **symbol table** which manages atoms. Especially the heap area is often accessed simultaneously by mutators and collectors. Thus the overhead for mutual exclusion affects the processing time. We have solved this problem by splitting the heap area to pages.

The heap area is divided into **heap pages**, each of which consists of 512 cells. A mutator receives free cells of one page by accessing the heap area at one time. Each heap page is managed by the heap table. The table is a set of three constituents; i.e., a **lock flag** which indicates that the heap page is allocated to a mutator, a **freehead** which points at the free list inside the heap page, and a **freetail** which points at the tail of the free list.

When a mutator needs cells, a currently unused heap page is chosen from the lock flag of the heap table. A page of cells are obtained by copying its freehead to a local variable of the mutator. Mutual exclusion is unnecessary when cells are needed, because the local variable is accessed. If all the cells of the page are consumed again, another page of cells are obtained using the heap table in the same fashion. The freetail is used to reduce mutual exclusion time for the collectors.

6.2   GC

Partial marking GC consists of the root insertion phase, the marking phase, and the sweep phase. Only the root insertion is performed by mutators. This section describes our implementation of each phase. Details of partial marking GC are found in [13, 14, 15].

6.2.1   Root insertion

A mutator holds its **root insertion stack** (root stack), on top of which a pointer to a root cell is stacked. GC root includes a symbol table, a constant table and a process structure. Among those, the symbol table, the constant table and the process structure of a Lisp process registered to the block queue are managed globally.

Each mutator pushes its context in the process structure of the Lisp process queued in the local queue onto the root stack. After all the mutators finish root insertion, the globally managed pointer is pushed.

6.2.2   Marking

Each collector holds its **marking stack** and marks all cells reachable from the root. Firstly a collector marks from the root insertion stack of the mutator whose ID is the same as the collector. When the marking is done from the stack, the marking continues from unprocessed root insertion stacks.

In the parallel GC paradigm, live cells might be collected if a mutator rewrites the pointer while a collector is marking. To avoid this situation, the mutator has to inform the collector every time the pointer is rewritten. A **pointer rewrite stack** is prepared to implement this information. When the pointer is changed during list processing, the cut pointer is pushed onto the rewrite stack. The collector to which the marking is assigned from the root insertion stack begins new marking from the rewrite stack. This marking task continues until no pointer remains on the stack.

The marking phase completes when all the collectors' marking comes to end.

6.2.3 Sweep phase

Sweeping is performed in pagewise manner. First, all heap pages are assigned to collectors. Each collector connects unmarked cells in each of assigned page and creates a free list. The free list is attached to the cdr part of the freetail in the heap table.

The sweep phase termintaes after the task described above is performed for every heap page.

7 Scheduler

A **scheduler** as LWP is introduced to manage mutators and collectors. The scheduler's task is to control GC phase switching and to insert roots handled globally by the system. The latter task might imply that mutators and collectors have to wait. Our experiment, however, shows that root insertion in the global area performed by the scheduler is only 1.3~5.5% of the pause period of mutators' GC root insertion (details are described later). We did not take other way where global area root insertion by the scheduler is divided to multiple mutators because of the large synchronization overhead.

7.1 GC phase switching

GC phase switching needs synchronization in our system, because multiple mutators and collectors are running. The scheduler manages the number and state of the currently running mutators and collectors. Each mutator and collector performs GC phase switching by communicating with the scheduler.

First the scheduler sends the start signal of root insertion to each mutator (Figure 2 ①). On receiving the signal, each mutator halts list processing and starts root insertion. When root insertion is done, each mutator sends the completion signal back to the scheduler and waits until all the root insertion phase is over. (Figure 2 ②). After receiving the completion signal from all the mutators, the scheduler performs the global root insertion. Then the scheduler sends the completion signal of the root insertion phase to each mutator. (Figure 2 ③). Each mutator resumes list processing on receiving the signal.

The scheduler sends the start signal of marking to collectors at the same time as the completion signal of root insertion to mutators (Figure 2 ④). After that, similar signals for the marking and sweep phases are exchanged. Barrier synchronization has been implemented in this manner.

In phase switching, as shown above, barrier synchronization is performed by communicating with the scheduler. In starting root insertion (Figure 2 ①) the scheduler

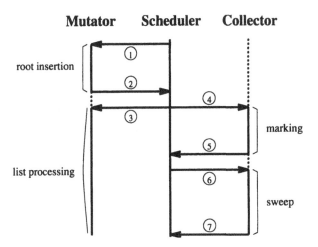

Figure 2: Switching of GC phase

sets the flag for each mutator. In other cases, communication with the condition variable is used.

8 Issues in paralleling list processing

In applying partial marking GC to a sequencial Lisp system, realtime processing with achieved in applications with less than 50% GC rate [1] when one collector is used. In the case of two collectors, the GC rate should be less than 60 % to achieve realtimeness[14].

It is also reported that parallelizing list processing with parallel GC improves both speed and realtimeness[11]. Realtimeness in this context means that list processing is not interrupted other than by root insertion, i.e. other than cell drought or synchronization. In partial marking GC, mutators must stop when root insertion occurs. Thus processing is interrupted. This interruption period, however, is less than 1/25 compared with non-parallel GC[11].

If the number of mutators and collectors is fixed, GC processing can not keep up with cell consumption in some applications, because parallel list processing consumes more cells.

Our experiment shows that the cell consumption rate varies from application to application. Even within one application, the consumption rate changes as processing proceeds. Since our system runs both mutators and collectors in parallel, the consumption rate might affect the entire system performance in the following ways.

1. When cell consumption is high

---

[1]GC rate represents the ratio of GC period to all the processing time in a Lisp system with stop-and-collect GC.

List processing might be interrupted because collectors' processing can not keep up with mutators'.

2. **When cell consumption is low**
   Due to running collectors more than needed, GC trigger rate rises per a unit time and list processing's interruption period by root insertion gets longer. Access conflicts to cells also grow up and processing time become longer.

The optimal number of mutators and collectors can not be decided uniquely because the number of CPUs is different among computers. Thus our system is equipped with a mechanism which determines the optimal number of mutators and collectors dynamically according to the cell consumption rate.

9   Dynamic CPU allocation

Our system is a parallel Lisp with parallel GC with a mechanism which decides CPU allocation dynamically to mutators and to collectors according to the cell consumption rate and the number of free cells. With this mechanism well balanced processing (in terms of processing speed and realtimeness) on a fixed number of CPU machine can be implemented for various applications.

9.1   Strategy of CPU allocation

We describe our strategy of CPU allocation in terms of two problems in the previous section.

CPU allocation is decided by the cell consumption rate, the sweep rate, the number of remaining free cells, and the number of CPUs. Our strategy is to minimize the number of GC processes as long as list processing is not interrupted due to cell drought and to minimize GC triggering. Although reducing the number of GC processes prolongs processing time needed for each GC, the number of GC triggering per a unit time decreases. Thus list processing delay due to GC is shortened.

9.2   Deciding CPU allocation

Figure 3 shows transition between mutators and collectors. GC_i represents start of the ith GC cycle and the horizontal axis is time. The regular lines represent mutators. The dotted lines do collectors. The number of lines corresponds to the number of CPUs. The parameters are set as follows (the ones in ith GC cycle):

M_i : the number of mutators

C_i : the number of collectors

U_i^j : the number of cells consumed by mutator j

K_i^j : the number of cells reclaimed by collector j

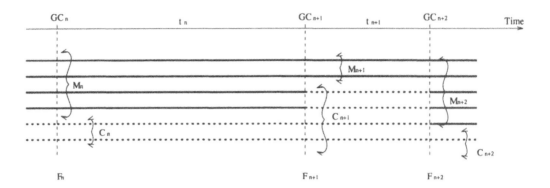

Figure 3: Temporal transition of the number of mutators and collectors

N : total number of CPUs $(= M_i + C_i)$

t_i : period for the GC cycle

F_i : the number of free cells when the GC cycle started

Our model to determine the number of mutators and collectors sets the following assumptions:

> **Assumptions 1 Unreclaimed rate in an area by two consecutive GCs is nearly the same.**

> **Assumptions 2 Processing time for GC is inversely proportional to the number of CPUs.**

> **Assumptions 3 Cell drought should not happen.**

> **Assumptions 4 The total number of mutators and collectors is constant.**

Assumption 1 tells that a GC cycle takes the same time when the number of collectors is unchanged. Assumption 2 means that $t_i C_i$ is constant. Thus,

$$t_n C_n = t_{n+1} C_{n+1} \tag{10.1}$$

The amount of cells consumed by mutators in the nth GC cycle is:

$$\sum_{k=1}^{M_n} U_n^k$$

If there is only one mutator, the mutator can consume the following (maximum):

$$Max(U_n^1, U_n^2, ..., U_n^{M_n})$$
$$= Max^k(U_n^k) \quad (\text{where } k = 1, 2, ..., M_n) \tag{10.2}$$

Thus the maximum number of cells consumed by one mutator can be defined by (10.2). Since the power of cell consumption is proportional to time and the number of mutators, U (the amount of cells consumed by a mutator at t_{n+1}) satisfies the following equation.

$$\frac{U}{Max^k(U_n^k)} = \frac{t_{n+1}}{t_n}$$

where t_n, t_{n+1} are GC times.

The discussion above yields the following relation:

$$U = Max^k(U_n^k)\frac{t_{n+1}}{t_n}$$

The total amount of cells consumed by the mutators in the $n + 1$st GC is:

$$U M_{n+1} \tag{10.3}$$

Processing efficiency requires as few GCs as possible. If GC is done when all the free cells are consumed, GC occurs at fewest times. That means that M_{n+1} should be set so that the number of cells in (10.3) is equal to the number of free cells. In other words, M_{n+1} should be set so that the following equation is satisfied.

$$U M_{n+1} = F_{n+1} \tag{10.4}$$

From equations (10.1) and (10.4) along with our assumption that the number of mutators and collectors is constant, M_{n+1} is defined as follows.

$$M_{n+1} = \frac{F_{n+1}N}{Max^k(U_n^k)C_n + F_{n+1}}$$

Since the number of mutators and collectors is one or more in our system, next equation should be satisfied.

$$1 \leq M_{n+1} \leq N - 1$$

Thus the number of optimal mutators is:

$$M_{n+1} = Max(1, Min(N - 1,$$
$$\frac{F_{n+1}N}{Max^k(U_n^k)C_n + F_{n+1}})) \tag{10.5}$$

When the right hand side of (10.5) is not an integral value, it should be truncated toward zero. (If truncated toward positive infinity, cell drought might happen more likely, thus Assumption 3 might get invalid.)

10   Implementing dynamic CPU allocation

The scheduler determines the CPU allocation to mutators and collectors dynamically by monitoring the cell consumption in each GC cycle. Each mutator and collector counts the number of generated and reclaimed cells. The scheduler compares the two numbers when the root insertion phase is completed and determines the CPU allocation.

A CPU is switched from a mutator to a collector is performed in the following way.

1. The scheduler registers the following processes to the local queue of mutator B. One is a Lisp process being evaluated on a mutator A which will be switched to collector. The other processes are the ones registered in the local queue of mutator A.

2. The scheduler sends a CPU switch signal to mutator A by setting the flag of mutator A.

3. Mutator A frees its area and sends a completion signal to the scheduler.

4. The scheduler terminates the LWP which handles mutator A and creates a new LWP which performs the collector task.

When switching the CPU allocation from a collector to a mutator, only steps from 2 to 4 are performed.

11   Performance evaluation of our system

Experiments have been conducted to evaluating our system in three points: the processing speed, realtimeness and the dynamic CPU allocation.

11.1   Experiments

Our system has been implemented on SPARCcenter 2000 running Solaris 2.4. The machine is loaded with 16 CPUs, 1G bytes memory, 20K bytes instruction cache memory, 16K bytes 1st data cache memory and 1M bytes external cash. In the experiments the numbers of mutators and collectors vary from 1 through 10 and 1 through 5, respectively. The following values were measured: how many times GC occurred, GC processing time for one GC, mutator's pause period by root insertion, mutator's root insertion time, and scheduler's root insertion time in the global area. Comparison is made with / without the dynamic CPU allocation.

11.2   Programs

1. Fibonacci number

Table 1: GC times and pause time of Fibonacci (1 collector)

Mutator #	1	2	4	8
Times	1541	874	521	290
Pause time(μs)	1004	1146	2421	5033

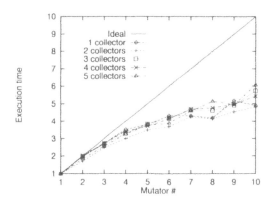

Figure 4: Speedup of Fibonacci

This program calculates the 35th Fibonacci number by generating 40 Lisp processes. Since Fibonacci number is a mathematical calculation, very few cells are consumed. Execution time is measured as the number of collectors varies from 1 through 5. Figure 4 shows the result. When one collector is used, the shortest time is measured. The horizontal axis represents the number of mutators and the vertical does the speedup ratio compared with one mutator. Linear improvement ratio would be ideal. Table 1 and Figure 7(a) show the number of GC triggering, one pause period of a mutator, and the GC time, respectively. When more than one collector is used, the result was worse than the case of one collector. The reason would be that unnecessary collectors cause more pauses of mutators due to more GCs and more conflicts in accessing data.

In terms of the number of GCs, it decreases more than execution time, because more mutators cause less overall execution time and longer GC period (Figure 7(a)). Figure 1 well confirms that.

2. N-Queens Problem

This program calculates an n-Queens problem by generating n Lisp processes. Because an n-Queens problem is a list processing application, it consumes a lot of cells. Our experiment is conducted in the case of **n=11** as the number of mutators varies from 1 through 10. Figure 5(b) shows the execution time. Figure 6 and Figure 5(a) show the number of GCs and one-time pause period

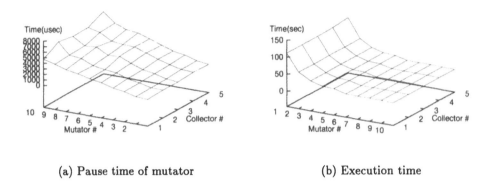

(a) Pause time of mutator   (b) Execution time

Figure 5: 11-Queens problem

(Figure 2 ①~③) and the root insertion time, respectively.

The shortest execution time is obtained when two collectors are employed. Figure 6(b) shows that fact.

11.3   Discussion

Here we analize the experiment results in terms of the number of collectors, the speedup gain rate, the size of the heap page, GC time, realtimeness of our parallel GC and time for root insertion.

11.3.1   The number of collectors

Figure 6(b) shows that less collectors are more efficient when the number of mutators is small in the 11-Queens problem. It also shows that processing speed slows down by one collector when the number of mutators gets larger. This means that free cells run out and list processing is interrupted when the number of mutators is large. Thus more collectors should be used. Figure 4 shows that one collector is enough even when many mutators are running in calculating the Fibonacci number. Thus the appropriate number of collectors varies from application to application.

11.3.2   Performance gain by the number of units

To evaluate the performance gain by the number of units, Amdahl's Law [1] is applied.

$$P = \frac{N(1 - S(N))}{S(N)(1 - N)} \qquad (10.6)$$

In (10.6), P represents the ratio of the paralleled portion (**parallel ratio**), N is the number of mutators, $S(N)$ shows the speedup ratio compared with the case when one mutator is used.

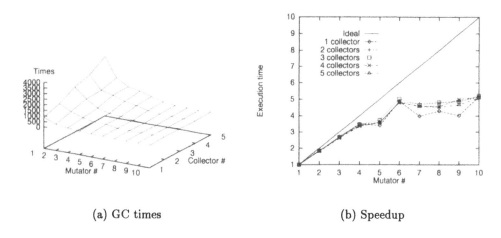

(a) GC times   (b) Speedup

Figure 6: 11-Queens

Figure 4 shows that the parallel ratio of Fibonacci is $P = 0.91$ for $N = 10$ and $S(10) = 5.5$. In Fibonacci calculation, speedup effect by more mutators appears because 40 fine-grain Lisp processes evaluated in parallel.

The result of Figure 6(b) is analized next. The granularity of generated processes is large in the 11-Queen problem and the processing time in which all the processes are running is short. For $N = 6$ a good result is obtained ($P = 0.96$) from $S(6) = 5$. For $N = 10$ the parallel ratio gets lower ($P = 0.88$) from $S(10) = 5$. The execution time becomes almost the same for both 6 and 10 mutators because one mutator can perform up to 2 processes (Our 11-Queens problem generates 11 Lisp processes). When 6 or more mutators are used, 1 or more mutators seem being kept idle. For $N = 11$ idle mutators should be small because each mutator performs one Lisp process. The parallel ratio in this case is $P = 0.94$ from $S(11) = 7$, which is an acceptable result.

11.3.3 Heap page size

One heap page is fixed to 512 cells (4096 bytes) in our system. This size was determined from the fact that the best execution time of 11-Queens problem was obtained when the page size was 4096 byte size from the tests between 512 and 16384 bytes.

11.3.4 GC cycle time

Figure 7(a) shows one GC cycle time for the Fibonacci number and 11-Queens problem. Table 2 shows collector's GC time with 10 mutators for the Fibonacci calculation.

The collector performs marking and reclaiming. In both tasks multiple collectors run almost independently. Thus, the linear gain can be expected. Our experiments

Table 2: Average GC cycle time of Fibonacci number

Collector #	1	2	4
GC time ($msec$)	225.1	112.6	50.49

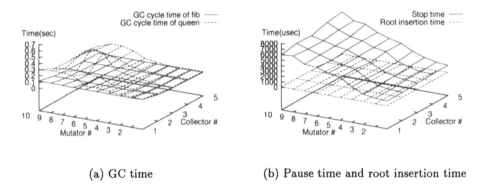

(a) GC time   (b) Pause time and root insertion time

Figure 7: Fibonacci number

confirmed that half execution time is achieved by double collectors.

In the 11-Queens problem, the use of more collectors does not necessarily reduce GC time, because cell consumption rate depends on time when GC is triggered. The reason for this is that the cell consumption speed depends on the coarse grain of processes.

11.3.5   Realtimeness in parallel GC

Improvement of realtimeness by parallel GC is estimated by pause time of a mutator in Table 1 and Figure 7(b).

Let's estimate GC time in sequential GC. The basic algorithm for our parallel GC is mark-sweep. GC time for sequential mark-sweep GC is equivalent to the case of one collector in parallel GC. Figure 7(a) can be considered as the chart of the sum of marking and sweeping of a collector in parallel GC. Therefore 195ms (marking) and 382ms (sweeping) are obtained from Figure 7(a).

Judging from Table 1 and Figure 7(b), the pause time of our parallel GC is between 1004~7750μs and 833~7152μs, respectively. Lots of CPUs are used when the pause time is long. From the discussion so far, the pause time is reduced to 1/25 ~ 1/194 and 1/53 ~ 1/459, respectively. Thus the pause time gets shorter over 25 times by our parallel GC and high realtimeness is achieved compared with stop-and-collect GCs.

11.3.6 Time for root insertion

Figure 5(a) compares time for root insertion only, the pause period for root insertion (Figure 2 ①~③) and time for root insertion in the global area. This figure shows that the root insertion by mutators takes 3.0~23%, the root insertion by the scheduler takes 1.3~5.5% compared with the pause period. The remaining time is consumed for synchronization between the mutators and the scheduler.

This time cost heavily depends on transfer speed between CPUs, the number of CPUs, and the operating system even when the same CPU is used. Our system uses the LWP system calls to achieve synchronization. The use of spin lock[2] would be another choice. Other efficient methods could improve realtimeness.

11.4 Experiments on dynamic CPU allocation

Here transition of CPU allocation and speeding up by dynamic CPU allocation are measured as the initial number of mutators and collectors varies.

The number of CPUs is fixed, which is the sum of mutators and collectors. The initial number of mutators and collectors is specifed when the system starts. In our experiment the number of CPUs is fixed to 11 and execution time is measured in the following two ways.

1. All the possible combinations are tried as the initial value. CPU allocation is fixed.

2. All the possible combinations are tried as the initial value. CPU allocation is dynamically decided by the method described in 9.2. Task switch between mutators and collectors is encouraged.

Tested programs are Fibonacci calculation, the n-Queens problem, and a sequent calculation of prover MALL (Multiltiplicative-Additive Linear Logic) [5]. The results are shown in Figure 8.

Figure 8 shows that dynamic allocation reduces the execution time in every application. This result asserts that the number of necessary collectors varies during execution.

Since Fibonacci calculation does not consume lots of cells, the difference between the fixed allocation and the dynamic allocation is insignificant when more mutators are used. In the 11-Queens problem, however, dynamic allocation attains less execution time than every fixed combination. Thus it may be concluded that dynamic allocation could dramatically reduce the execution time for cell-consuming applications. Furthermore, dynamic allocation outperforms every fixed case in the 11-Queens problem. That means that the cell consumption speed varies even in a single application. For such applications dynamic allocation is proved to be very effective.

---

[2]A method which uses busy-wait.

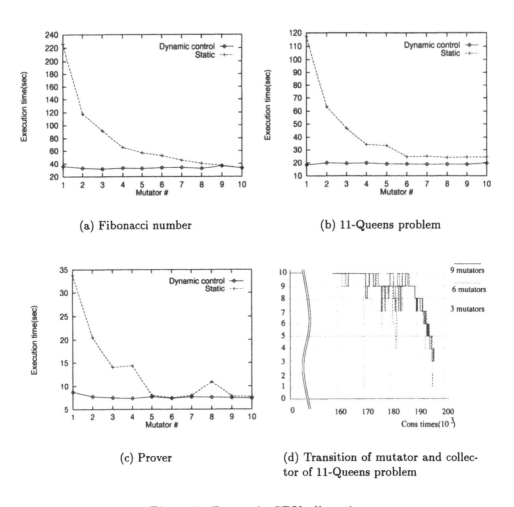

(a) Fibonacci number

(b) 11-Queens problem

(c) Prover

(d) Transition of mutator and collector of 11-Queens problem

Figure 8: Dynamic CPU allocation

In the case of the prover, execution time does not decrease much when 6 or more mutators are used in the fixed CPU allocation. This is because more parallel effect does not appear in this particular case. A different expression yields different parallel effect. When 8 mutators are allocated, execution takes longer due to the particular GC triggering timing. Dynamic allocation attains almost a minimum execution time of the fixed case.

From the experiments above, our dynamic CPU allocation of mutators and collectors attains the same or less execution time of the fixed CPU allocation.

Figure 8(d) shows transition of the CPU allocation in the 11-Queens problem. The vertical axis represents the number of mutators and the horizontal axis, time. For the experiments in Figure 8, transition of CPU allocation was measured for 3, 6, and 9 initial mutators. The number of mutators became 10 (maximum allocation) after a while regardless the initial value, because the remaining cells are counted to determine the allocation. That state continues for a while. Then more collectors are needed and list processing is interrupted due to free cell drought. This transition validates our parameter setting for CPU allocation.

12   Conclusion

We have focused on Lisp systems which run multiple list processing processes (mutators) and GC processes (collectors), and introduced a design of scheduler which controls the overall system. Our prototype on a parallel machine confirmed that execution time decreases by parallelizing list processing and that the pause period by GC gets less than 1/25. Thus we can confirm that parallelizing list processing as well as GC in a Lisp system decreases execution time in many applications.

We also added a mechanism which dynamically controls CPU allocation to mutators and collectors by monitoring cell consumption. We installed the strategy that more CPUs are allocated to list processing as long as list processing is not interrupted. Experiment results show that execution time with dynamic CPU allocation is less than or equal to fixed CPU allocation. Since the cell consumption rate differs among applications and it varies even in single application, dynamic allocation based on monitoring the consumption speed attained the best performance. Transition of CPU allocation also validated our parameter setting.

13   Future work

This paper confirmed improvement of processing speed by parallel list processing as realtimeness is maintained by parallel GC. Although experiments were done against major Lisp applications, more applications should be tested.

Our current parameter setting of CPU allocation is based on the strategy that list processing is performed by the maximum number of CPUs with least interruption of list processing. This parameter setting strategy should be reconsidered in the following points.

- Our system requires at least one mutator and one collector. If this constraint can be relaxed, CPU allocation can be done only by the remaining amount of free cells with zero collector initially.

- We can decrease overhead of access conflicts with idling mutators by deciding the number of mutators according to the parallelism of the application.

- We assumed that the performance is proportional to the number of collectors. The assumption is confirmed for the case with 1 to 3 collectors. Various applications should be tested with more collectors.

Acknowledgments

We thank Electrotechnical Laboratory for their kindly letting us use the computational resources. We are deeply indebted to Dr. Toshihiro Matsui, Mr. Tomotsugu Sekiguchi and NPB members at ETL.

Bibliography

1) G. Amdahl: Validity of the Single-Processor Approach to Achieving Large Scale Computing Capabilities, *Proc. AFIPS Conf.*, pp. 483–485 (1967).

2) H. G. Baker: List-processing in real time on a serial computer, *Commun. ACM*, Vol. 21, No. 4, pp. 280–294 (1978).

3) E. W. Dijkstra,L. Lamport,A. J. Martin, C. S. Scholten,E. F. M. Steffens: On-the-fly garbage collection: an exercise in cooperation, *Commun. ACM*, Vol. 21, No. 11, pp. 966–975 (1978).

4) R. P. Gabriel, J. McCarthy: Queue-based multi-processing Lisp, *ACM Symp. Lisp and FP*, pp. 25–43 (1984).

5) J.-Y. Girard: Linear Logic, *Theoretical Computer Science*, Vol. 50, pp. 1–102 (1987).

6) A. Goldberg and D. Robson: *Smalltalk-80 the language and its implementation*, Addison-Wesley, 1983.

7) Jr. R. H. Halstead: Implementation of Multilisp: Lisp on a multiprocessor, *ACM Trans. Programming Languages and Systems*, pp. 9–17 (1984).

8) T. Matsui and T. Sekiguchi: Design and Implemention of Parallel EUSLisp Using Multithread, *Trans. IPSJ*, Vol. 36, No. 8, pp. 1885–1896 (1995).

9) S. Jagannathan,J. Philbin: A foundation for an efficient multi-threaded Scheme system, *Proc. 1992 ACM Conf. on Lisp and FP*, pp. 345–357 (1992).

10) S. Takahashi and A. Maeda and Y. Tanaka and T. Iwai and M. Nakanishi: Parallel Lisp system equipped with paralle garbage collection, *IPSJ SIG NOTE*, Vol. 4, No. 4, pp. 19–24 (1995).

11) S. Takahashi and T. Iwai and A. Maeda and Y. Tanaka and M. Nakanishi: Parallel Lisp system equipped with paralle garbage collection, *Trans. IEICE*, Vol. J80–D–I, No. 3,pp. 247–257 (1997).

12) S. Takahashi and T. Iwai and Y. Tanaka and A. Maeda and M. Nakanishi: A Parallel Lisp System which Dynamically Allocates CPU to List Processing and GC Process, *Trans. IPSJ*, Vol. 38, No. 5,pp. 1050–1057 (1997).

13) Y. Tanaka,S. Matsui,A. Maeda,M. Nakanishi: Partial marking gc, *Proc. Intl. Conf. CONPAR94-VAPP VI*, pp. 337–348 (1994).

14) Y. Tanaka and S. Matsui and A. Maeda and M. Nakanishi: Parallel GC Using Parallel Marking and Its Performance Analysis. *Trans. IEICE*, Vol. J78-D-1, No. 12, pp. 926–935 (1995).

15) Y. Tanaka and S. Matsui and A. Maeda and M. Nakanishi: Partial Marking GC, *IPSJ SIG NOTE*, Vol. 94, No. 49, pp. 17–24 (1994).

16) N. Wirth: The design of a pascal compiler, *Software-Practice and Experience*, pp. 309–333,1971.

17) T. Yuasa: Real-time garbage collection on general-purpose machine, *Journal of Systems and Software*, Vol. 11 (1990).

Partial Marking GC: Generational Parallel Garbage Collection and its Performance Analysis

Yoshio Tanaka

National Institute of Advanced Industrial Science and Technology

Shogo Matsui

Kanagawa University

Atusi Maeda

University of Tsukuba

Masakazu Nakanishi

Keio University

ABSTRACT

In this paper, we describe the design and performance analysis of a new parallel *garbage collection (gc)* scheme called the *partial marking gc* which is a variant of generational gc. Partial marking gc is based on the *snapshot-at-beginning (snapshot)* algorithm, which is one of the most practical parallel mark-sweep gc algorithms. Partial marking gc reduces the time spent in marking and improves collection efficiency. Our analysis shows that the collection efficiency of the partial marking gc is 1.5 times better than the snapshot algorithm. The performance of the partial marking gc using one gc processor is equivalent to the snapshot algorithm using two gc processors. Our partial marking gc is easy to implement and provides an efficient and practical parallel gc algorithm.

1 Introduction

List processing systems automatically reclaim computer storage by *garbage collection* as part of their management of the free storage awaiting the requests from an allocation routine[17]. For instance, Lisp has one or more lists of free cells called a "free list"; and it retrieves a cell from the free list whenever an allocation routine such as *cons* is called. Traditionally, when free storage is exhausted, the garbage collector is executed. The garbage collector finds data objects[1] that are no longer in use and recycles their space for reuse by the running program.

When an application is running, objects are divided into *live objects* and *garbage objects*. A garbage object can not be reached by the program via any path of pointer traversals. Conversely, live objects can be reached. A garbage collector distinguishes between *live* and *garbage objects* and reclaims all garbage storage; the current program can then use the space. A typical garbage collector uses this "live" criterion, and defines it in terms of *root set* and *reachability* from these roots. The root set consists of global variables, local variables in the activation stack, and any registers used by active procedures. All objects reachable from the roots, meaning on any directed path of pointers from the roots, are considered live.

Garbage collection algorithms are classified according to how they identify live objects and garbage objects. Some common examples are the *reference counting*, the *mark-sweep*, the *copying* and so on. The parallel garbage collector presented in this paper is based on the mark-sweep algorithm, which consists of the following two phases:

1. **Marking phase** In the marking phase, the collector distinguishes live objects from garbage objects by *tracing*[2], and marks all reachable items. A typical marking implementation is done by altering bits within the objects. After the marking phase, all live objects will have been marked and can be distinguished from garbage objects.

2. **Sweep phase** The collector scans the memory space, finds the unmarked (garbage) objects and reclaims their space which is then linked onto the free list so that they are accessible to the allocation routines. The collector then clears the marks from the marked objects.

In many systems, programmers must explicitly reclaim heap[3] memory using a "free" or "dispose" statements; garbage collection frees the programmer from this burden. However, garbage collection causes long pauses in the processing procedure. In order to speed up the reclamation, various garbage collection algorithms have been studied. Generational garbage collection, which incorporates the concept of the lifetime of objects into its garbage collection, is one of the most efficient as the disruption time is very short. However, it does not eliminate the problem completely. Since these disruptions can be fatal for applications which require real-time processing, we must find and use garbage collection algorithms which cause no computation disruption.

One major attempt for eliminating this bottleneck is incremental/parallel tracing collection. In incremental garbage collection, small units of garbage collection are interleaved with small units of program execution. In the parallel garbage collection,

---

[1]We use the term object for any kind of structured data record, such as Lisp cons cells or C structs.

[2]Starting at the root set, the collector traverses the graph of pointer relationships.

[3]We use the term heap for the memory area for dynamic allocation.

the garbage collector (*collector*) and the executor of the program (*mutator*) run in parallel. Incremental garbage collection and parallel garbage collection can use the same algorithm. Although we propose and describe a new parallel garbage collection algorithm, it is possible to implement our algorithm in incremental garbage collection.

The difficulty with parallel garbage collection is that while the collector is tracing out the graph of reachable data structures, the mutator may change the graph. Figure 1 illustrates the problem.

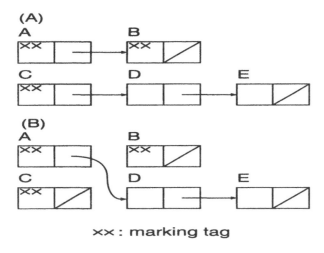

Figure 1: Violation of parallel garbage collection

Suppose the Objects **A**, **B**, and **C** have been scanned and marked by the collector (Figure 1-(A)). Now suppose that the mutator:

1. Changes the pointer from **A** to **B** to **A** to **D**.

2. Changes the pointer from **C** to **D** to a NULL pointer (Figure 1-(B)).

Now the collector can not mark objects **D** and **E** because when it reached the NULL pointer after object **C** it stops its traversal. As a result, although **D** and **E** are still alive, they will be reclaimed as garbage objects during the next sweep phase. In order to avoid this incorrect reclamation of live objects, a parallel garbage collection scheme must provide some way of keeping track of the changes to the reachable objects graph.

There are two basic approaches for coordinating the collector with the mutator. One is to use a *read barrier*, which detects possibly incorrect situation when the mutator attempts to refer a pointer to an unmarked object, and immediately shows the collector. The other approach is a *write barrier*, which detects it when the mutator attempts to write a pointer into an object. In general, a write barrier is cheaper than a read barrier because a read barrier has an unnecessary expense: it must check to see if the pointer is pointing to an unmarked object. The cost of these checks is high on conventional hardware, because they occur so frequently. Therefore, most parallel garbage collections use a write barrier scheme. Write barrier approaches fall into two different categories, *snapshot-at-beginning* and *incremental update*[2], depending on which aspect of the problem they address. Our parallel garbage collector is based on a snapshot method.

The snapshot algorithm has a well known disadvantage: the garbage objects disposed of during the marking phase are never collected in the subsequent sweep phase. Here, *collection ability* is defined as the number of reclaimed objects per unit of time, and *collection efficiency* is the ratio of collection ability of the parallel garbage collector to the collection ability of the stop-and-collect garbage collector. Hickey et al. reported that collection efficiency of the snapshot algorithm is about 0.5[4]. Although various parallel garbage collection algorithms have been studied, the application execution times and real-time performance have been unacceptable. It is strongly required that a practical snapshot-type parallel garbage collector has improved the collection efficiency.

As a step towards making parallel garbage collection practicable, we propose a *partial marking garbage collector*[14, 15]. Recently, general purpose multiprocessor systems have attracted widespread attention increasing the need for practical parallel garbage collection systems in real-time processing. A partial marking garbage collector is based on the snapshot algorithm, and it improves its collection efficiency by limiting the objects to be marked. In the following sections, its performance is applied to *EusLisp*[8, 9, 10], which is a *Common Lisp* based practical lisp system, and its real-time performance is reported.

2   Snapshot-at-beginning Algorithm

Snapshot-at-beginning algorithms use a write barrier to ensure that no objects ever become inaccessible to the garbage collector while collection is in progress. In this section, we describe the snapshot algorithm and its performance.

2.1   Snapshot Algorithm

Snapshot algorithms use a write barrier technique for coordination between the mutator and the collector. Conceptually, at the beginning of the garbage collection, a *copy-on-write* virtual copy of the graph of reachable data structure is made. That is, the graph of reachable objects is fixed at the moment garbage collection starts, even though the actual traversal proceeds incrementally.

One of the most famous snapshot collection algorithm is Yuasa's[19], and our implementation is based on Yuasa's snapshot collection. In our implementation, the snapshot collector uses three colors as tags for marking: *black*, *white*, and *off-white*. The objects subject to garbage collection are conceptually colored white. In the sweep phase, the collector reclaims the white objects. Black represents the color of marked objects, that is, the collector changes the tag of reachable objects to black in the marking phase. Off-white is a tag for free objects, and the tag of a newly allocated object is left off-white[4]. The mutator preserves the invariant that no black object hold a pointer directly to a white object. If the mutator replaces a pointer from a black object to a white one, it must coordinate with the collector.

The collector repeats a *GC cycle* which consists of a *root insertion phase*, a *marking phase*, and a *sweep phase*. In the root insertion phase, the collector collects a root set from the mutator – that is, pushes the root set onto the marking stack. In the marking phase, the collector traverses the graph and marks all reachable objects. The collector then scans the memory space and reclaims the space of garbage objects. In this way, the basic procedures of the collector are the same as an ordinary mark-sweep collector. However, the snapshot collection has the following two extra procedures:

- In the sweep phase, the collector reclaims the space for white objects. Black and off-white objects are not reclaimed and their tags are cleared, except for free objects. Because the tag of a newly allocated object is off-white, it is never reclaimed – even if it becomes an object unreachable from the roots.

- If a location is written to, the overwritten value is first saved and pushed onto a marking stack for later examination, meaning the overwritten pointer is colored off-white. In the example in figure 1, the pointer from B to D is pushed onto the marking stack when it is overwritten with the pointer to C. Thus, all objects live at the beginning of garbage collection will be reached through the collection's traversal, even if the pointers to them are overwritten. Since the root set have been pushed onto the marking stack, however, when a root is written over, it is unnecessary to pass the root to the collector.

The snapshot algorithm is very simple and can be easily implemented in both parallel and incremental garbage collection. If implemented as parallel garbage collection, the mutator must perform the root insertion and the notification of replaced pointers for coordination with the collector. However, the snapshot algorithm is more conservative than other algorithms, that is, an object allocated during collection and living at the beginning of the cycle will be reclaimed in the next cycle, even if it actually is a garbage object. Figure 2 demonstrates the disadvantage of the snapshot algorithm.

Just after the marking phase, tags of newly allocated objects are left as off-white. In the next sweep phase, as shown in the right of the figure, those objects (eight objects in the figure) are not reclaimed but changed their tags to white even if they are actually garbage objects. Because of the disadvantages described in this section, collection efficiency of the snapshot collection is about 0.5. As a result, the execution of the mutator is indeed frequently suspended in applications which consume many objects, because the collection of garbage objects by the collector can not catch up with the consumption of objects by the mutator[6].

---

[4]The tag of a newly allocated object may be black, depending on the implementation

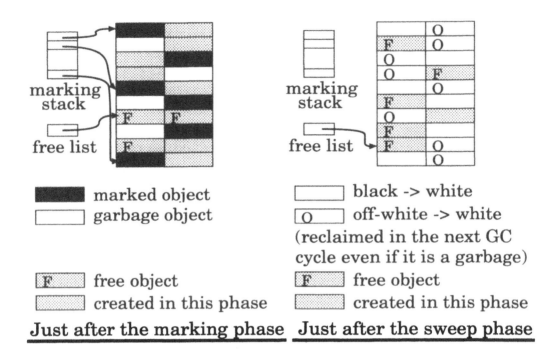

Figure 2: Disadvantage of the snapshot algorithm

3 Partial Marking Garbage Collection

The disadvantages of the snapshot collection just described limit the practical use of parallel garbage collection. Therefore, let's look at our new parallel garbage collection scheme called *partial marking garbage collection*, which improves collection efficiency and shows great potential for practical use.

3.1 Generational Garbage Collection

In 1983, it was found that most objects tend to live a very short time after generation, although a small percentage of them live much longer.[5]. While figures vary from language to language and program to program, usually between 80 and 98 percent of all newly-allocated objects die within a few million instructions, or before another megabyte has been allocated; the majority of objects die even more quickly, usually within tens of kilobytes of allocation. *Generational garbage collection* introduces the concept of the lifetime of objects into garbage collection. *Generation scavenging garbage collection*[16], which was proposed in 1984, is one of the most efficient generational garbage collection algorithms. It is based on copying garbage collection and avoids much repeated copying by segregating objects into multiple areas by age, and scavenging areas containing older objects less often than younger areas. Generation scavenging garbage collection takes only a few microseconds for one scavenging of the younger generation.

3.2 The Basic Idea

At the beginning of the sweep phase, unreachable objects can be divided into three categories according to their tags: *B type*, *O type*, and *W type*. The tags of *B type*, *O type*, and *W type* objects are black, off-white, and white respectively. As described above, *B type* and *O type* objects are never reclaimed in the subsequent sweep phase and they will be collected in the next sweep phase. Remember that almost all objects tend to live a very short time after generation; therefore most unreachable objects are *O type*, and the lack of ability to collect them immediately reduces the efficiency of the snapshot algorithm.

Partial marking garbage collection is based on the snapshot algorithm. It incorporates the concept of generational garbage collection into the snapshot algorithm. An object which is marked by the collector is considered to survive until the next GC cycle[18]. By leaving the tags of marked objects[5] as black in the sweep phase, marking for those objects can be omitted in the next marking phase. As a result, the time spent for marking is considerably reduced and unreachable *O type* objects will be reclaimed in the next sweep phase sooner. Thus, the partial marking garbage collection is designed to improve collection efficiency by reducing marking time.

A partial marking garbage collector uses two kinds of GC cycles: a *full cycle* and a *partial cycle*. The treatment of the black tag in the sweep phase determines the policy of the next GC cycle. The operations on the off-white and white tag are similar to those in the sweep phase of the snapshot algorithm. If the collector leaves the black tags of marked objects as black, the collector will not mark those objects in the next marking phase. As a result, the collector marks only the active objects which are allocated after the previous marking phase. This marking is called *partial marking*, and a GC cycle which contains a partial marking is called a *partial cycle*. An ordinary marking is called *full marking*, and a GC cycle which contains this marking is called a *full cycle*. Partial marking time is considerably less than that of full marking because there are fewer objects to be marked, and the collector can reclaim garbage objects which were unreachable *O type* objects that had not been reclaimed in the previous GC cycle. Figure 3 demonstrates the basic idea of partial marking garbage collection.

The upper left of the figure illustrates that in the full marking phase, all reachable objects are marked by the collector. Object tags which are allocated during the marking phase are left as off-white. At this point, the tags of objects are the same as in the snapshot algorithm shown in figure 2. In the subsequent sweep phase (upper right of the figure), *W type* objects are reclaimed and connected to a free list. Tags of marked objects are left as black, and off-white tagged objects are cleared (changed to white), except for free objects. In the partial marking phase (lower left of the figure), the collector marks only a few objects (two objects in this figure) which were allocated after the previous full marking phase, and completes the marking in a short time. As

---

[5]Black objects are also called marked objects

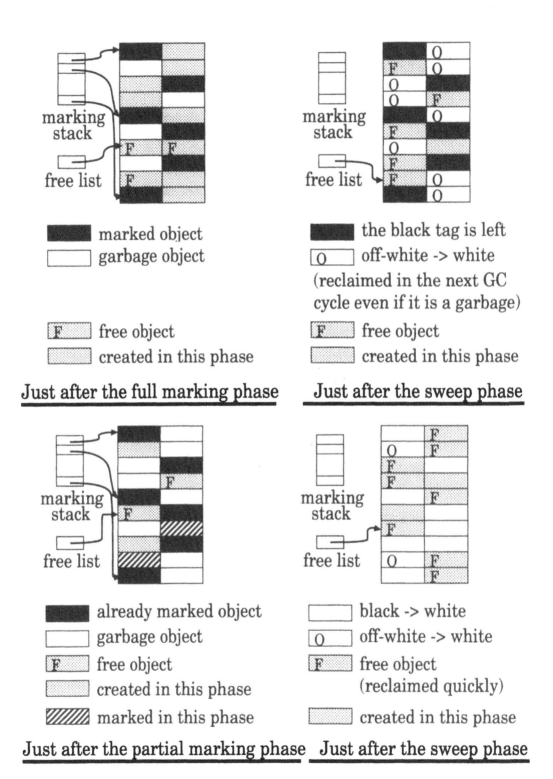

Figure 3: The basic idea of the partial marking garbage collection

a result, as shown in the lower right of the figure, many objects (eight objects in the figure) which were *O type* in the previous sweep phase can be reclaimed considerably more quickly compared to the snapshot collection. Although the snapshot collector can reclaim garbage objects which are alive and marked in the previous GC cycle, the partial marking collector can not reclaim them in a partial cycle. However, the idea of generational garbage collection indicates that the advantages of quicker *O type* reclamation outweighs the disadvantages.

The collector repeats a sequence which is comprised of a full cycle and some subsequent partial cycles. The objects marked during the full marking phase are equivalent to long lived objects in the generational garbage collection. Partial cycles are equivalent to scavenging the space for younger objects in generation scavenging garbage collections. A partial marking garbage collector is considered a generational garbage collector which scavenges old spaces frequently.

3.3   Coordination between the mutator and the collector

Since partial marking garbage collection is based on the snapshot algorithm, all objects alive at the root insertion are normally marked. However, a violation of the coloring invariant described in section 2.1 can occur in the following two cases:

1. During the full marking phase, the mutator writes a pointer to an off-white object into a marked object.

2. During the sweep phase in a full cycle, the mutator writes a pointer to an off-white or white object into a marked object.

Figure 4 illustrates an example of case 1.

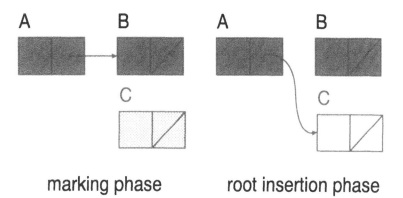

marking phase   root insertion phase

Figure 4: An example of an incorrect situation

In the marking phase, a pointer from A to B is changed from A to the off-white object C. In the subsequent sweep phase, the tag of C is then changed to white and the tag of A is left black. As a result, a pointer from a black object (A) to a white one (C) now exists at the root insertion of the partial cycle. Because the collector's traversal stops when it reaches a marked object, object C is not marked in the partial marking phase and will be reclaimed in the sweep phase. In both cases, a pointer from a black object to a white one exists at the root insertion phase, and the white object will be reclaimed unless there are other paths which include no black objects.

To avoid the violation of the invariant, partial marking garbage collection needs extra coordination between the mutator and the collector, which is not necessary in the snapshot algorithm. For example, when the mutator replaces the pointers and happens to fall into a situation described above, not only the overwritten pointers, but also the written pointers have to be passed to (pushed onto) the collector. In the first case, a black object never points to a white object at the beginning of the next partial cycle because a linked off-white object is changed to black during the full marking phase. And in the second case, although there are pointers from a black object to a white one, those white objects will be marked in the next partial marking phase by the collector's traversal from the pushed pointers. Figures 5 and 6 show the algorithms of the collector and the mutator of the partial marking garbage collection. The collector performs a full cycle and a partial cycle alternately.

An object has two pointer fields, car and cdr, and a tag field tag. N is the total number of objects in the heap. The system manages a linked list of free objects called *free list*. FREE.head and FREE.tail point to the head and the tail of the free list. NIL is a special pointer which indicates an empty object. The tag of a free object is off-white and its car part uses a special pointer f. The mutator notifies the collector of the pointer replacement through the marking stack. Push and pop are atomic operations for manipulation of the marking stack. Push stores an object specified by its argument onto the marking stack, and pop restores an object from the top of the marking stack. CYCLE is a flag which indicates whether the current GC cycle is partial or full. PHASE indicates the phase of the collector, and the mutator knows the current phase from it.

The following is a detailed description of each procedure:

- *GP_root_insert* pushes all roots onto the marking stack.

- *GP_mark* traverses the graph from the roots and marks all reachable objects.

- *GP_sweep_leave_mark* sweeps the heap and reclaims for unmarked objects. The tag of an off-white object is changed to white – except for free objects. The tag of a black object is left black. Thus, the next GC cycle will be a partial cycle.

- *GP_sweep_clear_mark* is the same as *GP_sweep_leave_mark* except that it changes the tag of a black object to white. Thus, the next GC cycle will be a full cycle.

- *GP_partial_marking_gc* is the main procedure of the collector. It sets the CYCLE and PHASE flags and repeats a full cycle and a partial cycle forever.

```
procedure GP_root_insert;
  begin
    push all roots onto the stack
  end;
procedure GP_mark;
  begin
    while the stack is not empty do
      begin
        n := pop;
        while (n ≠ NIL) and
              (n.car ≠ f) and
              (n.tag ≠ black) do
          begin
            n.tag := black;
            push(n.cdr);
            n := n.car
          end
      end
  end;
procedure GP_sweep_leave_mark;
  begin
    for i := 1 to N do
      if i.tag = white then
        GP_append(i)
      else if (i.tag = off-white) and
              (i.car ≠ f) then
        i.tag := white
  end;
```

```
procedure GP_sweep_clear_mark;
  begin
    for i := 1 to N do
      if i.tag = white then
        GP_append(i)
      else if i.car ≠ f then
        i.tag := white
  end;
procedure GP_partial_marking_gc;
  begin
    while true do
      begin
        CYCLE := full;
        PHASE := rootins; GP_root_insert;
        PHASE := marking; GP_mark;
        PHASE := sweep;
        GP_sweep_leave_mark;
        CYCLE := partial;
        PHASE := rootins; GP_root_insert;
        PHASE := marking; GP_mark;
        PHASE := sweep;
        GP_sweep_clear_mark
      end
  end;
procedure GP_append(i);
  begin
    i.tag := off-white;
    i.car := f;
    i.cdr := NIL;
    FREE.tail.cdr := i;
    FREE.tail := i
  end;
```

Figure 5: The algorithm of the partial marking collection (collector)

```
procedure LP_rplaca(m, n);              procedure LP_rplacd(m, n);
  begin                                   begin
   push(m.car);                            push(m.cdr);
   if CYCLE = full then                    if CYCLE = full then
    if (PHASE = marking) and                if (PHASE = marking) and
      (n.tag = off-white) then               (n.tag = off-white) then
    push(n)                                 push(n)
    else if (PHASE = sweep) and             else if (PHASE = sweep) and
          (n.tag ≠ black) then                   (n.tag ≠ black) then
    push(n);                                push(n)
    m.car := n                              m.cdr := n
  end;                                    end;
                                        procedure LP_cons(m, n);
                                          begin
                                           sleep while FREE.head = FREE.tail
                                           NEW := FREE.head;
                                           FREE.head := FREE.head.cdr;
                                           NEW.car := m;
                                           NEW.cdr := n
                                          end;
```

Figure 6: The algorithm of the partial marking collection (mutator)

- *GP_append* sets an off-white tag into a **tag** field and **f** into a **car** part of an object specified by the argument. Then, it appends the object to a free list.

- *LP_rplaca* replaces the **car** part of an object specified by the first argument, **m**, with an object specified by the second argument, **n**. It pushes the overwritten pointer (**m.car**). This is the same procedure as in the snapshot algorithm. Furthermore, it checks the phase and the cycle, and if they satisfy the condition described in the top of this section, the written pointer (**n**) is also pushed.

- *LP_rplacd* is the same as *LP_rplaca* except that *LP_rplacd* replaces the **cdr** part of an object.

- *LP_cons* is an allocation routine. It retrieves an object from the free list, and stores objects specified by the arguments into the **car** part and the **cdr** part of a retrieved object. The tag of the object is left off-white.

In the implementation of the algorithm, CYCLE and PHASE are the critical sections and mutual exclusive control is necessary to operate the flags. It should be noted that the mutator must not write over root pointers during the time the collector pushes the root set onto the marking stack.

4 Performance Analysis

Hickey et al. analyzed the performance of an *incremental update* garbage collection[4]. They focused on the condition of the *stable state* in which the mutator never suspends the computation because of the exhaustion of free objects. In this section, we analyze the performance of both partial marking collection and snapshot collection using the same methods of Hickey et al.'s analysis. We analyzed the performance based on the following model and assumptions:

model

All objects are of fixed size, and the data structure of each object is the same as that described in Figures 5 and 6, that is, an object has two pointer fields and a tag field. Let N be the number of objects and L be the number of live objects. We assume that the mutator allocates and disposes an object for every r units of time. Thus, the number of live objects, L, takes a fixed value. We assume that when the system starts, there are already L live objects. The collector marks an object for every m units of time in the marking phase, and scans an object for every s units of time in the sweep phase.

GC cycle

In the previous discussion, a GC cycle is defined as a sequence of root insertion, marking, and sweep phase. In our analysis, following Hickey et al.'s analysis method, we define a GC cycle as from the beginning of the sweep phase to the end of the marking phase.

garbage objects

In the incremental update algorithm, when the collector completes the marking phase, there are two types of unreachable objects according to their tags: *black* and *white*. Hickey et al. assume that the tags of all disposed objects by the mutator are black. This is a worst case scenario, assuming that all garbage objects will be reclaimed on and after the next GC cycle. In the snapshot algorithm, however, as described in section 3.2, there are three types of unreachable objects: *B type*, *O type*, and *W type*. In our analysis, we assume that the tag of a disposed object is either black or off-white, and the rate of *B type* disposed objects is fixed and expressed by b. This is also a worst case assumption, that is, all disposed objects will be reclaimed on and after the next GC cycle.

4.1 Performance Analysis of Snapshot Collector

Let T_{sweep} be the time taken for a sweep phase, and T_{mark} be the time for a marking phase. Because the time for a root insertion phase is much less than T_{sweep} and T_{mark}, we ignore the time for a root insertion in our analysis. Then, T_{cycle} which is the time spent for a GC cycle is expressed by

$$T_{cycle} = T_{sweep} + T_{mark} = sN + mL. \tag{11.1}$$

If the mutator never suspends the computation, the total number of generated objects in a GC cycle is fixed. We represent the value as G^{crit}. G^{crit} is expressed by

$$G^{crit} = \frac{T_{cycle}}{r} = \frac{sN + mL}{r}. \tag{11.2}$$

Now, the condition to preserve the stable state can be considered as follows:

- If the mutator never suspends the computation during the first GC cycle, there are G^{crit} garbage objects at the end of the GC cycle. Since all of those objects are either *O type* or *W type* objects, no objects will be reclaimed in the sweep phase of the second GC cycle.

- The collector supplies G^{crit} objects in every *ith* GC cycle, s.t. $i > 2$, which are disposed during $(i-2)th$ GC cycle. Therefore, if the mutator does not consume all free objects during the first two GC cycles, the mutator will never suspend the computation.

In short, the condition to preserve the stable state is that the mutator does not suspend the computation because of the exhaustion of free objects during the first two GC cycles. This condition is expressed by

$$G^{crit} \leq N - L - G^{crit}. \tag{11.3}$$

$(N - L - G^{crit})$ is the number of free objects at the end of the first GC cycle, which must be more than the number of consumed objects, G^{crit}, during the second GC cycle. Consequently, the condition to preserve the stable state is expressed by

$$G^{crit} \leq \frac{N - L}{2}. \tag{11.4}$$

4.2   Performance Analysis of Partial Marking Collector

We derive the condition for preserving the stable state in the partial marking garbage collection using the same manner as the snapshot algorithm. We assume that the collector performs a full cycle and a partial cycle alternately. Figure 7 illustrates the process flow of the partial marking garbage collector.

t1 to t9 indicates the starting time of each phase. Let T_{mark_f} and T_{mark_p} be the time for a full marking phase and a partial marking phase respectively. T_{mark_f} is equivalent to T_{mark}. The time for a sweep phase is also the same as the snapshot algorithm. Therefore, T_{cycle_f} which is the time spent for a full cycle is expressed by

$$T_{cycle_f} = T_{sweep} + T_{mark_f} = sN + mL = T_{cycle}. \tag{11.5}$$

Thus, the mutator allocates G^{crit} objects during a full cycle if it does not suspend the computation. In the next sweep phase (t3 to t4), the collector reclaims no objects. In the subsequent partial marking phase (t4 to t5), the collector tries to mark objects which were allocated on and after the previous full marking phase (t2 to t4) and

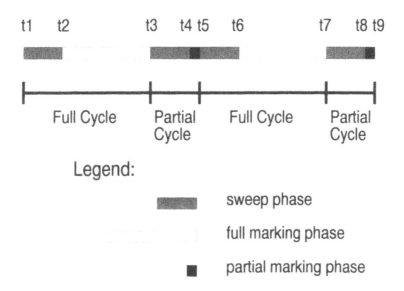

t1   t2   t3   t4 t5   t6   t7   t8 t9

Full Cycle   Partial   Full Cycle   Partial
                   Cycle   Cycle

Legend:

sweep phase

full marking phase

partial marking phase

Figure 7: Process flow of the partial marking garbage collector

alive at the root insertion (t4). Since the time between t2 and t4 is equivalent to the time between t1 and t3, the number of objects allocated during t2 and t4 is G^{crit}. Since the mutator consumes objects regularly, the number of *O type* objects which were disposed during t2 to t4 is $(1 - b)G^{crit}$, which is equivalent to the one during t1 to t3. Hence, the number of objects to be marked in the partial marking phase (t4 to t5) is $G^{crit} - (1 - b)G^{crit} = bG^{crit}$. Let H^{crit} be the number of objects allocated during a partial cycle when the mutator never suspends the computation. Let T_{cycle_p} and T_{mark_p} be the time for a partial cycle and for a partial marking phase respectively. Then, H^{crit} is expressed by

$$H^{crit} = \frac{T_{cycle_p}}{r} = \frac{T_{sweep} + T_{mark_p}}{r} = \frac{sN + mbG^{crit}}{r}. \tag{11.6}$$

Since the number of reclaimed objects, which were *O type* garbage objects at t3, in the third GC cycle (full cycle) is $(1 - b)G^{crit}$, more free objects must remain than $G^{crit} - (1 - b)G^{crit} = bG^{crit}$ at the beginning of the third GC cycle in order to preserve the stable state in the third GC cycle. If the mutator never suspends the computation during the third GC cycle, the collector reclaims enough objects ($bG^{crit} + H^{crit}$ objects) to maintain a stable state in the fourth GC cycle because the mutator consumes H^{crit} objects during the GC cycle. After all, in $(2n + 1)th$ GC cycle ($n > 1$), there are $bG^{crit}s$ objects at the beginning of the GC cycle and the collector reclaims $(1 - b)G^{crit}$ objects. Therefore, the mutator is able to consume G^{crit} objects during the time without suspending the computation. In $2nth$ GC cycle ($n > 2$), since the collector reclaims $bG^{crit} + H^{crit}$ objects, the mutator can allocate H^{crit} objects and the stable state is preserved. Consequently, the condition to preserve the stable state is that there remain more than bG^{crit} objects at the end of the first two GC cycles, that is, $N - L - (G^{crit} + H^{crit}) \geq bG^{crit}$. This condition is expressed by

$$G^{crit} \leq \frac{\frac{r-s}{r}N - L}{1 + \frac{m+r}{r}b}. \tag{11.7}$$

As described above, G^{crit} is the number of objects allocated during one GC cycle when the mutator never suspends the computation. Thus, it is considered as the parameter which indicates the speed (pace) of the consumption of objects by the mutator. Here, we suppose that $N = 5MB, L = 500KB, s = 0.1\mu sec, m = 0.5\mu sec$, and $r = 2\mu sec$. Figure 8 shows the relationship between b and the maximum value of G^{crit} to preserve the stable state.

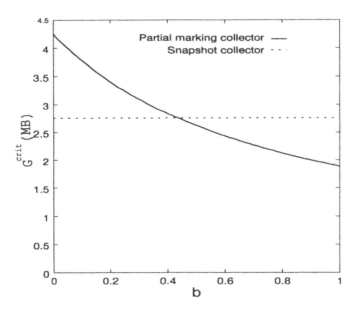

Figure 8: Maximum value of G^{crit} to preserve the stable state

The condition to preserve the stable state using the snapshot collector is that G^{crit} is less than 2.75MB, which is independent of b. On the other hand, the condition using the partial marking collector depends on the parameter b. Although b depends on the application, its value is expected between 0.02 and 0.2. Assuming that b is 0.2, the condition to preserve the stable state using the partial marking collector is that G^{crit} is less than 3.4MB. If b is 0.02, the maximum value of G^{crit} is about 4.15MB. By using the partial marking collector, the maximum object consumption speed by the mutator in the stable state is about 1.5 times compared to using the snapshot collector. When b exceeds 0.45, the performance of the partial marking collector is less than the snapshot collector.

5 Experimental Results

We implemented two Lisp systems based on Lisp-1.5 on the OMRON LUNA-88K: one system's collector is based on the snapshot algorithm, and the other is on the partial marking collector. The LUNA-88K is a quad-processor workstation whose operating system is MACH. The partial marking collector performs a full cycle and a partial cycle alternately. Since the mutator must not change the root set during a root insertion phase, in our implementation, the mutator suspends the computation while the collector executes *GP_root_insert*. Our system permits us to run one mutator and one or two collectors simultaneously. The number of collectors is specified by the command line argument. Using some benchmarks, we measured the performance of the partial marking collector and the snapshot collector. This section shows the performance of both collectors and a comparison with our performance analysis.

5.1 Evaluation of Parallel Garbage Collection

To evaluate the parallel garbage collector, we define *GC ratio* (R_G) and *improvement ratio* (I) as follows:

$$R_G = \frac{T_{seq.gc}}{T_{seq.total}}, \tag{11.8}$$

$$I = \frac{T_{seq.total} - T_{para.total}}{T_{seq.total}}, \tag{11.9}$$

where

$T_{seq.gc}$ is the time spent for garbage collection when the application is executed through the Lisp interpreter whose garbage collection scheme is a stop-and-mark-sweep collection (*seq-lisp*).

$T_{seq.total}$ is the execution time of the running application through *seq-lisp*.

$T_{para.total}$ is the execution time of the running application through the Lisp interpreter which provides parallel garbage collection (*para-lisp*).

R_G is the ratio of the garbage collection time to the total processing time. I is ratio of the speedup when using the parallel garbage collection system. They depend on the running application. The relationship between R_G and I indicates the ability of real-time performance and processing speed of the system. Here, we define the following parameters:

$T_{para.lp}$ is the time spent in list processing in *para-lisp*, which does not include the time while the mutator suspends the computation.

$T_{para.gc}$ is the time spent in garbage collection in *para-lisp*.

Then, $T_{para.total}$ and I are expressed by

$$T_{para.total} = max(T_{para.lp}, T_{para.gc}), \tag{11.10}$$

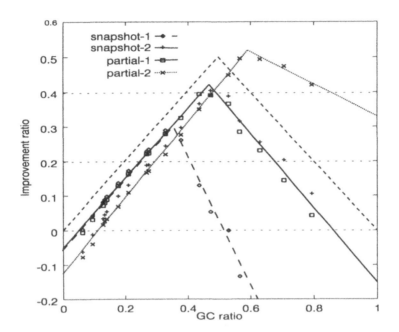

Figure 9: GC Ratio v.s. Improvement Ratio

$$I = min(\frac{T_{seq.total} - T_{para.lp}}{T_{seq.total}}, \frac{T_{seq.total} - T_{para.gc}}{T_{seq.total}}). \qquad (11.11)$$

We also define the following parameters:

$$T_{para.lp} = T_{seq.lp} + T_{para.oh}, \qquad (11.12)$$

$$O = \frac{T_{para.oh}}{T_{para.total}}, \qquad (11.13)$$

$$n = \frac{T_{para.gc}}{T_{seq.gc}}. \qquad (11.14)$$

$T_{para.oh}$ is overhead time of the mutator, O is the overhead ratio of the mutator, and n represents the overhead of the collector. Then I is expressed by

$$\begin{aligned} I &= min(\frac{T_{seq.total} - T_{seq.oh} - T_{para.lp}}{T_{seq.total}}, \frac{T_{seq.total} - nT_{seq.gc}}{T_{seq.total}}) \\ &= min(G - O, 1 - nG). \qquad (11.15) \end{aligned}$$

5.2   Experimental Results

Figure 9 shows the relationship between R_G and I. The benchmark program repeats consumption of an object. The number of repetitions is specified by its argument[6].

---

[6](defun eatcell (n) (cond ((= n 0) nil)
        (t (cons nil nil) (eatcell (- n 1)))))

In order to measure the improvement ratio under various GC ratios, we made an active list and varied its length.

The dotted line shows an ideal improvement ratio of a parallel garbage collection when one collector is executed. When R_G is less than 0.5, the reduced processing time by using the parallel garbage collector ($T_{seq.total} - T_{para.total}$) is equivalent to the time spent for garbage collection in *seq-lisp*. Therefore, the ideal improvement ratio is expressed by

$$I = R_G \qquad (R_G \leq 0.5). \qquad (11.16)$$

When R_G exceeds 0.5, the time spent for garbage collection is longer than that spent for list processing in *seq-lisp*. In this case, the mutator suspends the computation because the reclamation of objects by the collector can not catch up with the consumption of objects by the mutator, and $T_{para.total}$ is equivalent to $T_{seq.gc}$. Consequently, the ideal improvement ratio is expressed by

$$I = \frac{T_{seq.total} - T_{para.total}}{T_{seq.total}} = \frac{T_{seq.total} - T_{seq.gc}}{T_{seq.total}} = 1 - R_G \qquad (R_G > 0.5). \qquad (11.17)$$

In short, the continually increasing part of the graph indicates the stable state, that is, we can understand the maximum value of R_G from the peak of the graph, in which real-time processing is possible. The ideal improvement ratio is also derived from expression 11.15 when $O = 0$ and $n = 1$. We can derive O from the y-intercept of the graph. The slope of the decreasing part indicates n.

In the snapshot algorithm, when one collector is used (snapshot-1), real-time processing is possible until the GC ratio exceeds approximately 33%. O is about 5% and n is 2, which indicates that the snapshot collector needs two GC cycles for the reclamation of O *type* objects. I is less than 0 for $R_G > 0.5$, that is, the processing of *para-lisp* is slower than *seq-lisp* for such applications. When two collectors are executed, although O is 12%, applications can be processed in real-time until GC ratio exceeds about 50% (snapshot-2).

In partial marking collection, when one collector is used, free objects are never exhausted until R_G exceeds about 50%. The graph gives rough agreement with ideal processing and is almost the same as the snapshot collection when two collectors are used. O is about 5% and n is 1. The processing of *para-lisp* is faster than *seq-lisp* until R_G exceeds about 85%. The performance of the partial marking collection when one collector is used is equivalent to the snapshot collection where two collectors are used. The maximum value of I is about 40%, which means the processing time of applications in *para-lisp* is about 60% of the one in *seq-lisp*. When two collectors are executed, the mutator never suspends computation because of the exhaustion of free objects until R_G exceeds about 60%. O is about 12% and n is 0.5. Although I is negative where R_G is low because of the overhead of the mutator, we succeeded in improving the performance when R_G is low by controlling the execution of the collector, that is, the collector suspends executing the GC cycles until the amount of free objects falls below a certain threshold[13].

5.3   A Comparison with Analysis Results

The following compares the results of our analysis described in the previous section with experimental results. Using the parameters presented in the previous section, R_G is expressed by

$$
\begin{aligned}
R_G &= \frac{sN + mL}{r(N - L) + sN + mL} \\
&= \frac{sN + mL}{(r + s)N + (m - r)L}.
\end{aligned} \tag{11.18}
$$

When running the benchmark program, b can be approximated 0 because the benchmark disposes objects immediately after the allocation, and there are a few O *type* garbage objects which were used by the system. Therefore, G^{crit} can be expressed by

$$
G^{crit} = \frac{sN + mL}{r} \tag{11.19}
$$

for both snapshot collection and partial marking collection. In our experiments, s, m, N, and r depend on the system and running applications, and their values are fixed. Therefore, the only factor which decides the mutator's state (stable or not) is L. In the snapshot collection, the maximum value of L in the stable state ($L_{max.snapshot}$) is derived from expression 11.4 and 11.19 as follows:

$$
L_{max.snapshot} = \frac{r - 2s}{r + 2m} N. \tag{11.20}
$$

From $L_{max.snapshot}$ and expression 11.18, we can derive the maximum value of R_G in the stable state as

$$
G_{max.snapshot} = \frac{1}{3}. \tag{11.21}
$$

This is very close to the experimental results, which show that the maximum GC ratio in the stable state is about 33%.

Similarly in the partial marking collection, according to expression 11.7 and 11.19, the maximum value of L in the stable state ($L_{max.partial}$) is derived as

$$
L_{max.partial} = \frac{r - 2s}{r + m} N. \tag{11.22}
$$

From $L_{max.partial}$ and expression 11.18, we can derive the maximum value of R_G in the stable state as

$$
\begin{aligned}
G_{max.partial} &= \frac{rm - sm + sr}{2rm - sm + 3sr} \\
&= \frac{1}{2} - \frac{\frac{1}{2}s(m + r)}{2rm - sm + 3sr}.
\end{aligned} \tag{11.23}
$$

Considering the value of s, m, and r, $G_{max.partial}$ is approximated by 0.5 and it is very close to the experimental result. Since the benchmark used in our experiments is a tiny application and contains no operations for pointer replacement such as *rplaca* and *rplacd*, we conducted another experiment using workloads that included *boyer*[3] and *bit*[7] in which there are many long-lived objects and pointer replacement. The results are almost the same as in the previous experiments, that is, the maximum GC ratio in the stable state is about 33% and 50% when one collector is used for snapshot and partial marking collection respectively.

6 Partial Marking Garbage Collection on EusLisp

EusLisp is a *Common Lisp* based object-oriented programming language with geometric modeling facilities whose goal is an implementation of a 3D geometric modeler and its application to high-level robot programming. In order to extend the application fields in a more real-time oriented direction, EusLisp supports parallel and synchronous programming using the Solaris 2 operating system's multi-thread facility. Since the first version of EusLisp provided only a stop-and-mark-sweep collector, garbage collection limits the performance of real-time processing. Usually, it takes several hundred milliseconds for one garbage collection and mutators are forced to suspend in the meantime. This suspension becomes a grave issue for some applications such as image processing in frame rate and controlling servo mechanisms of actuators. In order to improve the real-time performance of EusLisp, we incorporate partial marking garbage collection into it. This section describes the design and the experimental results of that incorporation.

6.1 Design of Partial Marking Garbage Collector on EusLisp

We designed and implemented a multi-mutator and multi-collector Lisp as a prototype system of EusLisp using parallel garbage collection[11, 12]. Our system has some mutators and collectors which can run in parallel. Furthermore, the system controls not only the execution of the collectors, but also the number of the mutators and the collectors. That is, the system turns a collector into a mutator when there are enough free objects for computation, or turns a mutator into a collector when the mutators have consumed so many objects that garbage objects should be reclaimed quickly. In order to control multiple mutators and collectors, the system has a thread for scheduling. The scheduler thread watches the number of free objects and invokes the collectors if it falls below a certain threshold. It also decides the number of mutators and collectors according to such factors as the number of free objects and the pace of objects' consumption by the mutator.

We implemented partial marking garbage collection on EusLisp using the same strategy as in our prototype system. Since the mutator suspends computation during the root insertion phase, we focused on the time for root insertion. The process of root insertion consists of the following procedures:

---

[7]*bit* receives a list and returns a list of binary tree whose nodes are the elements of the list

step 1   A scheduler thread notifies the mutators to start the root insertion. All
collectors do nothing until they receive the next notification.

step 2   All mutators synchronize when they receive the notification.

step 3   All mutators push their root set onto the marking stack. Then, every
mutator suspends computation until it receives notification to resume.

step 4   A scheduler thread pushes the global roots onto the marking stack.

step 5   A scheduler thread orders the mutators and collectors to resume processing.

In our implementation, a scheduler thread uses a *signal* for notification. The time for
steps 1, 2, and 5 depend on the number of mutators. The time for step 3 depends on
the depth of the mutator's activation stack. Although the time for step 4 depends
on the number of global roots, it is usually fixed.

6.2   Experimental Results

Using various workloads, we measured the root insertion time for the various number of mutators on a Sun Microsystem's multiprocessor workstation (SPARC Center
2000, 16CPUs). We also broke down the root insertion time. Figure 10 shows the average root insertion time, notification time using a signal, and barrier synchronization
time.

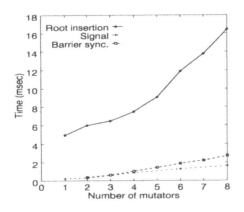
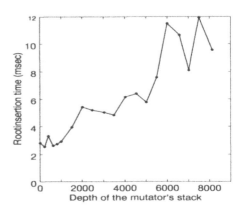

Figure 10: A relationship between the   Figure 11: Depth of the mutator's stack
number of threads and root insertion   v.s. root insertion time
time

As the number of mutators increased, the time for sending a signal and barrier
synchronization time increased. However, they are relatively short compared to the
root insertion time, that is, the greatest part of the root insertion time is considered
as the time spent for step 3. Figure 11 shows the relationship between the depth of
the mutator's activation stack and the root insertion time when only one mutator
is running. Although the root insertion time depends on the depth of the mutator's

stack, it varies from several milliseconds to 12 milliseconds. As described before, the stop-and-collect garbage collector forces the mutator to suspend for several hundred milliseconds. The suspension time of the mutator by garbage collection is considerably reduced by introducing partial marking garbage collection.

7 Related Work

Most parallel garbage collectors are based on the tracing (copying or mark-sweep) methods. It is relatively easy to make reference counting collectors parallel. However, there is a severe problem of effectiveness. Parallel tracing collectors based on read barrier need special hardware for efficient implementation. Without specialized hardware support, a write barrier appears to be easier to implement efficiently.

An approach using the incremental update algorithm is proposed by Boehm et al.[1]. Their algorithm uses virtual memory dirty bits as a coarse pagewise write barrier. All black objects in a page must be re-scanned if the page is dirtied again before the end of a collection. However, coarseness sacrifices real-time guarantees.

Matsui et al. proposed *complementary garbage collection*, which is a combination of incremental update collection and snapshot collection[7]. Although incremental update collectors are known to have higher collection ability than snapshot collectors, *root-set-scanning* procedure in incremental update collectors is much more complex and spoils the real-time ability. To avoid this problem, complementary collector replaces the procedure with a new non-stop procedure based on the snapshot collection. Consequently, complementary garbage collection can provide the same high collection ability as the incremental update collection, and the same high real-time ability as the snapshot collection.

8 Summary and Future Work

Snapshot algorithms have a well-known disadvantage: most short lived objects can not be reclaimed quickly. In order to solve this problem, we proposed a generational parallel garbage collection named *partial marking garbage collection*. Partial marking collection improves the collection efficiency by limiting the objects to be marked. Following Hickey et al.'s analysis, we analyzed the performance of a partial marking collection. It showed that the performance of the collection efficiency is 1.5 times that of a snapshot collection. The performance of a partial marking collection when one collector is used is equivalent to the snapshot collection using two collectors. We implemented a partial marking garbage collector and obtained experimental results which were quite agreeable with the value that had been obtained by our analysis. For a practical use of parallel garbage collection, we incorporated a partial marking collector into EusLisp. The suspension time of the mutator by garbage collection is considerably reduced and it is several milliseconds. In general, incremental update collection is considered to be more effective than snapshot collection because most short-lived objects are reclaimed quickly. Partial marking garbage collection solve the problem of the snapshot collection and can provide an efficient and practical system.

Although partial marking collection succeeded in reducing the suspension time of the mutator, it is in the order of several milliseconds. In order to reduce the root insertion time, we are now investigating an incremental root insertion strategy, in which root set are pushed onto the marking stack incrementally.

Acknowledgment

Dr. Toshihiro Matsui, who is a developer of EusLisp, helped us with the incorporation of the partial marking garbage collection into EusLisp. We designed and implemented a prototype system with Mrs. Satoko Matsuo and Mr. Teruo Iwai. Dr. Eiko Takaoka measured the performance of the partial marking collector on EusLisp. Mr. Francis O'Carroll checked the English manuscript. We wish to express our gratitude for their kind assistance.

Bibliography

1) H. J. Boehm, A. J. Demers and S. Shenker, Mostly Parallel Garbage Collection, *Proceedings of International Conference on PLDI'91*, ACM SIGPLAN Notices, Vol. 26, No. 6, 1991, pp. 157–164.

2) E. W. Dijkstra, L. Lamport, A. J. Martin, C. S. Scholten and E. F. M. Steffens, On-the-Fly Garbage Collection: An Exercise in Cooperation, *Commun. ACM*, Vol. 21, No. 11, 1978, pp. 966–975.

3) R. P. Gabriel, *Performance and Evaluation of Lisp Systems*, MIT Press, Cambridge, Massachusetts, 1985, pp. 116–135.

4) T. Hickey and J. Cohen, Performance Analysis of On-the-fly Garbage Collection, *Commun. ACM*, Vol. 27, No. 11, 1984, pp. 1143–1154.

5) H. Liberman and C. Hewitt, A Real-Time Garbage Collector Based on the Lifetimes of Objects, *Commun. ACM*, Vol. 26, No. 6, 1983, pp. 419–429.

6) S. Matsui, S. Teramura, T. Tanaka, N. Mohri, A. Maeda and M. Nakanishi, SYNAPSE: A Multi-micro-processor Lisp Machine with Parallel Garbage Collector, Lecture Notes in Computer Science, Vol. 269, Springer-Verlag, 1987, pp. 131–137.

7) S. Matsui, Y. Tanaka, A. Maeda and M. Nakanishi, Complementary Garbage Collector, *Proceedings of the International Workshop on Memory Management*, Lecture Notes in Computer Science, Vol. 986, Springer-Verlag, 1995, pp. 163–177.

8) T. Matsui, *EusLisp Reference Manual*, Electrotechnical Laboratory, Tsukuba, 1995.

9) T. Matsui and M. Inaba, Euslisp: An object-based implementation of lisp, *Journal of Information Processing*, Vol. 13, No. 3, 1990, pp. 327-338.

10) T. Matsui, Multithreaded Implementation of An Object Oriented Lisp, EusLisp, T. Yuasa and H.G. Okuno eds., *Advanced Lisp Processing Technology*, Gordon and Breach, 2000.

11) S. Takahashi, T. Iwai, A. Maeda, Y. Tanaka and M. Nakanishi, Parallel Lisp System Equipped with Parallel Garbage Collection, *Transaction of the Institute of Electronics, Information and Communication Engineers*, Vol. J80-D-I, No. 3, 1997, pp. 247–257.

12) S. Takahashi, T. Iwai, Y. Tanaka, A. Maeda and M. Nakanishi, A Parallel Lisp System which dynamically allocates CPU to list processing and GC process, T. Yuasa and H.G. Okuno eds., *Advanced Lisp Processing Technology*, Gordon and Breach, 2000.

13) Y. Tanaka, S. Matsui, A. Maeda, N. Takahashi and M. Nakanishi, Parallel Garbage Collection by Partial Marking and Conditionally Invoked GC, *Proceedings of International Conference on Parallel Computing Technologies*, Vol. 2, 1993, pp. 397–408.

14) Y. Tanaka, S. Matsui, A. Maeda, and M. Nakanishi, "Partial Marking GC", *Proceedings of International Conference on COMPAR 94 - VAPP VI*, Lecture Notes in Computer Science, Vol. 854, Springer-Verlag, 1994, pp. 337–348.

15) Y. Tanaka, S. Matsui, A. Maeda, and M. Nakanishi, Performance Analysis of Parallel Garbage Collection Using Partial Marking, *Journal of Systems and Computers in Japan*, Vol. 27, No. 8, 1996, pp. 29–38.

16) D. Ungar, Generation Scavenging: A Non-disruptive High Performance Storage Reclamation Algorithm, *ACM SIGPLAN Notices*, Vol. 19, No. 5, 1984, pp. 157–167.

17) P. R. Wilson, Uniprocessor Garbage Collection Techniques, Lecture Notes in Computer Science, Vol. 637, Springer-Verlag, 1992, pp. 1–42.

18) P. R. Wilson and T. G. Moher, "Design of the Opportunistic Garbage Collector", *Proceedings of OOPSLA '89*, 1989, pp. 23–35.

19) T. Yuasa, Real-Time Garbage Collection on General-Purpose Machines, *Journal of Systems and Software*, Vol. 11, No. 3, 1990, pp. 181–198.

12

Garbage Collection of an Extended Common Lisp System for SIMD Architectures

Taiichi Yuasa

Graduate School of Informatics
Kyoto University

Taichi Yasumoto

Faculty of Integrated Arts and Sciences
Aichi University of Education

ABSTRACT

We report the garbage collection of an extended Common Lisp system for SIMD (Single Instruction Stream, Multiple Data stream) parallel architectures. This system and its language is called TUPLE. The TUPLE language is an extension of Common Lisp with capabilities for SIMD parallel computation. By providing a large number of subset Common Lisp systems running in parallel, TUPLE supports parallel list processing. For this purpose, each processing element (PE) of the target machine has its own heap in its local memory. Therefore, we need parallelize garbage collection in order to improve the performance of parallel programs.

This paper describes the current implementation of the parallel garbage collection on the MasPar MP–1, a SIMD parallel computer with at least 1024 PEs. The presented techniques can be applied to other SIMD machines, since the discussions in the paper assume common features of SIMD architectures.

1 Introduction

TUPLE is an extension of Common Lisp [6] with functions for SIMD parallel computation. The TUPLE system is based on KCL [9] (Kyoto Common Lisp), a full-set Common Lisp system developed by the group including the first author. The TUPLE system is currently running on the MasPar MP-1, a SIMD parallel computer with at least 1024 PEs. While the original KCL is written partly in C and partly in Common Lisp, the TUPLE system on the MasPar is written partly in MPL [16], the extended C language on the MasPar, and partly in TUPLE itself.

The TUPLE system consists of a large number of subset Common Lisp systems, called PE subsystems, that run in parallel. In addition, there is a full-set Common system, called the front-end system, with which the user interacts to develop parallel programs.

Each PE subsystem has its own heap in its local memory. Since any object in a heap can be referenced from heaps of the other PEs, each PE subsystem cannot perform garbage collection independently. In addition, the garbage collection algorithm has to be designed carefully so that more PEs can participate in the computation at the same time. Without an efficient garbage collection algorithm that overcomes these difficulties, we could not obtain an efficient parallel list processing environment on SIMD architectures.

This paper reports the garbage collection algorithm of the TUPLE system. We first overview the memory management of the TUPLE system in Section 2. Then in Section 3, we propose a garbage collection algorithm that is suitable for SIMD architectures. We will discuss the efficiency of the algorithm, based on the results of some evaluation tests in Section 4. Details of the TUPLE language is beyond the scope of this paper (refer to [10]). In this paper, we sometimes use general Lisp terms prefixed with "PE." In such a case, the prefix "PE" means "in/for the PE subsystems", unless mentioned otherwise. For instance, "a PE variable" means a variable in the PE subsystems.

2   Memory Management of TUPLE

The MasPar MP-1 consists of two parts: the front-end UNIX workstation and the back-end. The back-end consists of the array control unit (ACU), which broadcasts instructions to PEs, and the PE array, where PEs are aligned in a two-dimensional array. Each PE does not have its own instruction stream, but executes instructions that are broadcast from the ACU. The memory size in the back-end is relatively small. The size of the data memory in the ACU is 128 Kbytes and the size of the memory in each PE is 16 Kbytes. Virtual memory is not supported on these memories.

Communication between two components of the MP–1 is relatively slow. Communication between the front-end and the ACU, between the front-end and a PE, and between the ACU and a PE, take about 600, 15000, and 20 times, respectively, more than a single word (four bytes) assignment in the front-end. Although the former two communications are extremely slow, it is possible to improve the effective speed by data buffering. PEs are connected by a mesh network for local communication and by a router for global communication. Communication through these networks is also slow. Fetching a word from a neighbor PE takes about 60 times more than an assignment. Therefore, it is important to avoid inter-PE communication during garbage collection.

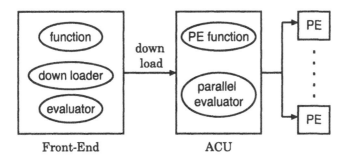

Figure 1: Implementation on MP–1.

2.1 Heaps

Roughly speaking, a TUPLE program consists of ordinary Common Lisp functions and *PE functions*. Ordinary functions are executed sequentially by the front-end system as in ordinary Common Lisp systems. Parallel computation is triggered by invoking a PE function from the front-end system, which then is executed in parallel by the PE subsystems. A PE function can receive arguments, invoke other PE functions, and return values, just as ordinary functions can.

In the implementation of TUPLE on the MasPar MP–1, PE functions are stored in the ACU, and parallel execution is controlled by the parallel evaluator in the ACU (see Figure 1). The PEs execute instructions that are broadcasted by the ACU. Each PE has its own memory space and operates on local data there. In the MasPar, the memory space in each PE is small, but each PE subsystem has enough functionality to perform parallel symbolic processing and list processing.

This structure of the TUPLE system requires three kinds of heaps:

- the *font-end heap* where ordinary Common Lisp objects are allocated

- the *PE heaps* where objects (including cons cells) of the PE subsystems are allocated

- the *ACU heap* where those objects common to all PE subsystems, such as PE functions, are allocated

Any object in one of these heaps can be referenced from any component of the MP–1 system. For example, an object in the front-end heap may be referenced from the ACU (e.g., as a constant value in a user-defined PE function) and PEs (e.g., by being passed as an argument to a PE function). Also, a cons cell in a PE heap may be referenced from the front-end (as a value returned from a PE function), the ACU, and the other PEs (by inter-PE communications).

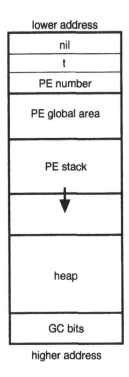

Figure 2: The PE data area.

2.2   Data Representation and Allocation

In addition to cons cells, each PE subsystem supports fixnums, short-floats, characters, and vectors. As in the original KCL, fixnums, short-floats, and characters are immediate data in TUPLE. Thus, these data objects are not allocated in any PE heap.

Figure 2 shows the data area of each PE that TUPLE handles directly. The run-time stack of MPL, the extended C language on the MasPar, is not shown in the Figure. The first words of the memory area are used to allocate three built-in constants: **nil**, **t**, and **penumber**. The value of **penumber** is an integer that uniquely identifies each PE. Next to these words is the PE global area, where user-defined global PE variables, constants, and vectors are allocated. This global area expands dynamically as the user defines PE variables etc. Next is the PE stack area where local PE variables are allocated and temporary values (including arguments to PE functions) are stored.

Then there is a heap area where PE cons cells are allocated. The total size of the data area is 8 Kbytes for the MasPar system that has 16 Kbytes of local memory per PE. Half of the data area is used as the heap. Since each cons cell occupies 8 bytes (i.e., 2 words), 512 cells are available per PE. Mark bits for PE cons cells are separately stored in the last part of the data area. Each mark bit corresponds to one of the 512 cells and 32 mark bits are packed into a single word. Thus we only need 16 words for the entire mark bits.

Cells in the ACU heap are homogeneous and each cell occupies four words. The first word of a cell is used as the data tag and the GC mark bit. Use of the remaining three words depends on the tag. In order to simplify the discussion of garbage collection, we assume that these three words have only pointers to cells in the ACU heap and the other heaps.

3 Garbage Collection

The original KCL uses the conventional mark-and-sweep algorithm. Free cells of the same size are linked together to form a free list. Some objects such as arrays are represented by a fixed-length *header cell* which has a pointer to the *body* of the object. For an array, for instance, array elements are stored in the body and the header cell contains various information on the array, such as the dimensions. Bodies are allocated in a special area called the *relocatable area* and are relocated during the sweep phase to make a large free space in the relocatable area. This implementation is closely related with the fact that KCL is written in the C language. Since bodies are always referenced via the header cells, we do not need to change the values of C variables that hold KCL objects, even when bodies are relocated. Note that the address of a C variable depends on the C compiler. Thus, this implementation of the original KCL increases the portability of the system.

Since TUPLE is written in MPL, a data-parallel extension of the C language, we essentially use the mark-and-sweep garbage collector for the back-end heaps. Since all cells in a back-end heap are homogeneous, we need only one free list for each heap, and no relocation is necessary once the size of the heap is fixed.

Recent sequential Lisp systems tend to adopt copying garbage collection. Copying garbage collection has two major advantages over mark-and-sweep garbage collection:

1. It does not cause fragmentation in the heap.

2. The execution time depends on the number of non-garbage cells, rather than the size of the entire heap space.

Mark-and-sweep garbage collection does not cause fragmentation in the implementation of TUPLE, because the size of memory cells in each heap is fixed. The second feature is not a large advantage for TUPLE, because the heap size itself is very small. Copying garbage collection requires twice as large a memory space than the total size of all allocatable cells. This will cause a serious problem for systems with a small amount of memory space. Therefore, mark-and-sweep garbage collection is more suitable for TUPLE.

The garbage collector of TUPLE is invoked when one of the free lists is exhausted or when the relocatable area of the front-end becomes full. As in KCL, the garbage collector consists of two phases:

1. the mark phase, when all cells in use are marked, and

2. the sweep phase, when each non-marked cell (i.e., garbage cell) is linked to a free list and each body whose header cell is marked is relocated.

The sweep phase can be executed for each component of the MasPar, independently of the other components, for the following reasons.

- Each garbage cell in a component is linked to a free list in the same component.

- There is no pointer that points to the body in the front-end directly from the back-end. Even when a body is relocated in the front-end, no back-end pointers need to be changed.

Therefore, we use the sweep phase routine of the original KCL without any modification. The sweep phase routine for ACU cells is obvious. It scans the entire ACU heap and simply links non-marked cells to the free list of the ACU. The similar routine works for cells in each PE heap, and this routine can be executed in parallel by all PEs, without any overhead such as PE synchronization.

The mark phase, on the other hand, is not so easy because it requires communications between the front-end and the back-end, and we had to exploit an efficient algorithm, which we report in the following subsections. We first explain the marking algorithm for PE cells, which is the most sophisticated part of the mark phase, and then we explain the entire mark phase of the current implementation of TUPLE on the MasPar.

3.1 Problems in Implementing the Mark Phase

As already seen, the implementation of TUPLE on the MasPar has the following unique features with regards to garbage collection. Most of these features can be shared with implementations of TUPLE on other SIMD machines.

1. It has multiple heaps: the front-end heap, the ACU heap, and a large number of PE heaps. The contents of a heap are independent of the other heaps.

2. Each cell in a heap may be referenced from a cell in another heap.

3. Inter-PE communication is relatively slow, and communication between the front-end and the back-end is extremely slow.

4. Each PE has a small amount of memory.

5. PEs can execute instructions in parallel, but only one instruction at a time.

The first and second features imply that garbage collection cannot be done separately for each heap and that communications are inevitable between the components during garbage collection. The third feature requires some mechanism to reduce communications during garbage collection. The fourth feature indicates that we cannot heavily rely on stacks and that it is difficult to use recursive algorithms. The last feature encourages us to develop a new parallel algorithm for garbage collection on PE heaps.

3.2 Marking PE Cells

In order to mark PE cells efficiently in parallel, we use a special bit called "the request bit" for each PE cell, as well as the ordinary mark bit. The request bits are used to remember those PE cells whose *car* and *cdr* fields are to be taken care of by the PE marking routine. Rather than recursively traversing pointers to PE cells, the PE marking routine repeatedly scans the PE heaps and sets on the request bits of those cells that are pointed to from within PE heaps. Here is the algorithm.

```
more := true;
while more do
    more := false;
    for i from 0 to M − 1 do
        if i.request then
            if not i.mark then
                mark_object(i.car);
                mark_object(i.cdr);
                i.mark := true;
                more := true;
            endif
            i.request := false;
        endif
    endfor
endwhile
```

where M is the number of cells in each PE heap, $i.request$ and $i.mark$ are the request bit and the mark bit, respectively, of the ith cell, and $i.car$ and $i.cdr$ are the *car* and *cdr* fields of the ith cell, respectively. Note that this algorithm is intended to be executed by all PEs in parallel. It is straightforward to implement this algorithm in a SIMD parallel language such as MPL. We will show later how the request bits are initialized, and how *mark_object* is implemented.

This algorithm requires no extra stack space and thus is suitable for marking on machines with very small amount of memory. Although the algorithm requires one request bit per PE cell, the size of memory required for the entire request bits of a PE is only $M/32$ words on 32-bit architectures. About the run-time efficiency of the algorithm, the algorithm requires M^2 time in the worst case. If every cell i $(0 < i < M)$ points to the cell $i − 1$, then the body of the **while** statement can mark only one cell per iteration. On the other hand, the ordinary recursive marking algorithm requires M time in the worst case. Remember, however, that our target is an SIMD architecture. Even if each PE can finish the marking in time M, the entire execution may require MN time in the worst case, with N being the total number of PEs, because of different shape of structures among PEs. In the current implementation of TUPLE on the MasPar with 1024 PEs, $M = 512$ and $N = 1024$. Thus the above algorithm is superior to the parallel version of the ordinary recursive algorithm, in the worst case.

3.3 Marking from PEs

The parallel subroutine *mark_object* receives an object x for each PE and behaves as follows.

1. If x is a pointer to a PE cell, then set on the request bit of the cell.

2. If x is a pointer to a front-end cell, then save it into the *FE buffer*. We will explain below how this case is handled.

3. If x is a pointer to an ACU cell, then call the ACU marking routine.

Note that the first two cases can be handled by PEs in parallel, but the last case cannot because the ACU marking routine can handle one pointer at a time.

In the second case, we use the buffer to temporarily store pointers to front-end cells, in order to reduce communications between the front-end and the back-end. This buffer consists of a single word per PE, and therefore the entire buffer can store as many pointers as the total number of PEs. When the entire buffer becomes full, all pointers in the buffer are block-transferred to the front-end and the front-end marking routine is invoked.

If a PE receives a pointer p to a front-end cell as the argument of *mark_object*, then it first tries to save p into its own buffer word w. However, the buffer word may already be occupied by some pointer that was saved by a previous call of *mark_object*. Even in that case, there may remain some free words in the buffer. Even if the entire buffer is full, we can still have a chance to find space in the buffer because some pointers in the buffer may be duplicated. These considerations suggest the possibility to defer control transfer to the front-end.

The algorithm below will be executed when there are more than one *occupied PEs*, that is, those PEs that received a pointer p to a front-end cell as the argument of *mark_object* and whose buffer word w is already occupied. In the algorithm, N denotes the total number of PEs. We assume that PEs are numbered 1 to N and the ith PE is denoted as P_i. By *free PEs*, we mean those PEs that received an object other than a pointer to a front-end cell as the argument of *mark_object* and whose buffer word w is not occupied yet.

1. Give a unique ordinal number *ord* to each occupied PE. Let N_s be the largest ordinal number, i.e., the total number of occupied PEs. Let s_i denote the PE number of the occupied PE with the ordinal number i.

2. Give a unique ordinal number *dest* to each free PE. Let N_d be the largest ordinal number, i.e., the total number of free PEs. Let d_i denote the PE number of the free PE with the ordinal number i.

3. For each occupied PE P_{s_i} such that $1 \leq i \leq min(N_s, N_d)$, save the pointer p into the buffer word w of the ith free PE P_{d_i}. This step consists of the following substeps.

   (a) For each occupied PE P_{s_i} such that $1 \leq i \leq min(N_s, N_d)$,

   $$tmp \odot ord \Leftarrow p$$

   (b) For each free PE P_{d_i} such that $1 \leq i \leq min(N_s, N_d)$,

   $$dest \odot ord \Leftarrow d_i$$

   (c) For each P_i such that $1 \leq i \leq min(N_s, N_d)$,

   $$w \odot dest \Leftarrow tmp$$

   Here, "$x \odot y \Leftarrow z$" means to assign the value of z to the variable x of P_y. This operation includes PE communication from the source PE to P_y.

4. If $N_d < N_s$, remove duplicated pointers in the entire buffer (which is full now) as follows.

   (a) Sort the pointers in the buffer so that the pointer value of the buffer word w of P_{i-1} becomes less than or equal to that of P_i for all i such that $1 < i \leq N$.

   (b) For each P_i ($1 < i \leq N$), if the pointer value in its buffer word w is equal to that of P_{i-1}, then clear w.

   Then repeat Steps 1 to 3 once more. After that, if $N_d < N_s$ again, then block-transfer the entire buffer to the front-end and invoke the marking routine of the front-end. On return from the front-end marking routine,

   (a) Clear the entire buffer.

   (b) For each occupied P_{s_i} ($N_d < i \leq N_s$),

   $$w := p$$

Operations in the algorithm are implemented efficiently on SIMD architecture such as the MasPar. We can use well-known $\log N$ time parallel algorithms for giving ordinal numbers in Steps 1 and 2 and for sorting the entire buffer in Step 4 (refer, for example, to [3]). In the MasPar, these algorithms are implemented as system libraries. Step 3 requires PE communications three times. These PE communications are performed through the global PE communication network such as hyper cube, and thus are highly efficient on many modern SIMD machines, including the MasPar.

Let us estimate the effects of buffering. Without buffering, the time to send M pointers is:

$$MT_{PF} \tag{12.1}$$

where T_{PF} is the time to send one word from a PE to the front-end. With buffering, the time to send M pointers from a PE to the front-end is:

$$B(M'') + KT_{PP}M' \tag{12.2}$$

where

T_{PP} is the time to send one word to a neighbor PE

$B(x)$ is the time to block-transfer x words between a PE and the front-end

M' is the number of checks to find an empty buffer $(M' < M)$

M'' is the number of different pointers among the M pointers $(M'' < M)$

K is a constant that is determined by the performance of the algorithms for giving ordinal numbers and sorting.

$B(M'')$ is the time to block-transfer different pointers to the front-end. $KT_{PP}M'$ is the time to search empty PE buffers M' times. (12.2) is equivalent to:

$$MT_{PF} \left(\frac{B(M'')}{MT_{PF}} + K\frac{T_{PP}}{T_{PF}} \frac{M'}{M} \right) \tag{12.3}$$

The subformula within parentheses determines whether the buffering is effective. The first term of the subformula represents the speedup obtained by block transfer. Since $B(M'') \ll M''T_{PF} < MT_{PF}$, the value of this term is much smaller than 1. The second term represents an overhead to find empty PE buffers. For the MasPar MP–1, $T_{PP}/T_{PF} = 0.004$ and M' is much smaller than M. Therefore, we can estimate that the value of the subformula is usually much smaller than 1, and that we can reduce the communication time by using buffering.

3.4   The Mark Phase

To simplify the algorithm, TUPLE always starts garbage collection with the top-level marking routine of the front-end. This routine scans the root locations in the front-end memory such as stack entries, and traverses pointers while marking all front-end cells it encounters. When it encounters a pointer to a cell in a back-end heap, it temporarily stores the pointer in a buffer and keeps going. There are two such buffers in the front-end: the *ACU buffer* for pointers to ACU cells and the *PE buffer* for pointers to PE cells. The buffers are used to reduce overhead of the communication between the front-end and the back-end.

When the ACU buffer becomes full, pointers in the buffer are block-transferred to the ACU and the marking routine of the ACU is invoked. On the other hand, when the PE buffer becomes full, the *requesting routine* is invoked, which sets on the request bits of those PE cells that are pointed to by the pointers in the PE buffer. When these routines return, execution of the top-level marking routine of the front-end resumes.

Note that the PE marking routine described in the previous subsection is never invoked during the top-level marking routine of the front-end. It is invoked only after all root locations in the front-end memory have been scanned. Thus all PE cells that are referenced from the front-end have been set their request bits on, at the first invocation of the PE marking routine. This reduces the number of repetition of the outermost loop of the PE marking routine.

The ACU marking routine traverses pointers and marks all ACU cells it encounters. When it encounters a pointer to a PE cell, it simply sets on the request bit of the PE cell. Again, this is necessary in order to defer the call to the PE marking routine so that as many PE cells as possible have been set on their request bits before the PE marking routine is invoked next time.

When the ACU marking routine encounters a pointer to a front-end cell, it does not invoke the front-end marking routine immediately. Rather, it saves the pointer into the FE buffer that is used to save pointers from PEs to the front-end. By using this buffer, rather than another buffer in the ACU memory, we have a chance to remove duplicated pointers to the front-end efficiently in parallel in the way described in the previous subsection.

As in the previous section, let us estimate the communication time, when we use buffering from the ACU to the front-end. Let M represent the number of pointers from the ACU to the PEs.

$$B(M'') + KT_{PP}M' + MT_{AP} \tag{12.4}$$

$$= MT_{AF}\left(\frac{B(M'')}{MT_{AF}} + K\frac{T_{PP}}{T_{AF}}\frac{M'}{M} + \frac{T_{AP}}{T_{AF}}\right) \tag{12.5}$$

T_{AP} represents the time to transfer one word from the ACU to a PE. T_{AF} represents the time to transfer one word from the ACU to the front-end. The other variables have the same meanings as in the previous section. The first two terms in (12.4) are the same as (12.2). The time to transfer pointers to front-end cells from the ACU to PEs is added as the third term in (12.4). For the MP–1, $T_{PP}/T_{AF} = 0.1$ and $T_{AP}/T_{AF} = 0.03$. Therefore, we can conclude that the communication time will be reduced to a large extent in ordinary cases.

3.5 Compaction of the PE Global Areas

The global area of each PE may contain (global) PE variables and PE vectors. (In this subsection, we treat PE constants as global PE variables, since the difference is inessential in the context of garbage collection.) Since these may become garbage, we have the chance to compactify the global area and leave space for more global PE variables and PE vectors. In addition, compaction of the global area makes more space for the PE stack.

The following design decisions of TUPLE makes it simple to compactify the PE global area.

- The words of PE local memories at the same address are used for the same purpose. They may constitute a single PE variable, or they may constitute elements of a PE vector with the same index.

- Each PE variable is referenced only via an ACU symbol cell. Thus if the ACU symbol cell becomes garbage, the PE variable also becomes garbage. When a PE variable is relocated, we need to replace only the pointer in the ACU cell.

- Each PE vector is also referenced only via a header cell in the ACU. Thus if the header cell becomes garbage, the entire PE vector becomes garbage. When a PE vector is relocated, we need to replace only the pointer in the ACU header cell.

In order to keep track of the ACU cell that points to each word in the PE global area, TUPLE has a table of backward pointers, in the ACU memory. Note that the size of the table is equal to the maximum size of the global area in each PE, which is 512 words for the current implementation on the MasPar with 16 Kbytes of local memory per PE. This size is negligible when compared with the total size of the ACU data memory. Note also that the table needs to be updated only during the sweep phase and when a new global PE variables or PE vector is being defined. Thus the maintenance of the table causes no run-time overhead.

As the result of compaction, the PE global area shrinks toward the lower address, and an open space is created between the global area and the stack area. This space is used as the stack area once the control returns to the top-level of TUPLE. That is, the pointer that indicates the bottom of the stack is reset to the first free word when the execution of the current top-level form is finished.

4   Performance Measurements

We are particularly interested in the effects of the following aspects of the proposed garbage collection algorithm.

1. parallel marking of PE cells

2. buffering for communication between the front-end and the back-end

3. repeated scanning of the PE heaps for marking PE cells

In order to evaluate the effects concerning these aspects, we implemented various garbage collection algorithms on TUPLE. For example, for the evaluation of parallel marking, we developed a version of TUPLE that is equipped with a sequential marking algorithm. We compared the two versions of TUPLE as follows. First, we setup the heaps with the same contents for these two versions, by running the same program. Then we forced the garbage collection and measured the execution time on each version. This execution time is the total time for marking and sweeping cells in the front-end, the ACU, and the PEs.

The benchmark program we used to setup the heaps is to construct a binary search tree in each PE [10, 12]. Each node of the tree is represented by three PE cells as illustrated in Figure 3. We repeatedly invoked the PE function bs-add, which adds one node into one of the trees in PEs. During garbage collection, all node cells are regarded as "used cells." These benchmark tests are performed on the MasPar MP–1 with VAXstation 3520 as the front-end and with 1024 PEs in the back-end.

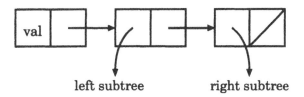

Figure 3: A node of a binary search tree.

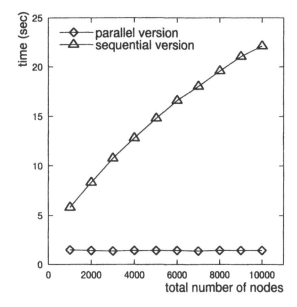

Figure 4: Effects of parallel marking of PE cells.

4.1 Effects of Parallel Marking

For this evaluation, we developed a version of TUPLE that is equipped with a sequential marking algorithm, and compared with it the version with the proposed algorithm. Figure 4 shows the execution time for garbage collection on these two versions. The x-coordinate represents the number of times **bs-add** is invoked, i.e., the total number of nodes in all trees.

In the parallel version, the execution time is almost constant, whereas the execution time in the sequential version increases as the number of tree nodes increases. The difference is quite large. For 10,000 nodes, the sequential version takes 16 times more than the parallel version. The reason is that, in the parallel version, even if the number of nodes becomes n times more, the execution time for cell marking takes only $n/1024$ times more, because of parallel execution by 1024 PEs.

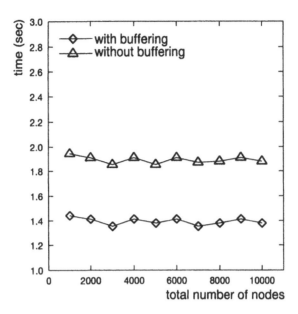

Figure 5: Effects of buffering (no pointer to FE from PEs).

4.2   Effects of Buffering

In order to evaluate the effects of buffering for communication between the front-end and the back-end, we developed a version of TUPLE that does not perform buffering, and compared with it the version with the proposed algorithm. Figure 5 shows the execution times on these two versions.

Although trees in PEs do not contain pointers to objects in the front-end, there exist pointers between the ACU and the front-end because the definitions of some built-in PE functions and benchmark functions contain pointers to front-end objects. In each versions of TUPLE, the execution time is almost constant. However, the version with buffering is about 1.36 times faster than the version without buffering. This difference reflects the effects of buffering for communication between the ACU and the front-end, since there is no pointer between the front-end and each PE. This difference would increase as we define more PE functions.

In this evaluation, there exist about 300 pointers between the front-end and the ACU. Since the total size of the buffer in PEs is 1024 words, all pointers are stored in the buffer and then block-transferred at the same time. The benchmark results indicate that, even with the communication overhead between the ACU and the PEs, our buffering method is still effective.

In order to evaluate the effects of buffering for communication between the PEs and the front-end, we modified the benchmark program so that each tree node has an additional cell, which contains a pointer to a symbol in the front-end. For the other respects, the benchmark program is the same as before. Figure 6 shows the

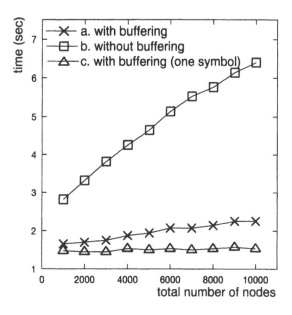

Figure 6: Effects of buffering (with pointers to FE from PEs).

benchmark results. Benchmark *a* is with buffering and benchmark *b* is without buffering. In these benchmarks, each additional pointer points to a different symbol in the front-end. Benchmark *c* is also with buffering, but all additional pointers point to the same symbol in the front-end.

For benchmarks *a* and *b*, the execution time increases as the number of tree nodes increases, but benchmark *b* takes much more time than benchmark *a*. For 10,000 nodes, benchmark *b* takes about 2.6 times more than benchmark *a*. This proves the efficiency of our buffering method.

For benchmark *c*, the execution time is almost constant. This is because our garbage collection algorithm removes duplicated pointers by sorting pointers in parallel. Although parallel sorting itself consumes some execution time, this overhead is small enough, compared with the gain that is obtained by using parallel sorting.

4.3   Effects of Repeated Scanning

In order to evaluate the effects of repeated scanning of the PE heaps for marking PE cells, we developed a version of TUPLE that is equipped with a typical recursive marking algorithm. We call this version as the *recursive version*. In this section, we call the version with the proposed algorithm as the *scanning version*. Figure 7 shows the execution times on these two versions.

Benchmark *a* is on the recursive version and benchmark *b* is on the scanning version. Benchmarks *c* and *d* are also on the recursive and the scanning versions, respectively, but these benchmarks mark cells only in a single PE (the PE with the

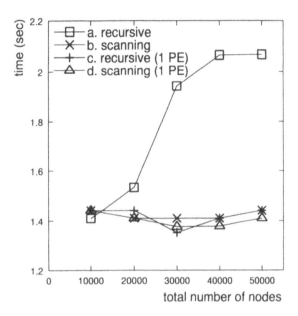

Figure 7: Effects of repeated scanning.

processor number 0). For benchmark *a*, the execution time rapidly increases as the number of nodes increases, whereas the execution time for benchmark *b* is almost constant. As the trees grow up, each tree forms its own shape, and there exist various shapes of trees in the PEs. This variation of tree shapes makes the recursive version (benchmark *a*) much slower than the scanning version (benchmark *b*). While the garbage collector is marking cells in the left subtrees, those PEs that do not have left subtrees are inactive (i.e., idle), and vice versa. The result of benchmark *c* proves this. If the garbage collector marks cells in only one PE, then the execution time of the recursive version is almost the same as that of the scanning version.

5   Conclusions

We have reported the garbage collection algorithm for an extended Common Lisp system for SIMD architectures. The algorithm effectively reduces the communication overhead between the front-end and the back-end, by using parallel sorting and buffering. Also, the algorithm repeatedly scans the PE heaps for marking PE cells, rather than using conventional recursive marking algorithms. This scanning method is particularly effective when the structures of PE cells are different among PEs.

The scanning method has one problem. When many pointers point in the direction that is opposite to the direction of scanning, then we have to repeat scanning many times. This is because the cell that is pointed to by such a pointer is marked during the next scan. In the worst case where all *n* pointers point to the same direction and the heap is scanned in another direction, each heap scan can mark only one cell and thus we have to scan the heap n times to mark all cells.

Remember that, in our implementation of TUPLE, all mark bits and request bits are collected together in areas that are separated from the heap area where all cells are allocated. This implementation solves the above problem to some extent. In the MasPar MP–1, one word is 32-bit wide. The heap scanning algorithm can process 32 consecutive cells with a single integer operation. For example, it can check whether all request bits of 32 cells are off, by testing whether the word for the 32 request bits is zero. In the worst case we mentioned above, each heap scan should be very fast, since almost all words for request bits are zero. In general, as the number of iterations of heap scanning increases, the time for each scanning decreases. Thus the total time for cell marking should not be very long, even in the worst case.

This implementation of our garbage collector shows that an algorithm that is efficient on sequential machines is not always efficient on parallel machines, in particular on SIMD machines. Even if an algorithm looks inefficient, it may give a high performance when it is suitable for the platform architecture. Our experiments give such an example.

Acknowledgements

Toshiro Kijima joined the design of the parallel algorithm and gave us many useful suggestions based on his experiences of designing and implementing his extended C language for SIMD parallel computation. The project of TUPLE is supported partly by Sumitomo Metal Industries., Ltd. and partly by Digital Equipment Corporation.

Bibliography

1) Okazawa, T.: Design and Implementation of a Common Lisp System Extended for Massively Parallel SIMD Computer. Master's thesis (in Japanese), Toyohashi Univ. of Tech. (1992).

2) Padget, J.: Data-Parallel Symbolic Processing. *Proceedings of the DPRI symposium*, Boston (1992).

3) Quinn, M.: *Designing Efficient Algorithms for Parallel Computers*. McGraw-Hill (1987).

4) Sabot, G.: Introduction to Paralation Lisp. Technical Report PL87-1, Thinking Machines Corporation (1987).

5) Sabot, G.: *The Paralation Model: Architecture Independent Parallel Programming*. MIT Press (1988).

6) Steele, G.: *Common Lisp the Language*. Digital Press (1984).

7) Steele, G., Hillis, D.: Connection Machine Lisp: Fine-Grained Parallel Symbolic Processing. *Proc. 1986 ACM Conf. on Lisp and Functional Programming* (1986).

8) Wholey, S., Steele, G.: Connection Machine Lisp: a dialect of Common Lisp for data parallel programming. *Proc. Second International Conf. on Supercomputing* (1987).

9)   Yuasa, T.: Design and Implementation of Kyoto Common Lisp. *Journal of Information Processing*, Vol.13, No.3 (1990).

10) Yuasa, T.: TUPLE - An Extension of KCL for Massively Parallel SIMD Architecture - Draft for the Second Edition. available from the author (1992).

11) Yuasa, T.: TUPLE: An Extended Common Lisp for Massively Parallel SIMD Architectures. *Proceedings of the DPRI symposium*, Boston (1992).

12) Yuasa, T., Yasumoto, T., Nagano, Y., Hatanaka, K.: TUPLE: An Extended Common Lisp for Massively Parallel SIMD Architectures (in Japanese). *Trans. of IPS Japan*, Vol.35, No.11 (1994).

13) Connection Machine Lisp Reference Manual. Thinking Machines Corporation (1987).

14) Introduction to Data Level Parallelism. Technical Report PR86-14, Thinking Machines Corporation (1986).

15) *Lisp Reference Manual. Thinking Machines Corporation (1988).

16) MasPar Parallel Application Language (MPL) User Guide. MasPar Computer Corporation (1991).

The Design and Analysis of the Fast Sliding Compaction Garbage Collection

Motoaki Terashima

Mitsuru Ishida

Hiroshi Nitta

Graduate School of Information Systems
The University of Electro-Communications

ABSTRACT

The design and analysis of fast sliding compaction GC (Garbage Collection) called FSC is presented and its implementation on PHL (Portable Hash Lisp) is reported. FSC is "stop–and–collect" type GC and adopts a fast pointer adjustment scheme and $O(A)$ time compaction scheme using a sorting technique, where A is all object size in use. FSC has the excellent features such as: (1) it performs sliding compaction fastest among most known sliding compaction GC, (2) it requires an additional space less than a thirty-second part of a heap, (3) it is applied to "generation". FSC has been successfully implemented on PHL being ported to many machines. The performance evaluation of different GC schemes obtained from experimental data shows excellence of FSC such that the time ratio of FSC to copying collection GC is ordinarily within 1.5.

1 Introduction

Automatic storage management which is called GC (Garbage collection) is essential to implementations of programming languages that handle dynamic data structures[7]. GC techniques have been improved for nearly forty years since the invention of programming languages such as Lisp and Algol, and now it is even more important to develop efficient GC schemes for large memory systems.

In this paper we present the design and analysis of fast sliding compaction GC called FSC. FSC is "stop–and–collect" type GC and performs its task fastest among most known sliding compaction GC including Morris's GC scheme[14], LLGC[18] and SMC[22]. The latter two are invented in a series of our GC development. The sliding compaction GC is also called sliding compactors, and its merit is space economy in managing variable-sized data objects as compared with the GC based on a copying collection scheme, or the so-called copying collection GC[9]. Another merit of sliding compaction GC is its property of "GOP" (Genetic Order Preserving)[20] which means that allocated order of every data object once established in a storage space (or a heap) is kept unchanged forever. This results from its sophisticated way of object relocation: all data objects in use are gathered up into one end of the heap called the *bottom* so that their allocated order is preserved and no "hole" of unused space is made (see Figure 1). The GOP enables us to make effective use of such allocated order in searching and sorting of data objects as seen in an implementation of Warren Abstract Machine[2] that needs to preserve the order of any two choice points[4].

We use some terms and quantities described in the following. A data object, d, is an element of a countably infinite set, D, of objects ($d \in D$), and is instantiated as a collection of contiguous machine words, or "fields" in our terminology. Each field being located in the heap can be addressed using non-negative integer, I, such that for a field, f, its address is given as $Adr(f)$ ($\in I$). The field that precedes f, if any, is addressed as $Adr(f) - 1$, and the field that follows f is $Adr(f) + 1$.

There is a special data object, r, that is the "root" of all data objects being in use ($r \in D$). Each data object is classified into two groups, a set of "active" data objects and another set of "inactive" data objects, depending on whether the data object is effectively referred to by r or not. The former is retained by the GC because it is in use, while the latter becomes garbage, and it is reclaimed by the GC. A field that is used for an active data object is called an "active field", and a field for an inactive data object is an "inactive field". A cluster is a brick of successive active fields such that adjacent clusters are separated by inactive field(s). The head of a cluster is defined as the field whose location is lowest among its fields.

A forward pointer is a pointer, p, that refers from its start node, f_p, to a destination node, $f_{\bar{p}}$, that is located higher than the start node, namely, $Adr(f_p) < Adr(f_{\bar{p}})$. To the contrary a "backward repointer" is a pointer that refers from its start node to another node that is located lower than the start nodes, $Adr(f_p) > Adr(f_{\bar{p}})$. Address constants, *bottom* and *top*, are the lowest and the highest addresses of the heap, respectively. Three quantities, S, A and N, express the number of total fields of the heap, the number of all active fields and the number of clusters, respectively. Then the load factor, α, is defined as A/S.

FSC has the following specific features:

1. It performs sliding compaction with a time proportional to A plus $Ng(N)$, where $logN \leq g(N) \leq N$.

2. It requires an additional space whose size is less than $S/32$ in order to make an offset table and two address tables inclusively.

3. It is applied to "generation" [13, 23] straightforwardly by virtue of data objects being allocated in order of age.

The sliding compaction GC is typically made of three phases; marking, pointer adjustments and data relocation. The time required by the marking phase is proportional to A, but the latter two seemed very expensive in time due to multiple scans of the heap. Therefore many interesting schemes have been proposed so that the time required by these phases becomes proportional to A by using a sorting technique[5, 15, 18, 22].

FSC also makes use of sorting to obtain the head of each cluster in order, so that all clusters can be scanned straight by skipping every inactive fields. The term $Ng(N)$ is an additional cost for sorting N addresses of all heads. This excellent feature is similar to LLGC and SMC, but unlike them FSC makes use of an offset table[20] for fast pointer adjustments. Since most data objects are made of two or more fields as seen in symbols and blocks etc. and each cluster is made up of one or more active data objects, the number of clusters is less or equal to that of active fields ($N \leq A$). In addition our experimental data show that the relation, $N \ll A$, is satisfied. Consequently the second term, $Ng(N)$, can be ignored, and FSC requires a time proportional nearly to A. In fact its actual processing time becomes the shortest among most known sliding compaction GC with $O(A)$ time space.

The additional space that is called W-space is used for two address tables, namely the first and second address tables, and the offset table. W-space is located at the highest address of the heap. The size of W-space is set to the offset table's size that is less than $S/32$, and it changes dynamically at run time. The first address table holds addresses that are gathered as a 'candidate' of the head of each cluster at marking of every active data objects. Then 'genuine' heads of all clusters (N addresses) are chosen from the table, and they form the second address table.

The addresses of the heads are sorted in increasing or decreasing order, which requires a time proportional to $Ng(N)$ as described above. The sorted addresses are utilized in scanning the heap by skipping every bricks of inactive fields effectively, because they indicates both start points (i.e., the heads) and order of clusters. Such a scan requires $O(A)$ time space, not $O(S)$

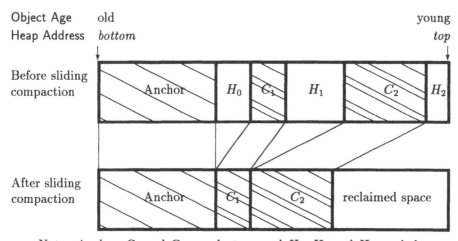

Note : Anchor, C_1 and C_2 are clusters, and H_0, H_1 and H_2 are holes.

Figure 1: Action of Sliding Compaction.

W-space may overflow when the first address table becomes larger than it. This occurs in case of a large load factor or high fragmentation of clusters, though it is rare to see these cases. FSC can proceed to sliding compaction as conventional sliding compaction GC, even if such overflow occurs.

The offset table is used to adjust pointers. It contains an integer value as an entry, called "offset register". Each entry corresponds to a "subspace", a brick of successive fields that is typically 32 field long. All subspaces are disjoined and they form the heap. Each offset register has a total number of inactive fields from *bottom* to the head of the subspace to which the offset register corresponds. The offset value to adjust a pointer can be obtained from an offset register and a single subspaces. The latter means to scan part of the subspace. In FSC, a mean value of the number of its fields being scanned is only 4.

FSC as well as other sliding compaction GC generates the anchor by virtue of GOP. The anchor is a special cluster of data objects being alive over several GC invocations and remaining unchanged at *bottom*. Obviously, the anchor is free from relocation and every pointers referring to it don't need adjusting. The offset table has no entries corresponding to both the anchor and the following brick of inactive fields (e.g., H_0 in Figure 1). Consequently, its size is $(S - S_A)/32$, where S_A is the number of such fields

Recently, applications based on Lisp have become very large, and they require a lot of storage space for their execution. Therefore, they need a more efficient execution time and working space for GC. This is the design goal of FSC.

The design and software implementation of FSC are described in Section 3. Data representation of PHL (Portable Hashed Lisp) on which FSC has been successfully implemented is also described in Section 3. Analysis of FSC is described in Section 4 using experimental data.

2 Background

2.1 Sliding Compaction vs. Copying Collection

As described in Section 1, sliding compaction GC is no longer inferior to copying collection GC for its time space. Moreover, the former is invoked less frequently than the latter, because the latter provides a half heap, the so-called "semi-space", for use at a time. If the load factor, A/S, is large, sliding compaction GC is superior to copying collection GC, and quite effective; it performs sliding compaction even if the load factor is larger than 0.5. If the load factor is very small, sliding compaction GC may be inferior to copying collection GC, because the latter can usually copy a single field datum two or more times faster than the former relocates such a datum, and this overcomes its demerit of the frequency: about two times frequent than the former. Therefore a value exists in the load factor at which they balance well, though the value varies with the condition of the computer system such as access time of the main memory and cache memory, architecture, etc. Further discussion on this point is given in Section 4 with our experimental data.

2.2 Sorting Technique in GC

Introduction of a sorting technique into GC schemes is not new in itself. Sliding compaction GC schemes making use of a sorting technique have been proposed for ten years[5, 15, 18, 22]. They commonly collect and sort addresses of active data objects or clusters in order to make them $O(A)$ in time space. Carlsson, et al. proposed use of *Linear Probing Sort*, and asserted that the time cost for the sorting is reduced to $O(A)$[5]. But no experimental results were shown, and it requires additional storage that could keep at least $2A$ pointers.

Sahlin proposed a method clustering active data objects, and got $O(N \log N)$ sliding compaction GC[15]. It requires no other additional storage, but needs traversal of active data objects twice and then sorting of listed N entries. They are more time costly than linear searching and linear sorting that FSC do alternatively, because their accessing patterns are scattered around the whole storage space.

Suzuki and the first author proposed new type GC called LLGC and showed its experimental data [18]. LLGC also adopts sorting and clustering. Clustering reduces the number of the elements for sorting to N. LLGC adopts an original algorithm for relocation, which do not need other bits than marking for each fields and additional storage space.

The first author, et al. proposed a successor to LLGC, that is called SMC[22]. SMC is similar to LLGC except for data relocation that makes use of Morris's GC scheme. It requires a special bit called Morris's "shift bit" for each field that holds a pointer. Several architectures require us to set least significant two bits of such a (byte pointer) field to zeros for data alignment, so that one of them can be used as a shift bit and the other is a mark bit. The Morris's GC scheme performs sliding compaction by scanning the heap twice, but the existence of shared active data objects makes it costly in time, as described in Section 4. Again we adopt an original algorithm of data relocation in FSC.

Koide and Noshita proposed GOP copying collection GC[12], which also uses sorting. It requires additional time cost in sorting active data objects. However copying collection GC itself differs from our framework.

2.3 Generation

One successful improvement in GC time cost is generational GC that takes life time of each data object into account[13, 23]. Each data object is classified by age as "old object" or "young object" in the generational GC. If young objets become garbage more than old objects, which is the assumption used in the generational GC, the GC can save much time by focusing its scavenge on young objects rather than all data objects. Most of generational GC is based on a copying compaction scheme, and provides two or more distinctive areas of the heap in order to group data objects together by age.

One problem with these generation GC is "forward pointer(s)" that refer to "young object(s)" from "old object(s)" crossing a space boundary. This is solved by the use of remembered set[23] that is an additional storage space kept for forward pointer(s) that need processing as root(s). Another problem is "tenured garbage", namely, a group of old object(s) that became garbage but remains in the heap. Many schemes have been proposed to reduce it effectively[1, 3, 8, 24]. However, their common approach is to adjust the "promotion threshold" not rigidly but expediently, that is the age when young objects are promoted to old objects, by using very specific and complicated mechanism.

Sliding compaction GC relocates all active data objects towards *bottom*. Therefore, a specific order of data objects is established in the heap, if an allocator employed consistently get fields for new data objects in order from *bottom* towards *top*. They are "younger" towards *top*, and contrary they are "older" towards *bottom*, because a data object, *d*, is created recently than any data objects that are located between *bottom* and *d*. If a node is created after its successor as seen in a typical implementation of a CONS operation of Lisp, backward pointers may appear in the heap but no forward pointer appear initially. A forward pointer is generated as a side effect of SETF–like operations such as SET and RPLACA. Figure 2 shows a CONS data object of Lisp that was created in that way, where all pointers will go towards *bottom* as backward pointers. If it forms a single cluster, the head is a field addressed as a_0.

MOA[19] is ambitious in the sense that it achieved "generation" on SMC. MOA as well as other sliding compaction GC generates the anchor by virtue of their GOP property. Obviously, GC don't need to relocate the anchor and to adjust the pointers toward it, which contributes to save GC's processing time. Moreover, MOA tries to distinguish a part of the anchor where there are no forward pointer(s) referring to other cluster(s), because such a part is free from GC processing. This can be easily done with only two pointers, though "write-barrier" is needed at SETF like operations similar to other generational GC. The time efficiency largely depends on its nature as shown in MOA's experimental data.

3   Implementation

This section presents the design and implementation of FSC on PHL which is a dialect of Lisp.

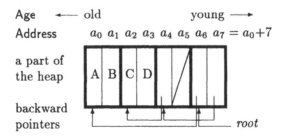

Note : a_5 addressed field is NIL.

Figure 2: CONS data object of ((A . B) (C . D)).

3.1 PHL and its Data Representation

PHL[21] is designed as a compiler–based portable Lisp system compatible with Common LISP[17]. PHL provides a large storage space such as 512 (2^{29}) MB, in which many data type objects are located. PHL has been successfully ported to various machines with different architectures such as Sparc, R4000/5000, Alpha, Pentium, because its source codes are written in C and PHL itself.

A data object of PHL is instantiated using fields, and our current implementation supports not only 32 bit long fields but also 64 bit long fields for 64 bit MPU machines[16]. The field is divided into two parts, namely, a tag part and an address part. They correspond to the upper 3 or 2 bits and the lower 29 or 30 bits, respectively, in case of 32 bit long fields. The tag is what is called "pointer tag".

Table 1 shows data representation of PHL: the tag and address parts. CONS data, symbols and blocks are reference data types. Their address part is 29 bit long and represents a heap address by the byte, in which their object is located. This can provide 512 MB of the storage space. Each object is located at a distance from a word boundary, so that the lower two bits are usually set to zero. One of these bits is used for a marking bit at GC, and the other bit is reserved for future.

Short reals, short integers and character codes are immediate data types. Their address part represents their value as an immediate datum using 27 (in case of short reals) or 28 bits fully. The lower two bits of their address part are reserved and usually set to zero similar to reference data types. These two bits cannot be used for coding the immediate data value, so that there is slight overload on specific operations of both short integers and character codes by additional 'bit shift' operations. However primitive operations of marking and unmarking as well as predicates of examining the sate of a marking bit of each field are written in simple and short codes, which contributes to the speedup of GC.

The short real data have an exponent of 8 bits and a mantissa of 19 bits. The latter is only 5 bits shorter than the mantissa of single precision floating-point numbers. Their size is larger than those of minimum exponent and mantissa of 'short floating-point number' that should have an immediate representation in Common LISP. It is also adequate to execute REDUCE 3[11] floating-point applications saving much space of the heap.

Table 1: Data representation of PHL (32 bit field)

Data types	Field		External form
	tag	address part	examples
CONS data	000	.... xy	(a . b)
Symbols	001	.... xy	ab
Blocks	010	.... xy	"ab" 123456789
Short reals	011	.... xy	1.0
Short integers	10	.... xy	−99999999 99999999
Character codes	11	.... xy	#\a

Note: 'x' denotes a marking bit.

'y' denotes a bit reserved for future use.

Short integers have a 28 bit long address part that can represent integers between $\pm 10^8$ (one hundred million). This value becomes the radix in case of long numbers being made as blocks. Similarly character codes have a 28 bit long address part where 7 bit ASCII character(s) are coded up to 4 characters. Character strings are also made as blocks using this form. Other features of PHL are not presented here for space economy.

3.2 Basic Idea

In this section we describe the basic idea that brought forth time efficiency of FSC.

3.2.1 Two-pass Scans

FSC performs sliding compaction by scanning clusters (or the heap) twice, while conventional sliding compaction GC usually scans the heap three times corresponding to offset table making, pointer adjustment and relocation processes. As Morris's scheme adopts a backward scan and a forward scan, two scans seem to be more efficient in time than three scans in case a larger heap is provided for use.

The key to a reduction of scans is the division of a pointer adjustment process into two parts: backward pointer adjustment and forward pointer adjustment processes. The former is joined to the offset table making process that scans clusters first, and the latter is joined to the relocation process that scans clusters second.

A backward pointer in a field can be adjusted, when the field is scanned first. This results from the fact that the offset table has been made partially so that the offset register corresponding to a subspace to which the backward pointer points is available. A forward pointer in a field can be adjusted when the the field is scanned again. This result from the fact that the offset table is made perfectly after the first scan and that the field to which the forward pointer points and higher fields remain unchanged so as to be able to check their marking bits.

3.2.2 Application of Genetic Order

The heads of all clusters are given as 'genuine' addresses. They are chosen from candidate addresses that have been gathered at marking of every active data objects. The candidate addresses are classified into two groups, namely, genuine addresses pointing to the heads of clusters and redundant addresses each of which points to a part of a single cluster (not the head). Since both of them are stored in the first address table, it is desirable to avoid storing the redundant addresses as much as possible for space and time economy.

As described in Section 2, a specific order of data objects is established upon their allocation such that any node is created after its successor. On condition that such an order is preserved from both GC and LISP operations, a sequence of nodal addresses becomes orderly that is obtained by visiting any CONS data object in "post order": CAR, CDR and then the node. A CONS data object of Figure 2 generates a sequence of a_0, a_2, a_4, a_6, for instance.

upper 5 bits	lower 27 bits	Contents
00000		unique offset value
1 x x x x		internal offset value is encoded

Note: 'xxxx' denotes an internal offset value.

Figure 3: Refined offset register (32 bit field)

To the contrary, each field of a CONS data object should be marked in "pre order": the nodal fields, CAR and then CDR so that its preceding field may be marked before. This enables us to stop storing an redundant address that points to a field whose preceding field is already marked. When this marking rule is applied to the same CONS data object described above, a_0 is an only address that needs storing. Therefore, we adopt a mixed strategy for visiting order: node (marking only), CAR, CDR and node (storing an address only). The fields of symbols and blocks are scanned forward (from their lowest field), because there is no established criterion on them.

3.2.3 The Offset Table

The idea of the offset table is already presented in the paper[20]. For a given pointer, p, if p's destination node, $f_{\vec{p}}$, is to move toward *bottom* by relocation, p needs adjusting for consistency with the number of inactive (non-marked) fields counting from *bottom* to $f_{\vec{p}}$. Such a number corresponds to the distance that $f_{\vec{p}}$ moves for upon relocation, and called the "offset value" of p. The problem is how to obtain it quickly.

One practical approach is to use the offset table, as described in Section 1. The offset value of a pointer, p, can be obtained by adding the value of the offset register to which $f_{\vec{p}}$'s subspace corresponds and the number of inactive field(s) of the subspace from its first (0-th) field to $f_{\vec{p}}$.

It is clear that a binary search scheme is applicable to each scan of the subspace. To say more precisely, if $f_{\vec{p}}$ is located in a lower part of the subspace, namely, $(Adr(f_{\vec{p}}) - bottom) \bmod 32 \leq 15$ in case of a 32 field subspace, the scan begins at its 0-th field and goes forward. Otherwise the scan begins at its last (31-st) field and goes backward. In this case, another offset register is used that corresponds to the next subspace. This makes a mean value of the number of scanned fields 8.

Moreover FSC adopts a refinement of the scheme described above. An extra value called 'internal offset value' is encoded in each offset register, that represents the number of inactive fields from 0-th field to 15-th field of the subspace to which the offset register corresponds. The internal offset value uses upper 5 bits of the offset register (see Figure 3). The MSB denotes that the internal offset value is coded (by 1) or not (by 0). The lower 27 bits are used for (ordinary) offset value. Note that the heap size represented by 27 bits words (fields) address is the same as 29 bits byte address.

The offset register contains a unique offset value in case of MSB=0. The unique offset value is applicable to all data objects in a subspace to which the offset register corresponds. In other words, every pointers pointing to such a subspace have the same offset value, and fortunately there is no need to scan the subspace any more.

In case of MSB$\neq$0, a quoter of the subspace is scanned at the most. The starting points are 15-th and 16-th fields in addition to 0-th and 31-st fields. For the former two, the internal offset value is also used. Obviously a mean value of the number of scanned fields decreases to 4, a half of 8.

The refined scheme described here contributes largely to speed up the pointer adjustment. Our experimental data shows that the refined scheme carries out each pointer adjustment faster than both Morris's scheme and 'marking bit map' scheme[20].

3.2.4 W-space

LLGC, SMC and MOA that were invented in a series of our GC development all make use of an additional space to store addresses of active fields. They maintained the additional space effectively so that it is kept below 10% of S (LLGC) or 5% of S (SMC and MOA) for space economy.

FSC also manages the additional space called W-space effectively. The prime purpose of using W-space is to make the offset table whose size is $S/32$ (about 3% of S) at most. W-space is allocated in the heap (32 bit long field), so that the address of *top* varies with the size of W-space. The size that will be used for next FSC invocation is determined by the following formula considering the current situation. The new W-space size $W^{i+1}(i \geq 0)$ is:

$$
W^{i+1} = \begin{cases} (S - S_A)/32 & \text{if the offset table is larger than W-space.} \\ W^i - 0.5\,E & \text{if the offset table is smaller than a half of W-space } (W^i/2). \\ W^i & \text{otherwise} \end{cases}
$$

where W^i and E are the current W-space size and its unused space for the offset table, and $W^0 = S/32$.

3.3 FSC Processes

FSC performs the following processes sequentially: marking, ordering, offset table making and relocation. In this subsection these processes are described in detail.

3.3.1 Marking

The marking process marks all active data objects for their fields by tracing them from roots of a value stack and OBLIS. It also makes the first address table in lower side of W-space by adding new candidate address to it (see Figure 4 (a)). Each data object is traced in a specific order according its data type as described in section 3.2.2.

The maximum size of the first address table is fixed at the W-space size. Therefore addresses that need storing may be full to its capacity. If the first address table overflows, the table is abandoned. No addresses are stored newly, and the ordering process is skipped. This makes FSC conventional sliding compaction GC. If the address table is made successfully, FSC continues the ordering process.

3.3.2 Ordering

The ordering process makes the second address table in higher side of W-space and sorts addresses in this table (see Figure 4 (b)). An address, a, that is located in the highest field of the first address table is removed and then examined. If $a-1$ addressed field is inactive (non-marked), a is stored in the second address table using its first (the lowest) field, because a is the head of a cluster. Note that when the second address table becomes one field larger the first address table becomes one field smaller. There is no conflict of them. Finally the second address table contains N addresses that point to heads of all clusters. The task of making the second address table requires a time proportional to A at most.

Quick sorting is applied to N addresses stored in the second address table. Our quick sorting makes use of the remainder of W-space as a 'explicit' stack. If the stack size is less than N, insertion sorting is executed instead of quick sorting. It is clear that both require $O(Ng(N))$ time space. Consequently, the time cost of this process is the sum of $O(A)$ and $Ng(N)$.

3.3.3 Offset Table Making

This process makes the offset table and adjusts every backward pointers scanning the clusters once. This scan requires a time proportional to A, if the sorted addresses described above are available. The offset table grows in chase of 'vacant lot' of the second address table that is no longer used, as seen in Figure 4 (c). Therefore the second address table may be destroyed (addresses are rewritten with offset values).

If useful addresses were rewritten, that point to clusters being not yet scanned, some inactive fields and clusters have to be scanned till a useful address is found in remains of the second address table. If the second address table was not made, all fields of the heap have to be scanned from *bottom* to *top*

The offset values of backward pointers can be obtained using part of the offset table that has been made. Its last entry corresponds to the current cluster being scanned, so that every pointers that point to the same (current) cluster can be adjusted fastest.

The W-space size changes dynamically at run time considering its previous utilization. If the anchor unfortunately disappeared or drastically decreased in size, the W-space may be smaller than the offset table being required. In this case the offset table is made partially for higher subspaces (at *top* side). The garbage that may remain at *bottom* side is reclaimed at next FSC invocation.

A chain called "a–link" is also made simultaneously using a pointer stored in an inactive field between clusters in order to connect them. A–link is used at the relocation process, which makes the heap scan $O(A)$ in time space similar to the sorted addresses. Finally the roots of a stack and OBLIS are adjusted.

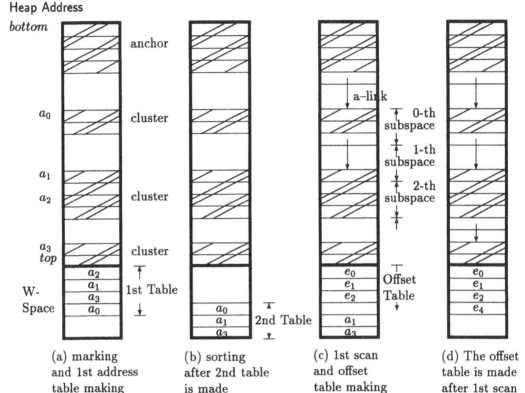

Note: The order of addresses in the 1st address table of (a) is an example.
e_i ($i \geq 0$) is an offset register corresponding to i-th subspace.
The W-space size is somewhat exaggerated for the purpose of illustration.

Figure 4: Action of FSC.

3.4 Relocation

The relocation process performs to unmark and relocate all active objects. All forward pointers of clusters are adjusted using the offset table. Every clusters are scanned once. When an inactive field is encountered that follows a cluster, the scan is simply transferred to the next cluster pointed to by a pointer in the inactive field.

4 Analysis of FSC

Our FSC has been successfully implemented on PHL that now runs on many machines of different architectures. Among them the machine used here is a workstation called Sony NEWS-5000 (its MPU is R4400SC/50 MHz). Three type GC, namely, FM (successor of SMC), FSC and copying collection GC is coded as the GC of PHL. Benchmark programs are TPU[6], Boyer[10] and a REDUCE 3.4[11] test program.

Table 2:   Performane evaluation of three type GC.

		0.10	0.15	0.20	0.25	0.30	0.40	0.80
		TPU						
S (MB)		0.10	0.15	0.20	0.25	0.30	0.40	0.80
G (sec.)	FM	0.48	0.26	0.19	0.17	0.13	0.08	0.04
	FSC	0.25	0.15	0.10	0.08	0.06	0.05	0.02
	Copy	0.18	0.11	0.07	0.06	0.04	0.03	0.02
n FM, FSC, Copy		26	15	10	8	6	4, 5, 5	2
A (MB)	FM	0.0317	0.0314	0.0301	0.0304	0.0314	0.0351	0.0288
	FSC	0.0321	0.0326	0.0309	0.0336	0.0312	0.0336	0.0277
	Copy	0.0324	0.0315	0.0306	0.0320	0.0306	0.0352	0.0300
G/nA $\left(\frac{sec.}{MB}\right)$	FM	0.582	0.551	0.631	0.698	0.685	0.570	0.694
	FSC	0.323	0.306	0.290	0.298	0.316	0.293	0.354
	Copy	0.214	0.232	0.229	0.244	0.208	0.213	0.333
Ratio FSC/Copy		1.59	1.32	1.27	1.22	1.51	1.38	1.06
		BOYER						
S (MB)		0.625	0.65	0.70	0.75	0.80	1.00	1.60
G (sec.)	FM	1.46	1.50	0.96	1.02	0.78	0.58	0.33
	FSC	1.21	1.10	0.99	0.88	0.72	0.43	0.31
	Copy	0.60	0.49	0.42	0.42	0.32	0.23	0.14
n FM, FSC, Copy		6, 7, 6	6, 6, 5	4, 5, 4	4	3	2	1
A (MB)	FM	0.4123	0.4265	0.3990	0.4179	0.4094	0.4240	0.4765
	FSC	0.4229	0.4207	0.4193	0.4165	0.4016	0.4160	0.4627
	Copy	0.4175	0.4083	0.3987	0.4186	0.4104	0.4237	0.4814
G/nA $\left(\frac{sec.}{MB}\right)$	FM	0.590	0.586	0.601	0.610	0.635	0.684	0.693
	FSC	0.408	0.435	0.472	0.528	0.597	0.517	0.669
	Copy	0.240	0.240	0.251	0.256	0.259	0.271	0.291
Ratio FSC/Copy		1.70	1.81	1.88	2.30	1.90	1.90	2.40
		REDUCE 3.4						
S (MB)		0.66	0.70	0.80	0.90	1.00	1.20	1.60
G (sec.)	FM	4.33	3.44	1.94	1.60	1.00	0.72	0.33
	FSC	2.57	1.90	1.26	0.96	0.77	0.45	0.26
	Copy	1.77	1.34	0.84	0.56	0.44	0.29	0.16
n FM, FSC, Copy		14,15,13	11,11,10	6, 7, 6	5, 6, 4	3, 4, 3	2	1
A (MB)	FM	0.5234	0.5250	0.5221	0.5228	0.5220	0.5300	0.5271
	FSC	0.5234	0.5229	0.5224	0.5237	0.5257	0.5278	0.5267
	Copy	0.5222	0.5229	0.5230	0.5204	0.5200	0.5304	0.5268
G/nA $\left(\frac{sec.}{MB}\right)$	FM	0.591	0.595	0.619	0.612	0.638	0.679	0.625
	FSC	0.327	0.330	0.345	0.367	0.366	0.426	0.503
	Copy	0.261	0.256	0.268	0.269	0.282	0.273	0.304
Ratio FSC/Copy		1.25	1.29	1.29	1.36	1.30	1.56	1.65

Note. FM : Fast sliding compaction GC based on Morris's scheme.
Copy : Copying collection GC (S indicates a semi-space size).

These three programs largely differ in GC's behavior. Boyer is a typical program that generates many long-life data objects intermittently. REDUCE test program generates many data objects being shared for a long time. The results of their execution are shown in Table 2, varying the storage space size, S, including the additional space such as W-space. Note that S corresponds to a semi-space size for copying collection GC. The data obtained are G (the total GC time), n (the number of GC invocations) and A.

The average GC time, G/n, of FSC, FM and copying collection GC ('Copy' in Table 2) is nearly level due to their $O(A)$ time space feature. However, the values of G/nA differ slightly in these programs. We call the value GC unit time hereafter. FM takes more time to process a single active field than FSC, while copying collection GC takes less time than FSC. FSC has a good effect on both TPU and REDUCE execution. The ratio of FSC to copying collection GC is within 1.5 for their execution.

Figure 5 shows the behavior of FSC and Morris's scheme more visually. The latter is used as a representative of conventional sliding compaction GC. The x-axis indicates the load of quick sorting by the quantity $N \log N/A$, and the Y-axis GC unit time, namely, G/nA.

Variations of GC unit time are plotted for the execution of three test programs. When the load of sorting is relatively low (less than 25 per KB), all GC unit time remains nearly low level in case of FSC, while it seems to increase linearly in case of Morris's scheme ('plus' symbols in the figure). Note that variations of GC unit time of Morris's are plotted in a position whose x-axis value is the same as FSC's (white tiny circles in the figure) using the same storage space. Since the unit of the x-axis is nearly S, this proves the well-known fact that conventional sliding compaction GC requires $O(S)$ time space.

When the load of sorting is relatively high, GC unit time becomes larger like a step function as seen in Boyer. This indicates that FSC is not so good at processing such a program in a relatively large storage space, though FSC is faster than most conventional sliding compaction GC.

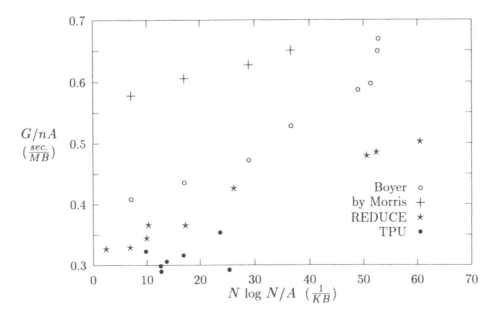

Figure 5: Correlation of $N \log N/A$ and G/nA.

5 Concluding Remarks

We introduced new GC, called FSC, which performs its task fastest among most known sliding compaction GC. FSC is a successor of LLGC and SMC that were invented in a series of our GC development. FSC has many excellent features to realize time and space economy. The time efficiency of FSC as well as other GC that makes use of a sorting technique largely depends on the cost of the sorting as described here.

When the load factor is relatively small, FSC can process a single active field nearly one and a half times as long as copying collection GC can do. The application of FSC to both generation and real-time GC is an interesting theme for future research.

Acknowledgments

We are indebted to all our colleagues, too many to be listed here, who have worked and/or are working with us in implementing, testing and refining many versions of FSC on various machines. Special thanks are due to Tsuyoshi Sasahara and Keishi Sato for their devoted contribution to this research.

Bibliography

1) A. W. Appel: Simple Generational Garbage Collection and Fast Allocation, *Software Practice and Experience*, 19, (2), 171–183 (1989)

2) K. Appleby, et al.: Garbage collection for Prolog based on WAM, *Comm. ACM*, 31, (6), 719–741 (1988).

3) D. A. Barrett and B. G. Zorn: Garbage collection using a dynamic threatening boundary, *ACM Conference on Programming Language Design and Implementation*, 301–314 (1995).

4) Y. Bekkers, O. Ridoux and L. Ungaro: Dynamic Memory Management for Sequential Logic Programming Languages, *IWMM'92*, 82–102, LNCS. 637, Springer-Verlag, September 1992.

5) S. Carlsson, C. Mattsson and M. Bengtsson: A fast expected-time compacting garbage-collection algorithm, *ECOOP/OOPSLA '90 Workshop on Garbage Collection in Object-Oriented Systems*, 1990, also available from ftp.diku.dk:/pub/GC90/Mattson.ps.

6) C. L. Chang: The unit proof and the input proof in theorem proving, *JACM*, 17, (4), 698–707 (1970).

7) J. Cohen: Garbage collection of linked data structures, *ACM Computing Surveys*, 13, (7), 341–367 (1981).

8) A. Demers et.al.: Combining generational and conservative garbage collection, *17th ACM Symposium on Principles of Programming Languages*, 261–269 (1990).

9) R. R. Fenichel and J. C. Yochelson: A Lisp Garbage Collector for Virtual Memory Computer Systems, *CACM*, 12, (11), 611–612 (1969).

10) R. P. Gabriel: Performance and evaluation of Lisp systems, Stanford University, CA., 1980.

11) A. C. Hearn: *REDUCE User's Manual, version 3.4*, The Rand Corporation, CA., 1988.

12) H. Koide and K. Noshita: On the Copying Garbage Collector which Preserves the Genetic Order (in Japanese), *Transaction of Information Processing (IPSJ)*, 34, (11), 2395–2400 (1993).

13) H. Liebeman and C. Hewitt: A real-time garbage collector based on the lifetimes of objects, *Comm. ACM*, 26, (6), 419–429 (1983).

14) F. L. Morris: Time- and Space-Efficient Garbage Collection Algorithm, *Comm. ACM*, 21, (8), 662–665 (1978).

15) D. Sahlin: Making Garbage Collection Independent of the Amount of Garbage, Research Report R86008, SICS, Box 1263 S-163 13 SPÅNGA SWEDEN, 1987.

16) K. Sato, T. Aoki and M. Terashima: A new PHL system implemented on Alpha-chip, Technical Report of *IEICE*, COMP97-94, *IEICE*, 57–64 (1998).

17) G. L. Steele, Jr.: *Common LISP, 2nd ed*, Digital Press, MA., 1990.

18) M. Suzuki and M. Terashima: Time- and space-efficient garbage collection based on sliding compaction, *Transaction of Information Processing (IPSJ)*, 36,(4), 925–931 (1995).

19) M. Suzuki, H. Koide and M. Terashima: MOA — A fast sliding compaction scheme for a large storage space, *IWMM'95*, 197–210, LNCS. 986, Springer-Verlag, September 1995.

20) M. Terashima and E. Goto: Genetic order and compactifying garbage collectors, *Information Processing Letters*, 7, (1), 27–32 (1978).

21) M. Terashima and Y. Kanada: HLisp — Its Concept, Implementation and applications, *Journal of Information Processing (IPSJ)*, 13, (3), 265–275 (1990).

22) M. Terashima, M. Ishida and T. Sasahara: Fast compactifying garbage collection (in Japanese), *Transaction of Information Processing (IPSJ)*, 36, (11), 2681–2689 (1995).

23) D. Unger: Generation scavenging, A non-disruptive high performance storage reclamation algorithm, *ACM Conference on Practical Programming Environments*, 157–167 (1984).

24) D. Unger and F. Jackson: An adaptive tenuring policy for generation scavengers, *ACM Trans. on Programming Languages and Systems*, 14, (1), 1–27 (1992).

14

Automatic Recompilation on Macro Redefinition, by Making Use of Weak Conses

Tsuneyasu Komiya

Graduate School of Informatics
Kyoto University

Taiichi Yuasa

Graduate School of Informatics
Kyoto University

Akihiro Fushimi

NTN Corporation

ABSTRACT

Many Lisp systems have both an interpreter and a compiler. In such systems, compilation of those functions that contain macro calls sometimes causes a trouble. The interpreter always uses the latest macro definition since macro forms are expanded at execution time. On the other hand, the compiler expands macros at compile time and thus uses those macro definitions that exist at compile time. Therefore, when a function is compiled, all macros that the function references must have already been defined. If a macro is redefined, the change cannot be reflected to compiled functions since macro forms have already been expanded. As the result, the behavior of a compiled function may be different from an interpreted function, depending on the time of macro definition. In this paper, we propose a mechanism to guarantee that a compiled function behaves in the same way as the interpreted function. A Lisp system with this mechanism uses a dependence graph of functions and macros. When a macro is redefined, the system automatically recompiles those functions that depend on the macro. The proposed mechanism can avoid redundant recompilation and discard unnecessary information for recompilation, by making use of weak conses.

1   Introduction

Many Lisp systems have both an interpreter and a compiler. In such systems, the interpreter can invoke a compiled function from an interpreted function, and a compiled function can invoke an interpreted function. This allows efficient program development. The programmer can develop a program interactively by using an interpreter while compiling well-debugged functions to speed-up test runs.

When we use both an interpreter and a compiler, compilation of those functions that contain macro calls sometimes causes a trouble. In Lisp, a macro form (a list whose first element is a macro name) is translated (or macro-expanded) into another form by the macro-expansion function associated with the macro name, and then the result of expansion is evaluated, instead of the original form. The interpreter always uses the latest macro definition since macro forms are expanded at execution time. On the other hand, the compiler expands macros at compile time and thus uses those macro definitions that exist at compile time. Therefore, when a function is compiled, all macros that the function references must have already been defined. If a macro is redefined, the change cannot be reflected to compiled functions since macro forms have already been expanded.

As the result, the behavior of a compiled function may be different from an interpreted function, depending on the time of macro definition and redefinition. This problem may be solved by:

1. avoiding use of the compiler during program development, or

2. recompiling all those functions that depend on a macro, each time the macro is redefined.

The former solution would reduce efficiency of program development since it increases the time for test run. The latter solution, if done manually, is tiresome and error-prone. Furthermore, the latter solution contains a difficult problem when a function object is referenced from a data structure. Even after the function is recompiled, the data structure still references the original function object, rather than the new function object.

In this paper, we propose a mechanism to guarantee that a compiled function behaves in the same way as the interpreted function. A Lisp system with this mechanism uses a dependence graph of functions and macros. When a macro is defined (or redefined), the system automatically recompiles those functions that depend on the macro. The proposed mechanism can avoid redundant recompilation and discard unnecessary information for recompilation, by making use of weak conses [4, 5, 6, 7, 8].

The rest of this paper is organized as follows. In Section 2, we show a typical situation in which the behavior of an interpreted function is different from the behavior of the compiled function. We present our fundamental ideas of automatic recompilation in Section 3, and propose the use of weak conses to represent the dependence graph in Section 4. Then, in Section 5, we present an implementation of automatic recompilation, which is actually incorporated into a Scheme [1, 2, 3] system, called TUTScheme [4].

2 Interpreted Functions vs. Compiled Functions

A compiled function may behave differently from the interpreted function, depending on the time of macro definition. As an example, consider the following definitions of a macro M and a function F. Here, we use the notation of Common Lisp [9] for macro and function definitions.

```
(defmacro M (n) ···)
(defun F (x) ··· (M y) ···)
```

The expression (M y) in the body of function F is a macro form. If F is compiled *after* M is defined, the form (M y) will be expanded as a macro form since M is known to be a macro name, and the result of expansion will be compiled. On the other hand, if F is compiled *before* M is defined, the form (M y) will be compiled as a function call since M is not known to be a macro name at compile time. Moreover, even if F is compiled *after* M is defined, redefinition of M cannot be reflected to the compiled function of F, because the macro form (M y) has already been expanded when F was compiled. Such a trouble does not occur as long as F is executed by the interpreter, since macros are expanded at execution time.

We try to solve this problem, by *automatic recompilation*. For the above example, the system automatically recompiles F each time M is defined or redefined. In the following sections, we discuss how such automatic recompilation is implemented.

Unfortunately, even if a function has been compiled with the latest macro definitions, this does not always mean the compiled function behaves in the same way as its interpreted version. This is because macro mechanisms of Lisp are very powerful. Lisp macros are allowed to do any computation during macro expansion. They can rely on the global status of the Lisp system. A typical example is as follows.

```
(defmacro M1 () (if x 'a 'b))
```

The result of a macro expansion of M1 depends on the global variable x. If the value of x is true, then the macro form (M) will be expanded to a. Otherwise, the form will be expanded to b. When compiling a function F that uses this macro, the compiler ought to use the value of x at that time. When F is interpreted, the result of macro expansion varies, as the value of x changes during execution.

We are not interested in tackling with such "dynamic" macros like M1. In fact, the recent definition of the ISO Lisp standard ISLISP [13] excludes dynamic macros. In the following discussions, we assume all macros are "static." Precisely, a macro M is static if it satisfies the following condition: Given an arbitrary macro form (M ···) of M, the result of its macro expansion is always the same (in the sense of the Lisp predicate `equal`), as long as no functions and macros used in expansion are redefined.

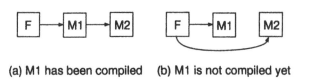

(a) M1 has been compiled   (b) M1 is not compiled yet

Figure 1: Two dependence graphs.

3   Automatic Recompilation

Our automatic recompilation mechanism guarantees that a compiled function behaves in the same way as the interpreted function. A Lisp system with this mechanism uses a dependence graph of functions and macros. When a macro is redefined, the system finds the set of those compiled functions and macros that depend on the macro, by using the dependence graph. Then the system automatically recompiles these functions, so that they can use the latest macro definition.

Actually, a compiled macro may also need to be recompiled, if it depends on the (re)defined macro. In addition, redefinition of a function may also cause recompilation of other functions/macros, if it is used for macro expansion. Thus the dependence graph should contain not only function-macro relations, but also macro-function, function-function, and macro-macro relations.

A compiled function/macro F is said to *depend* on a function/macro G, if G was called during the compilation of F. Here, by "calling a macro", we mean "calling the expansion function of the macro." Also, by "compiling a macro", we mean "compiling the expansion function of the macro." Note that this definition of dependence depends on whether or not functions/macros are compiled. Consider, for example, the following definitions.

```
(defun F () (M1))
(defmacro M1 () (M2))
(defmacro M2 () 'a)
```

If M1 is not compiled yet, compilation of F will call (the expansion function of) M1, which then calls M2 to execute its body. Therefore, F depends on both M1 and M2. If, however, M1 has already been compiled, the macro form (M2) has already been expanded. Thus, compilation of F will call M1, but M2 will not be called during the compilation. In this case, F depends on M1 but not on M2. Figure 1 shows the dependence graphs of these two cases. In the first case, as is clear from Figure 1 (a), F indirectly depends on M2. Thus, redefinition of M2 will cause recompilation of F, as well as recompilation of M1. In the second case, since M1 does not depend on M2, redefinition of M2 will cause recompilation of F, but not recompilation of M1 because M1 is not yet compiled.

The dependence graph changes dynamically each time a function/macro is defined, redefined, or compiled. For example, in Figure 1 (a), if M1 is redefined (but

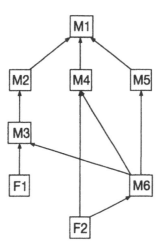

Figure 2: More complicated dependence graph.

not compiled yet), the link from M1 to M2 will disappear. In Figure 1 (b), if M1 is compiled, M2 will be linked from M1 after the compilation.

The order of recompilation is important when there are more than one functions/macros to be recompiled. Consider, for example, Figure 1 (a). As mentioned already, when M2 is redefined, both F and M1 must be recompiled. Since M2 has been redefined, the current compiled expansion function of M1 is obsolete. If F were recompiled first, then F would be compiled using this obsolete expansion function. The new compiled function of F would be the same as the previous compiled function, which does not reflect the redefinition of M2. In this case, therefore, M1 should be compiled first, and then F should be compiled using the new compiled expansion function.

The above discussion suggests that, before recompiling a function/macro F, all those compiled functions/macros on which F depends must have been recompiled. A recompilation order that satisfies this condition can be obtained by topologically sorting the subgraph that consists of those functions/macros that need to be recompiled. For example, suppose that M1 in Figure 2 is redefined. All the other functions/macros in the Figure must be recompiled, since they depend on M1 directly or indirectly. By topologically sorting these functions/macros, we will obtain, for example, the following correct order of recompilation.

    M2   M3   F1   M4   M5   M6   F2

Topological sorting is possible only when the subgraph is acyclic, i.e., when there is no closed loop in the subgraph. A closed loop is formed when a macro is defined whose expansion function recursively calls itself directly or indirectly. If this is the case, that macro cannot be successfully recompiled, because its recompilation uses the obsolete compiled expansion function.

In realistic applications, macros are sometimes defined "recursively." That is, a macro may be defined so that the result of expansion contains a macro form of

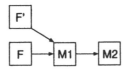

Figure 3: The dependence graph after redefinition of F.

that macro. Such a recursive macro definition does not cause any closed loop in the dependence graph, because compilation of the macro does not call its own expansion function. Also, even if a function is defined recursively, it causes no closed loop. Although it is theoretically possible to define a macro that causes a closed loop, the authors have never encountered such a macro definition in real programs. Thus, we would like to use the following rule.

Rule. Whenever a function/macro is compiled, the system checks if there will arise a closed loop in the new dependence graph. If it will, the system warns to the programmer and rejects the compilation.

Note that the rejected function/macro can still be executed by the interpreter.

The effect of automatic recompilation is different from manual recompilation by the programmer. Manual compilation creates a new function object associated with the function name, while automatic recompilation changes the contents of an existing compiled function object. This is because the function object may be referenced from a data structure. By changing the contents of the function object rather than creating a new function object, the data structure can reference the changed function object rather than the obsolete function object.

4   Dependence Graph with Weak Conses

Suppose that the function object of F in Figure 1 (a) is referenced from a data structure. In this case, if F is redefined and compiled, the dependence graph should change as shown in Figure 3. In the figure, F' is the new compiled function of F. The reason why F should remain in the dependence graph is that we suppose that the function object of F is referenced from the data structure.

When the system changes the dependence graph or automatically recompiles functions/macros, it is difficult to check efficiently whether the function object of F is actually referenced from a data structure. Therefore, we have to assume that all function objects are referenced from a data structure. Thus if a function is redefined, the previous function will remain in the dependence graph. However, this assumption may often cause redundant recompilation and unnecessary information for recompilation, since the function object may actually be obsolete, i.e., it may not be referenced from any data structure. By using weak conses to represent the

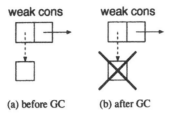

Figure 4: Weak cons.

dependence graph, we can discard unnecessary information and avoid redundant re-compilation. Weak conses are data structures which consist of the same components as cons cells. The car of a weak cons holds its pointer "weakly," while the cdr holds its pointer in the normal way. If the data in the car of a weak cons is not held normally by other data structures, it will be collected by the garbage collector (see Figure 4). By representing a dependence graph with weak conses, the system can automatically collect the obsolete function object at garbage collection time. For example, in Figure 3, if the function object of F is not referenced from any data structure, F will be collected by the garbage collector. We show the details of an implementation of a dependence graph with weak conses in Section 5.2.

5   Implementation

In this section, we present our implementation of automatic recompilation in TUT-Scheme [4], which is a Scheme system based on an incremental compiler and is developed by the authors. Our automatic recompilation system is written almost in Scheme, and the functions for changing the contents of a function object are implemented as primitive functions.

Macros in TUTScheme are similar to Common Lisp macros [9] rather than macros in "Revised[4] Report on Scheme [3]." In TUTScheme, it is possible to define a macro at only top-level, and the macro-expansion function is stored into the symbol whose name represents the macro name.

5.1   Incremental Compiler

In the system that has an incremental compiler, when a form is input at the top-level loop, the system immediately compiles the form and then executes its compiled codes. The incremental compiler can speed-up a program execution without spoiling interactive program development. For that reason, there are many systems based on incremental compilers [4, 6, 7, 8, 10, 11]. However, since these systems often do not have an interpreter, the trouble of macro redefinition will occur in these systems. On the other hand, some interpreter-based systems destructively replace a macro form with its expanded form at the time of the first macro-expansion [12]. In such systems, if

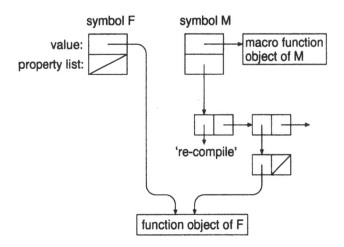

Figure 5: A representation of dependence graph, by making use of cons.

once the macro form in an expression is replaced with its expanded form, a change of the macro after that replacement cannot be reflected to the expression. Thus the automatic recompilation mechanism is also useful in those systems.

5.2   Implementation of Dependence Graph

In order to implement a dependence graph in TUTScheme, we make use of property lists of symbols. If X names a function or a macro, the symbol X has a property "recompile," and its value is a list of function objects which were compiled by calling the function/macro X during their compilation.

When a function/macro is (re)defined, the system appends its new function object to the property **recompile** of each symbol that names the function/macro that had been called during the compilation of the (re)defined function/macro. Note that although we do not append the symbol representing the function/macro name, if the function object is recompiled, the symbol will reference the new function object rather than the original function object. In Figure 5, we show a dependence graph when the function F calls the macro M.

The list which is the value of the property **recompile** is constructed by using weak conses. If the list is constructed by using normal cons cells, it may cause redundant recompilation and unnecessary information as described in Section 4. For example, in Figure 5, if the function F which calls the macro M is redefined, the property of the symbol M holds both the new function object and the original function object as shown in Figure 6. After that, if M is redefined, the original function object is recompiled even if it is not referenced from any data structure.

On the other hand, if the list is constructed by using weak conses, the original function object can be collected by the garbage collector, if it is not referenced from any data structure (see Figure 7). Note that the new function object of F is not

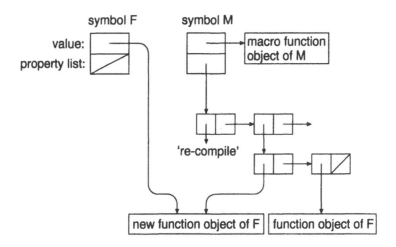

symbol F

value:
property list:

symbol M

macro function
object of M

're-compile'

new function object of F   function object of F

Figure 6: The dependence graph after redefinition of F.

collected since this is referenced from the symbol F.

Once the function object that is held by a weak cons is collected, this weak cons becomes useless. Such weak conses can be removed while the system traverses the list.

5.3 Recompilation

The data structure of a function in TUTScheme consists of the following elements.

- a function name

- a source code (a lambda expression)

- the compiled code

- a start address of the compiled code

- a vector of Scheme objects which are operands of the byte-codes

- an environment (a list which consists of values of closed variables)

- the number of arguments

When the system recompiles a function, the system gets the source code from the function object and compiles it. Then the system replaces the compiled code, the start address, and the vector in the function object with new ones.

If the environment of a function object is not empty, i.e., if the function is a closure, its source code must be recompiled under the environment information (such as local variable names) that was used when the closure was created. Thus the system need to save the environment information in somewhere. Furthermore, if a function

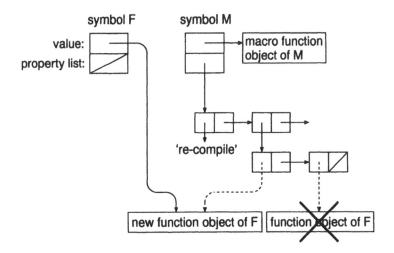

Figure 7: A representation of dependence graph, by making use of weak cons.

is recompiled, the set of closed variables in the function may be changed. In order to allow such changes, the environment of the function object must include all visible local variable bindings. This means that these local variables are regarded as closed variables.

In TUTScheme, however, a reference to a closed variable will be slower than to an unclosed variable since a binding of a closed variable will be allocated in the heap, while a binding of an unclosed variable will be allocated on the control stack. In TUTScheme, there are three kinds of local variable references:

1. References to closed variables

2. References to local variables that may be assigned by set!

3. References to local variables that are not assigned nor closed

In the first kind of references, the value of a variable is obtained by accessing the environment list, or by getting and accessing the cell that is stored on the control stack and has the value of the variable. In the second kind of references, the value of a variable is obtained through the cell on the control stack as well as in the first kind of references. In the last kind of references, the value of a variable is obtained by directly accessing the value on the control stack. The reason why the binding of an assigned variable is allocated in the heap is to support first-class continuations. In stack-based implementations of Scheme including TUTScheme, continuations are implemented by saving the contents of the control stack into the heap when a continuation is created and by restoring the control stack from the heap when the continuation is called. Thus, we need to allocate the binding of assigned variable in the heap so that the call frames both on the control stack and in the continuation object share the same binding in the heap.

```
(define (eval exp)
  (if (not (definition? exp))
      (bcload-eval (compile exp))
      (let ((name (definition-name exp))
            (result (bcload-eval (compile exp))))
        (if (function? (get-symbol-value name))
            (begin
              (record-caller
                (get-symbol-value name)
                (get-calling-function/macro))
              (for-each recompile (lookup name))))
        result)))
```

Figure 8: **Eval** for automatic recompilation

If the environment of a function object must include all visible local variable bindings, the method of the references to the unassigned or unclosed variables in the visible local variables are changed to the method of the first kind of references. This change reduces the performance of the variable references. For that reason, in our TUTScheme implementation, we abandon automatic recompilation of closures and thus an obsolete compiled closure will be used instead of the newly recompiled closure.

On the other hand, heap-based implementations of Scheme, which allocate call frames in the heap rather than on the control stack, can support recompilation of closures without reducing the performance of variable references.

5.4   Eval for Automatic Recompilation

The function **eval** in TUTScheme can be roughly written as follows.

```
(define (eval exp) (bcload-eval (compile exp)))
```

The function **compile** compiles an expression and returns the compiled expression. The function **bcload-eval** generates the byte-codes from the compiled expression, executes it by a byte-code interpreter, and returns a result. The **eval** for the automatic recompilation is defined as Figure 8. This **eval** is the same as the original **eval** if a given expression is not a definition. Otherwise, after the execution of **exp**, the value of the defined variable is examined whether it is a function (including an expansion function). If it is a function, the dependence graph is updated by using **record-caller** and **get-calling-function/macro**. The function **record-caller** takes two arguments, a function and a list of symbols, and appends this function to the property **recompile** of each symbol, if the property of the symbol does not yet have the function. The function **get-calling-function/macro** returns a list of functions/macros which had been called during the compilation of **exp**. In order to implement this function, the function **compile** is different from the original **compile**. This **compile** records those called functions/macros in somewhere during the compilation of **exp**. Then, those functions/macros that depend on the defined function/macro are found by **lookup**, and they are recompiled by **recompile**. The function **lookup** returns a topologically sorted list of those functions/macros. In our implementation, **recompile** notifies the programmer that a function/macro has been recompiled, so that the programmer can find wrong order of definitions and prevent errors when the program is executed on the other system that does not have the automatic recompilation mechanism. **Eval** finally returns the result of **exp**.

6 Conclusions

In this paper, we showed a typical situation in which the behavior of an interpreted function is different from the behavior of the compiled function, and proposed a mechanism to guarantee that a compiled function behaves in the same way as the interpreted function. Then we showed the proposed mechanism can avoid redundant recompilation and discard unnecessary information for recompilation by making use of weak conses. If a compiler is implemented with this mechanism, the programmer can use the compiler without taking care of the order of function/macro definitions, and find wrong order of definitions. This mechanism is especially effective for systems based on incremental compilers since those systems often do not have an interpreter.

Bibliography

1) Yuasa, T.: *Introduction to Scheme* (in Japanese), Iwanami Shoten (1991).

2) IEEE Standard for the Scheme Programming Language, IEEE (1991).

3) Clinger, W. and Rees, J., editors.: Revised[4] Report on the Algorithmic Language Scheme, MIT AI Memo 848b, MIT (1991).

4) Yuasa, T., et al.: TUTScheme Reference Manual (in Japanese), Toyohashi University of Technology (1994).

5) Terada, M.: Storage Management with Extended Weak Pointer (in Japanese), *Trans. Information Processing Society of Japan*, Vol. 34, No. 7, pp. 1610–1617 (1993).

6) MIT Scheme Reference Manual, Edition 1. 0 for Scheme Release 7. 1 (1991).

7) Kelsey, R. and Rees, J.: Scheme 48 (1992).

8) Rees, J. A., Adams, N. L. and Meehan, J. R.: The T Manual Fifth Edition — Pre-Beta Draft —, Computer Science Department, Yale University (1990).

9) Steele, G. L. et al.: *Common Lisp: The Language*, pp. 143–152, Digital Press (1984).

10) Bartley, D. H. and Jensen, J. C.: The Implementation of PC Scheme, *Proc. 1986 ACM Conference on Lisp and Functional Programming*, pp. 86–93 (1986).

11) ILOG: ILOG Talk Reference Manual Version 3.0, ILOG Inc. (1994).

12) Jaffer, A.: manual for scm (1993).

13) Information technology—Programming languages, their environments and system software interfaces—Programming language ISLISP, ISO/IEC 13816 (1997).

15

Applying Distortion-Oriented Technique to Lisp Printer

Hideki Koike

Graduate School of Information Systems
University of Electro-Communications, Tokyo

ABSTRACT

Computer users must interact with large amounts of information through video displays which are physically limited in size. The authors proposed a fractal-based method for information display control which can simultaneously display the details near user's focus and major landmarks away. This paper describes an application of this method to the Lisp printer. In general, the Lisp printer controls the display of a Lisp object by focusing on the depth of the object and number of siblings at each depth. However, with this method: (1) the total amount changes considerably corresponding to the target object; (2) it also changes considerably when each threshold is incremented or decremented; (3) it is hard to adjust two thresholds. We implemented a Lisp printer based on our fractal-based method, and showed its effectiveness through the comparative experiment to the traditional printer. We, moreover, extended this printer to a focus-oriented printer which uses another feature of our method, the integration of details and contexts.

1 Introduction

Information systems are now playing an important role as social infrastructure. Advances in computer hardware and software made it possible to manipulate a huge amount of information. However, communication from computer to human is mainly done through computer displays. Computer users must interact with such a huge amount of information through displays which are physically limited in size. This so-called "small screen problem[8]" has become one of major issues in computer-human interaction. In order to solve this problem, a number of techniques have been proposed, which are roughly divided into two categories: (1) large workspace approaches and (2) information reduction approaches.

Large workspace approaches. One of such examples that use physical large displays is MIT's Dataland[4]. Dataland uses a video projector to display various information on the wall. Virtual reality systems with head-mounted displays[5] are such examples that use virtual large displays. They display computer generated images in 360 degrees around users. However, if the amount of displayed objects continually increases, they will again face the same information overloading problems as normal displays. Text scrolling is another traditional and popular technique. Users can see a part of a text that is too large to fit in the display, through a small window and can see any part of the text by moving the window up and down. It is, however, desirable for users to be able to see their focus as well as major landmarks further away in particular applications (e.g., a program editor) as we describe in later sections.

Information reduction approaches. Techniques to display detail near a focal point and only important landmarks further away are called distortion-oriented approaches[11]. They are now getting popular in information visualization researches. One of such examples is Furnas's generalized fisheye views (GFV)[6]. GFV is applied to information structures that are represented as trees and makes it possible to display user's focus and contexts. However, since GFV does not consider the number of branches at each node, the display amount considerably changes when users move their focus of attention.

The author proposed another distortion-oriented algorithm called FractalView[9] which uses a fractal function to calculate the degree of importance of each node. FractalView can display focus and contexts and can minimize the difference in the display amount when users change their focus of attention.

This paper describes a Lisp printer which is an application of FractalView. The goal of the paper is to implement an application of FractalView and to show its effectiveness. Although we did not intend to make a complete Lisp printer, our prototype is practical and is superior to traditional Lisp printers in some points. The next section briefly describes the FractalView algorithm. Section 3 points out issues in traditional Lisp printers and proposes the FractalView Lisp printer. Section 4 shows session examples with both printers. Section 5 describes a focus-oriented printer. Section 6 discusses the problems of our approach. Section 7 is a conclusion.

2   FractalView

As is well known, a word "fractal" was proposed by B. Mandelbrot[12] and it represents self-similar objects in a broad sense. For example, a triadic Koch curve which is frequently referenced as an example of fractal figures has strict self-similarity. On the other hand, natural objects, such as coastline, trees, clouds and so on, are not strictly self-similar. It is, however, observed that they have statistical self-similarity. The fractal is a measure of complexity in mathematics and is used to model various natural phenomena in physics. In engineering fields, fractal is mostly associated with applications in image synthesis[2] or image processing.

FractalView applied the concept of fractal to information structures. When we draw fractal figures, we use a certain level of abstraction of them because real frac-

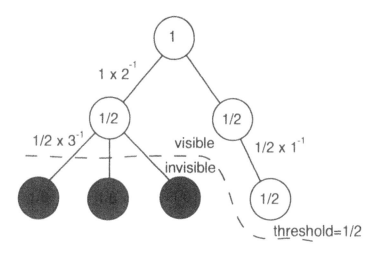

Figure 1: An example of propagation.

tal figures are obtained in the infinite state. This approximation mechanism is an abstraction of the complex object with a certain scale which is set by an observer. FractalView makes it possible to display an abstraction of information structures by regarding information structures as complex object.

FractalView algorithm is summarized as follows. Suppose each node x in a logical tree structure has a value Fv_x. Each Fv_x is calculated by using the following equation.

$$\begin{cases} Fv_{focus} & = & 1 \\ Fv_{child\_of\_x} & = & r_x \times Fv_x \end{cases} \tag{15.1}$$

$$r_x = CN_x^{-\frac{1}{D}}$$

where N_x is the number of siblings at node x; D is an appropriate constant value; and C is a constant value satisfying $0 < C \leq 1$.

Figure 1 shows an example of the propagation when $C = 1$ and $D = 1$. Then, we decide to display the nodes which have greater Fvs than a threshold and hide others. The main features of this algorithm are:

- details near a focus and only landmarks away are displayed;

- the total amount of displayed object is nearly constant when users change their focuses of attention;

- this amount can be set flexibly.

The detail of the algorithm is described in the paper[9], where FractalView is applied to the structured program editor. FractalView is also applied to the visualization of a huge tree in another paper[10].

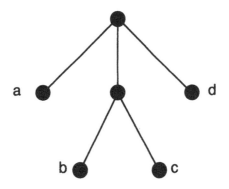

Figure 2: A tree which represents an s-expression (a (b c) d).

3   Lisp printer

3.1   Traditional algorithm

To print a large Lisp object, abbreviation is often used. The main reasons to use the abbreviation are (1) to fit the object in a display screen, (2) to enable users to concentrate on a focused element.

The traditional abbreviation algorithm focuses on the tree structure of an s-expression. For example, (a (b c) d) is represented as a tree shown in Figure 2. The printer decides which elements to be displayed by focusing on the depth of the tree and the number of elements at a given level. In Common Lisp[14], two global variables, *print-level* and *print-length*, control the display. The *print-level* controls how many levels deep a nested data object will print. The *print-length* controls how many elements at a given level are printed. This algorithm is widely used in many Lisp systems.

There are, however, some drawbacks in this algorithm. In the following discussions, we use two s-expressions. One is deeply nested and is represented as a binary tree,

((((1 2)(3 4)((5 6)(7 8)))(((1 2)(3 4))((5 6)(7 8)))))).

The other is a simple s-expression,

(1 2 3 4 5).

The former is bound to the variable **nested**, and the latter is bound to the variable **simple**.

The first problem is that the amount of the displayed object considerably differs depending on the target object. For example, if *print-level* is 4 and *print-length* is 2, **nested** and **simple** are printed as follows.

> nested

((((1 2)(3 4))((5 6)(7 8)))(((1 2)(3 4))((5 6)(7 8))))

> simple

(1 2 ...)

Although all elements of **nested** are printed, only two elements of **simple** are printed.

This problem seems to be solved by changing *print-level* to 5. It succeeds in local, but produces a side-effect in global. For example, if another s-expression which is represented as a 5 branch tree with 3 levels deep is printed with the same *print-level* and *print-length*, 125 atoms are printed. Thus, if *print-level* is increased, the amount of displayed object increases exponentially with the number of branches.

The second problem is that the displayed amount changes drastically by changing each threshold. Remember that all elements of **nested** are printed if *print-level* is 4 and *print-length* is 2. If *print-length* is changed to 1, only one atom is printed.

> nested

((((1 ...) ...) ...)...)

On the other hand, if *print-level* is changed to 3, no atom is printed.

> nested

(((# #) (# #))((# #) (# #)))

The third problem is that there are two thresholds that users manipulate. The users have to adjust two thresholds to get their desirable display. Then, when they want to print another s-expression, they have again to adjust these two thresholds.

The problems in the traditional Lisp printer are summarized as follows:

- the displayed amount differs considerably corresponding to the target object although the same thresholds are used;

- the displayed amount drastically changes when one of the thresholds is increased or decreased;

- it is difficult to adjust two thresholds.

3.2   FractalView printer

Since each Lisp object is represented as a tree, it is possible to apply the FractalView algorithm. In Figure 2, a focus is set to the root node and each node's Fv is calculated

```
procedure FRACTAL_PRINT (x:s-expression; scale : real);
begin
    if scale < threshold
       if x is atom
          print '?';
       else
          print '%';
    else
       if x is atom
          print x;
       else begin
          nelem := length of x;
          newscale := scale × nelem⁻¹;
          for each i in x do
             FRACTAL_PRINT(i, newscale);
       end;
end;
```

Figure 3: The FractalView printer's algorithm.

by using equation 15.1. First, the Fv_{focus} is 1. The root has two children and therefore each Fv is calculated as follows:

$$2^{-1/1} \times 1 = \frac{1}{2}$$

In the same way, the first child of the root has three children, the Fvs of the children are:

$$3^{-1/1} \times \frac{1}{2} = \frac{1}{6}$$

An atom and a cons which have smaller value than a threshold is abbreviated as '?' and '%', respectively. Figure 3 shows an algorithm. As you can see in Figure 3, the computation time depends on the displayed amount, not on the whole size of the s-expression. Therefore, it is possible to display the large s-expression in short time.

In Figure 2, there are three thresholds (1,1/2,1/6). It seems that there is no flexibility of choosing thresholds. However, when we print an s-expression with larger size or with a different number of branches, the number of thresholds will increase. The FractalView printer is currently implemented on MIT Scheme[7] and on Common Lisp.

4   Example Sessions

To evaluate our method, we chose two s-expressions shown in Figure 4 and Figure 5, both of which are picked from a Scheme textbook[1]. The former is an example

```
    (define-machine fib
(registers n val continue)
(controller
   (assign continue fib-done)
 fib-loop
   (branch (< (fetch n) 2) immediate-answer)
   (save continue)
   (assign continue afterfib-n-1)
   (save n)
   (assign n (- (fetch n) 1))
   (goto fib-loop)
 afterfib-n-1
   (restore n)
   (restore continue)
   (assign n (- (fetch n) 2))
   (save continue)
   (assign continue afterfib-n-2)
   (save val)
   (goto fib-loop)
 afterfib-n-2
   (assign n (fetch val))
   (restore val)
   (restore continue)
   (assign val
           (+ (fetch val)(fetch n)))
   (goto (fetch continue))
 immediate-answer
   (assign val (fetch n))
   (goto (fetch continue))
 fib-done))
```

Figure 4: An s-expression with many siblings.

```
    (define (+terms L1 L2)
(cond ((empty-termlist? L1) L2)
      ((empty-termlist? L2) L1)
      (else
       (let ((t1 (first-term L1))
             (t2 (first-term L2)))
         (cond ((> (order t1) (order t2))
                (adjoin-term
                 t1
                 (+terms (rest-terms L1) L2)))
               ((< (order t1) (order t2))
                (adjoin-term
                 t2
                 (+terms L1 (rest-terms L2))))
               (else
                (adjoin-term
                 (make-term (order t1)
                            (add (coeff t1)
                                 (coeff t2)))
                 (+terms (rest-terms L1)
                         (rest-terms L2)))))))))
```

Figure 5: An s-expression which is deeply nested.

```
      1 ]=> (set! print-length 27)
;Value: 27
1 ]=> (set! print-level 3)
;Value: 3
1 ]=> (normal-pp branched-list)          ; (A)
(define-machine
 fib
 (registers n val continue)
 (controller    % fib-loop
   %             % %
   %             % %
   afterfib-n-1 % %
   %             % %
   %             % afterfib-n-2
   %             % %
   %             % immediate-answer
   %             % fib-done))
;No value
1 ]=> (normal-pp nested-list)            ; (B)
(define (+terms 11 12) (cond % % %))
;No value
1 ]=> (set! print-level 4)
;Value: 3
1 ]=> (normal-pp nested-list)            ; (C)
(define
 (+terms 11 12)
 (cond (% 12) (% 11) (else %)))
;No value
1 ]=> (normal-pp branched-list)          ; (D)
(define-machine
 fib
 (registers n val continue)
 (controller
  (assign continue fib-done)
  fib-loop
  (branch % immediate-answer)
  (save continue)
  (assign continue afterfib-n-1)
  (save n)
  (assign n %)
  (goto fib-loop)
  afterfib-n-1
  (restore n)
  (restore continue)
  (assign n %)
  (save continue)
  (assign continue afterfib-n-2)
  (save val)
  (goto fib-loop)
  afterfib-n-2
  (assign n %)
  (restore val)
  (restore continue)
  (assign val %)
  (goto %)
  immediate-answer
  (assign val %)
  (goto %)
  fib-done))
;No value
```

Figure 6: An example session with the traditional printer.

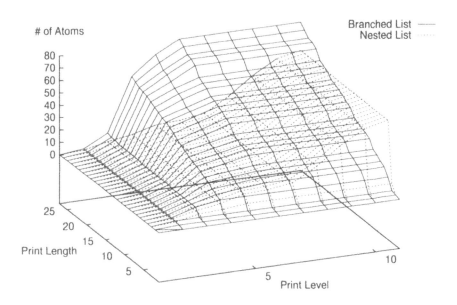

Figure 7: The relation between print-level, print-length, and the number of printed atoms.

that has many branches and is bound to the variable **branched-list**. The latter is an example that is deeply nested and is bound to the variable **nested-list**.

Figure 6 shows an example session with the traditional algorithm. In the figure, "1]=>" is a prompt produced by Scheme. Function **normal-pp** is the printer. To print **exp**, we call (**normal-pp ex**). The display is controlled by two variables **print-length** and **print-level** whose initial values are 27 and 3, respectively. **Nested-list** and **branched-list** are printed as shown in Figure 6(A) and 6(B), respectively. It is observed that **nested-list** prints more atoms than **branched-list** does. When **print-level** is increased to 4, the displayed amount of **nested-list** is not changed so much (Figure 6(C)). It still prints less amount than Figure 6(A). However, by incrementing **print-level**, most of the elements in **branched-list** are printed (Figure 6(D)). Note that it is impossible to get the medium amount between these two. Decreasing **print-level** is also not desirable because it causes to treat labels at the same level (e.g., **controller**, **fib-loop**, **afterfib-n-1**, etc.) unfairly.

Figure 7 shows a relation between **print-level**, **print-length**, and the number of printed atoms. **Nested-list** is sensitive when **print-length** is small and **branched-list** is sensitive when **print-level** is small.

On the other hand, Figure 8 shows an example session with the FractalView printer. The display is controlled by the variable **fractal-threshold**. In order

```
    1 ]=> (set! fractal-threshold 0.003)
;Value: .01
1 ]=> (fractal-pp branched-list)                    ; (A)
(define-machine
 fib
 (registers n val continue)
 (controller    (? ? ?) fib-loop
  (? % ?)       (? ?)   (? ? ?)
  (? ?)         (? ? %) (? ?)
  afterfib-n-1 (? ?)    (? ?)
  (? ? %)       (? ?)   (? ? ?)
  (? ?)         (? ?)   afterfib-n-2
  (? ? %)       (? ?)   (? ?)
  (? ? %)       (? %)   immediate-answer
  (? ? %)       (? %)   fib-done))
;No value
1 ]=> (fractal-pp nested-list)                      ; (B)
(define
 (+terms l1 l2)
 (cond
  ((empty-termlist? l1) l2)
  ((empty-termlist? l2) l1)
  (else (let ((? %) (? %)) (? % % %)))))
;No value
1 ]=> (set! fractal-threshold 0.0017)
;Value: .003
1 ]=> (fractal-pp nested-list)                      ; (C)
(define
 (+terms l1 l2)
 (cond
  ((empty-termlist? l1) l2)
  ((empty-termlist? l2) l1)
  (else
   (let
    ((t1 (? ?)) (t2 (? ?)))
    (cond (% %) (% %) (? %))))))
;No value
1 ]=> (fractal-pp branched-list)                    ; (D)
(define-machine
 fib
 (registers n val continue)
 (controller    (? ? ?)              fib-loop
  (? % ?)       (save continue)      (? ? ?)
  (save n)      (? ? %)              (goto fib-loop)
  afterfib-n-1 (restore n)           (restore continue)
  (? ? %)       (save continue)      (? ? ?)
  (save val)    (goto fib-loop)      afterfib-n-2
  (? ? %)       (restore val)        (restore continue)
  (? ? %)       (goto (? ?))         immediate-answer
  (? ? %)       (goto (? ?))         fib-done))
;No value
```

Figure 8: An example session with the FractalView printer.

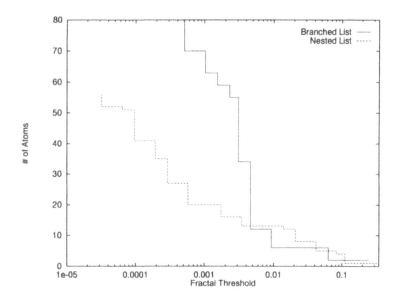

Figure 9: The relation between fractal-threshold and number of printed atoms.

to get the similar view to Figure 6(A), `fractal-threshold` is initially set 0.003. With this settings, `nested-list` is displayed as Figure 8(B). Note that the displayed amounts of Figure 8(A) and Figure 8(B) are closer than those of Figure 6(A) and Figure 6(B).

Moreover, it is possible to change the threshold smoothly. When `fractal-threshold` is changed to 0.0017, users can increase the display amount a little as shown in Figure 8(C) and Figure 8(D).

Figure 9 shows a relation between `fractal-threshold` and the number of printed atoms. There is not much difference between two when `fractal-threshold` is more than 0.03.

5 Focus-Oriented Printer

When a larger object is printed, it is convenient to print detail near the focused atom and to abbreviate distant atoms. In the previous examples, the focus was always set on the root node. By moving the focus, another feature of FractalView is utilized, that is, the integrated view of local details and contexts.

As an extension of the FractalView printer described in the previous section, a prototype focus-oriented printer was implemented. The printer takes an s-expression as an argument and constructs a tree structure. The tree structure is held until the next s-expression is given. When the user's focus moves, F_v of each node is recalculated by using equation 15.1. Currently, there are five commands, `print`, `up`, `down`, `next`, and `previous`, and they are used to print the s-expression, to move focus to its parent, to move focus to the eldest brother, to move focus to the next sibling, and to move focus to the previous sibling, respectively.

Figure 11 shows an example session with the focus-oriented printer. As a sample s-expression, we use the s-expression shown in Figure 10. Initially, the focus is set on the root. If a **print** command is invoked, an abbreviated view of the nested **sqrt** is obtained (Figure 11(A)). In this view, the function name, its arguments, and the body of **sqrt** is printed . The details of three internal functions, however, are abbreviated.

Next, the user invokes a **down** command to move his focus to **define**, two **next** commands to move his focus to the definition of **good-enough?**, and a **print** commands to print result (Figure 11(B)). This time the user can see the focused function **good-enough?** in detail. Moreover, the user issues a **next** command to move his focus to the function **improve** and he can see this function in detail (Figure 11(C)).

As shown in this example, FractalView can display details near the focus and only landmarks further away. As well, the difference between views before and after changing focus is minimized. It is difficult to get such effects with the traditional printer.

6   Discussions

One of major issues when FractalView is applied to the Lisp printer is that it does not always print the name of function or macros. In Common Lisp, if ***print-length*** is 2 or beyond, the function names are always printed. With FractalView, if there are many siblings at the same level of the function name, these elements are abbreviated.

This, however, does not mean superiority of the traditional printer. Because to set ***print-length*** to more than or equal to 2 might cause the overflow of the screen with some Lisp objects. If this overflow is allowed, we can change our algorithm so that it always prints the function names.

A main goal of this paper is not to show a complete Lisp printer, but to show FractalView's ability of controlling the display amount by applying it to the Lisp printer. To make such a printer that controls the display amount by understanding user's intention, knowledge engineering approaches will be necessary. Such algorithms, however, will become more complex and will require more computation time. On the other hand, the FractalView printer is implemented by using such a simple algorithm as shown in Figure 3 and is as practical as the traditional printer. Moreover, the FractalView printer is superior than the traditional printer in its ability of controlling the display amount, setting threshold flexibly, and displaying focus and context.

The FractalView printer is effective particularly in Scheme. Scheme can allow programmers to define functions inside a function like Pascal. This causes that each function tends to have larger size and more branches than in Common Lisp. The functions in Common Lisp also tend to be larger if they use many local variables inside **let**, **do**, and so on. In this paper, we chose Lisp as a target language. It

```
    (define (sqrt x)
  (define (good-enough? guess x)
    (< (abs (- (square guess) x)) .001))
  (define (improve guess x)
    (average guess (/ x guess)))
  (define (sqrt-iter guess x)
    (if (good-enough? guess x)
        guess
        (sqrt-iter (improve guess x) x)))
  (sqrt-iter 1 x)))
```

Figure 10: A sample Scheme program.

```
    1 ]=> (print)                                      ;(A)
(define
 (sqrt x)
 (define (? ? ?) (? % ?))
 (define (? ? ?) (? ? %))
 (define (? ? ?) (? % ? %))
 (sqrt-iter 1 x))
;No value
1 ]=> (begin(down)(next)(next)(print))            ;(B)
(define
 (? ?)
 (define (good-enough? guess x) (< (? %) .001))
 (? % %)
 (? % %)
 (? ? ?))
;No value
1 ]=> (begin(next)(print))                         ;(C)
(define
 (? ?)
 (? % %)
 (define
  (improve guess x)
  (average guess (? ? ?)))
 (? % %)
 (? ? ?))
;No value
```

Figure 11: An example session with focus-oriented printer.

is also possible to apply the FractalView algorithm to structured editors for other structured programming language such as C or Pascal.

7 Conclusion

This paper presented an application of our distortion-oriented technique, FractalView, to the Lisp printer. The FractalView printer makes it possible to minimize the differences of the display amount in different Lisp objects. It also makes it possible to change the display amount more smoothly than the traditional printer. Moreover, the focus-oriented printer which prints details near the focus and distant landmarks was shown.

Bibliography

1) Abelson, H., Sussman, G. J. and Sussman, J.: *Structure and Interpretation of Computer Programs*, MIT Press (1985).

2) Barnsley, M. F., Jacquin, A., Malassenet, F., Reuter, L. and Sloan, A. D.: Harnessing Chaos for Image Synthesis, *Computer Graphics*, Vol. 22, No. 4, pp. 131–140 (1988).

3) Barstow, D. R.: A Display-Oriented Editor for Interlisp, *Interactive Programming Environments* (Barstow, D. R., Shrobe, H. E. and Sandewall, E.(eds.)), McGraw-Hill (1984).

4) Bolt, R. A.: *The Human Interface*, Lifetime Learning Publications, Belmont, Calif. (1984).

5) Feiner, S. and Beshers, C.: Worlds within Worlds Metaphors for Exploring n-Dimensional Virtual Worlds, *Proceedings of the ACM SIGGRAPH Symposium on User Interface Software and Technology (UIST'90)*, ACM Press, pp. 76–83 (1990).

6) Furnas, G. W.: Generalized Fisheye Views, *Proceedings of the ACM Conference on Human Factors in Computing Systems (CHI'86)*, ACM Press, pp. 16–23 (1986).

7) Hanson, C.: *MIT Scheme Reference Manual* (1991).

8) Henderson, Jr., D. A. and Card, S. K.: Rooms: The Use of Multiple Virtual Workspaces to Reduce Space Contention in a Window-based Graphical User Interface, *ACM Trans. on Graphics*, Vol. 5, No. 3, pp. 211–143 (1986).

9) Koike, H.: Fractal Views: A Fractal-Based Method for Controlling Information Display, *ACM Trans. on Information Systems*, Vol. 13, No. 3, pp. 305–323 (1995).

10) Koike, H. and Yoshihara, H.: Fractal Approaches for Visualizing Huge Hierarchies, *Proceedings of 1993 IEEE/CS Symposium on Visual Languages (VL'93)*, IEEE CS Press, pp. 55–60 (1993).

11) Leung, Y. K. and Apperley, M. D.: A Review and Taxonomy of Distortion-Oriented Presentation Techniques, *ACM Trans. on Computer Human Interaction*, Vol. 1, No. 2, pp. 126–160 (1994).

12) Mandelbrot, B. B.: *The Fractal Geometry of Nature*, W.H.Freeman and Company, New York (1982).

13) Mikelsons, M.: Prettyprinting in an Interactive Programming Environment, *ACM SIG-PLAN Notices*, Vol. 16, No. 6, pp. 108–116 (1981).

14) Steele, Jr., G. L.: *Common Lisp the Language*, Digital Press, Bedford, Mass, 2nd edition (1990).

Index

Printed and bound by CPI Group (UK) Ltd, Croydon, CR0 4YY

23/10/2024

01778249-0003